CRIME AGAINST WOMEN

CRIME AGAINST WOMEN

Editors

ASHA SHUKLA
JAYA PHOOKAN

SERIALS PUBLICATIONS PVT. LTD.
New Delhi (INDIA)

Edition: 2015

ISBN: 978-81-8387-696-4

The views and opinions expressed in this book are author(s) own and the facts reported by him/her have been verified to the expert possible. The copyright owner/Editors and the publishers are not in any way liable for the same. The papers in the Book have been arranged alphabetically by author's name

SERIALS PUBLICATIONS (P) LTD.
4830/24, Prahlad Street, Ansari Road
Darya Ganj, New Delhi-110002 (India)
Phone : 23245225, 23272135
E-mail: serials@mail.com

CONTENTS

Foreword by Smt. Bhamathi Balasubramaniam ix

Preface xiii

List of Contributors xvii

1. Violence Against Girl Child and Women: 1
Issues and Concern
Asha Shukla & Jaya Phookan

2. Violence Against Women :Causes and Concern 24
Aradhana & Mahesh Bhargava

3. Violence Against Women and Girls : 39
The Improvised Life of a Girl Child
Archana Sahay

4. Cyber Crimes Against Women 53
Bhamathi Balasubramaniam

5. Jurisprudence of Women Empowerment and 75
Domestic Violence: The Laws and Flaws
Bir Pal Singh

6. Crime Against Women ....
Kusum Tripathi

7. Competency of Laws for Protection of Women Against Violence: A Need to Strengthen the Laws 122
Neelu Rawat

8. Management of Data on Crime Against Women (CAW): A Sociological Analysis 135
P M Nair

9. DNA Fingerprinting in Solving Crime against Girl Child and Women 147
Pankaj Shrivastava, Toshi Jain & S. K. Tiwari

10. Violence Against Unborn Girl Child: Female Foeticide-A Crime against Society 160
Parul Gaur and Lalit Mohan Sharma

11. Crime against Women- Wake up Call 187
Renu Sharma

12. Reading Into Crime Against Women In India: Some Issues and Perspectives 208
R. G. Dastidar

13. Private and Public Dichotomy about Domestic Violence: The State of the Art Literature on Issues and Concerns 227
R. K. Mohanty

14. A String of Stifled Womanhood (Suicides by Economically Independent Girls — An Issue of Concern) 269
Sudha Arora

15. Evolving Role of Women Cell 283
Suman Nalwa

16. ACID ATTACK: An Anti Woman Burning Social Mentality : An Analysis 300
Syed Mubin Zehra

17. Declining Child Sex Ratio in India 312
Upasana Behar

18. SECUREPIC: Securing Pictures on Social Networking Sites 332
Vasima Khan

19. Sexual Harassment in the Workplace 344
Vinita Bhatnagar

FOREWORD

Across the world, violence against women is recognised as a symptom of unequal gender- based power relations.In India regressive patriarchal values, which define socially and culturally determined norms, perptuate gender hierarchies. They are deeply embedded in society, community and family, which disproportionately penalise women and girls, which begins even before birth by killing female fetuses.India has one of the lowest sex ratios in the world with approximately 35 million women "missing". Research indicates that 12% of this gap is found at birth which increases to 25% in childhood.

The NCRB statistics indicate that an Indian woman is most unsafe in her marital home with 43.6% of all crimes against women being "cruelty" inflicted by those in her marital home. The findings of a recent survey carried out by India's National Commission for Women, shows that 88.9 percent of honor killings are perpetrated by family members. Violence against women is perpetrated not only, or even mostly, by strangers but also from agents of the state, spouses and family members. Of the 24,923 rape incidences in India in 2012, 98% of the offenders were known to the victim, which is higher than the global average of approximately 90%.

According to NCRB, registered rape cases in India have increased by almost 900 percent over the past.The total number of reported rapes rose to 33,707 in 2013 from 24,923 in 2012. An average of 92 women are raped in India every day. Numbers of trafficked women are also high, and 90 percent of India's trafficking in persons occurs within national borders. Rape and violence against women are, proverbially, among the most under-reported crimes. The UN Office on Drugs and Crimes records that in 2010, there were only 1.8 cases of rape reported per thousand people in India; in Germany it was 9.4, in Norway the figure was 19.2, in the United States it was 27.3 and in Sweden it was 63.5 per thousand. The presence of more women police officers might help in dealing with the problems. Unfortunately there are only 84,479 women police personnel in India, constituting only 5.33% of the total police force.

After the December 2012 gang-rape in Delhi, the Indian Government set up the Justice Verma Committee. The Committee submitted its report recommending wider inclusion of the definition of rape, changes to the medico-legal examination procedures of the rape victims and the prosecution of members of armed forces/uniformed personnel under ordinary criminal law in the case of rape.In response the Parliament passed the Criminal Law (Amendment) Act 2013 which provides for amendment of the IPC, Evidence Act and the CrPC. Some of the positive measures in these amendments included recognizing acid attacks, sexual harassment, voyeurism, stalking and trafficking of persons as criminal acts under the amendments to the IPC. Exclusive fast track courts were set up to deal with cases of sexual violence against women. Additionally a women's distress helpline number, 1091 was launched in various Indian cities.The Parliament also enacted the Sexual Harassment of Women at Workplace (Prohibition, Prevention and Redressal) Act 2013.

Despite rising awareness, change on the ground has been slow. The result was evident from the yet again rape of a young woman by a taxi driver in Delhi, which has again left the city and the country shocked and traumatised, searching for answers on how to end this tide of crimes against women.

The book on Crime Against Women edited by **Prof. Asha Shukla** and **Dr. Jaya Phookan** deals with the various issues and forms of crime against women, which includes status of crime against women and girl child in India, domestic violence, gender based discrimination, declining child sex ratio and female foeticide, acid attack, rape/gang rape, cyber crime, human trafficking, laws and acts related to crime against women, role of police, management of data related to crimes against women etc. I congratulate the editors for their unsparing efforts and initiative in bringing out this publication.

The contributors of the book are eminent scholars, academicians, committed policy makers, renowned IPS and IAS officers, NGO personnel who have made a difference by highlighting, advocating, researching and imparting training on the issues. I hope that this book will enable the readers to understand the issues more deeply and comprehensively. The book provides a balance between practical and theoretical issues. I have no doubt that this book will be a valuable reference tool and guiding light. This book is an essential reading for criminologists, sociologists, psychologists, academicians, scholars, police personnel, women activists, social workers and everybody concerned with the issue of crime against women and human rights.

B, Bhamathi, IAS
(presently Administrative Member in the Central Administrative Tribunal, Mumbai Bench, Mumbai in the rank and status of a High Court Judge)

PREFACE

Violence Against Women is a violation of Human rights that manifests itself in number of ways like Murders, honour killing, rapes, dowry deaths, molestation cases, Female Foeticide, Sexual Harassment at workplace, Importation of girls/Trafficking, Kidnapping and abduction, Domestic Violence, Suicide , acid attack etc. There are many instances of crime especially against women go unreported in India. Violence and Crime Against Women is a result of traditional patriarchal structure and gender relations that assumes men to be superior to women. Although many initiatives have been taken to improve the status of women, the constitutional dream of gender equality is miles away from becoming a reality. There is need to combat the crime against women which exists in various forms. Many recent efforts like amendments in key provisions of Criminal procedure Code, enactment of Sexual Harassment (prevention, protection and Redressal) at Workplace Act, 2013, have been made in this regard but lot more needs to be done . The laws and Acts, provision for protection and safety of women alone cannot solve the problem. There is need to change the mindset and attitude towards women and challenge the patriarchal set up.

The present book addresses the issue of violence and crime against women, looks for reason behind these crimes and gender discrimination which exists in society.The book also deals with various discourses on crime against women and strategies to combat the problem. The book consists of nineteen chapters dealing with different issues related to crime against women. Various issues which have been discussed in the book are: Issues and forms of Violence Against Women and Girls, Cyber Crimes Against Women, Management of Data on Crime Against Women (CAW), DNA Fingerprinting in Solving Crime against Girl Child and Women, Violence Against Unborn Girl Child: Female foeticide-A Crime against Society, Declining Child Sex ratio in India, Domestic Violence , Acid Attack, Sexual Harassment at Work Place ,discourses on Crime Against Women In India, , Laws and Acts For Protection of Women Against Violence etc.

Women's Studies Department, Barkatullah University, Bhopal is seriously working on the issue of violence and crime against women through its extension activities, seminars, gender sensitization training programmes and through teaching also.

At the very Outset, I am very thankful to Smt. Bhamathi Balasubramaniam for writing the foreword of this book. I am thankful to **Prof. M. D Tiwari,** Vice Chancellor, Barkatullah University, Bhopal for his guidance and cooperation in publication of this book.

This book would not have been possible without his support and guidance.

The contributors of the book are eminent scholars, academicians, renowned police personnels , NGO personnels, feminist writers who have dealt with the issue of violence and crime against women through firsthand experience as well as research. I am thankful to all of them for their contribution.I would like to thank especially to Dr. P.M.Nair, Mrs. Bhamathi Balasubramaniam, Mrs. Renu Sharma, Dr. Sudha Arora, Prof.Mahesh Bhargava, , Kusum Tripathi, Mr. Pankaj Srivastava, Dr. Syed Mubin Zehra for their valuable insights, suggestions and Contribution in the book.

I thank from bottom of my heart to the co-editor of book, **Dr. Jaya Phookan** for her ideas, constant support and efforts. I sincerely appreciate her efforts for supporting me in editing of the book. I thank the staff and my colleagues at the Women's Studies Department for their support and encouragement. I thank my family members for being a constant source of encouragement and support to complete the book.

I express my deep sense of gratitude to University grants commission (UGC) as this books has been published from the grant of UGC.

I would like to thank the team of Serials Publications, New Delhi for their cooperation and support in publication of this book.

Bhopal **Prof. Asha Shukla**

LIST OF CONTRIBUTORS

Prof. Asha Shukla, Head, Women's Studies Department, Barkatullah University, Bhopal (M.P).

Dr. Jaya Phookan, Assistant Professor, Women's Studies Department, Barkatullah University, Bhopal (M.P).

Aradhana, Assistant Professor in Psychology, DAV College for Women, Ferozepur Cantt (U.P).

Dr. Mahesh Bhargava, Chairperson, Harprasad Institute of Behavioural Studies, Agra (U.P).

Archana Sahay, Director, Aarambh and Childline(Collab), Bhopal (M.P).

Bhamathi Balasubramaniam, IAS, Presently Administrative Member in the Central Administrative Tribunal, Mumbai Bench, Mumbai in the Rank and Status of High Court Judge.

Dr. Bir Pal Singh, Assistant Professor, National Law Institute University, Bhopal (M.P.).

Kusum Tripathi, Feminist Writer and Activists, Mumbai (Maharashtra).

Dr. Neelu Rawat, Assistant Professor, Department of Sociology, Dr. Harisingh Gour University Sagar (M.P.).

Dr P M Nair, IPS, New Delhi, Expert on Anti-Human trafficking and related issues in India and Abroad.

Mr. Pankaj Shrivastava, Scientific Officer and Assistant Chemical Examiner to Govt. of MP, DNA Unit, State FSL, Sagar (M.P).

Toshi Jain, Research Scholar, DNA Unit State FSL, Sagar (M.P).

S. K. Tiwari, Director, State FSL, Sagar (M.P.).

Dr. Parul Gaur, Ph.D., State Quality Monitor, Mid-day Meal Programme, Vindhyanchal Bhawan, Bhopal (M.P)

Dr. Lalit Mohan Sharma, Company Secretary, Madhya Pradesh Poorv Kshetra Vidyut Vitran Co. Ltd., Jabalpur (M.P).

Mrs. Renu Sharma, Retd District Judge, Bhopal (M.P).

Prof. R. G. Dastidar, Department of Sociology, Barkatullah University, Bhopal (M.P).

Dr. R. K. Mohanty, OES-I, Reader in Sociology, BPSPA, Bhubaneswar-751 (Odisha).

Sudha Arora, Feminist writer and a Counsellar based in Mumbai (Maharashtra).

Suman Nalwa, Additional Deputy Commissioner, In Charge of Special Police Unit for Women and Children, New Delhi.

Dr. Syed Mubin Zehra, Social Analyist /Columnist / Author, New Delhi.

Upasana Behar, Social Activist and Associated with "Urban and Rural Growth Academy" Bhopal (M. P).

Vasima Khan, Computer Science & Engg., Assistant Professor, Computer Science & Engg., UIT, RGPV, Bhopal (M.P).

Dr. Vinita Bhatnagar, Associate Professor, Department of Humanities, UIT, RGPV, Bhopal.

1

VIOLENCE AGAINST GIRL CHILD AND WOMEN: ISSUES AND CONCERN

Asha Shukla and Jaya Phookan

Violence against girl child and women can be seen as an extreme form of discrimination—the root cause of this violence is gender inequality and the belief that boys are more valuable than girls. This discrimination and violence starts even before birth, with an alarming rise in female foeticide in the last decade. What is even more alarming is that sex-selective abortions have increased among the more educated and economically better-off Indians in relatively wealthy states such as Delhi, Punjab, Maharashtra (which includes India's financial capital, Mumbai) and Haryana. While sex-selective abortion is illegal in India, the 2011 Census shows an alarming decline in the child sex ratio in India which dropped in 2011 to 914 from 927 in 2001. The decline in the sex ratio in the age group 0-6 years is an extremely distressing trend. Nearly three million girls, one million more than boys, were "missing" in 2011 compared with 2001 and there are now 48 fewer girls per 1,000 boys than there were in 1981 according to Children in India (2012) Report of the Central Statistical Organization, Government of India.

Although according to the 2011 census, the sex ratio between men and women indicated 940 women to a 1000 men which is a definite improvement over the 2001 census where the ratio was 933:1000. However, India still has one of the lowest sex ratio in the world with approximately 35 million women missing. The highest number of missing women is in the north-western states of Punjab, Rajasthan and Haryana etc. Research indicates that 12% of this gap is found at birth which increased to 25% in childhood (Anderson and Ray, 2012).

"Missing Women"-a concept developed by Amartya Sen (1990, 1992)-refers to the observation that in parts of the developing world, notably in India and China, the ratio of women to men is suspiciously low. Sen translated those skewed sex ratios into absolute numbers by calculating the number of extra women who would have been alive (say in China or India)if these countries had the same ratio of women to men as in areas of the world in which they purportedly receive similar care. Sen estimated that more than 100 million women were "missing", presumably from inequality and neglect leading to excess female mortality . In this context,Das Gupta (2005) states that "the evidence indicates that parental preferences overwhelmingly shape the female deficit in south and East Asia."

The preference for boys is also reflected in the gender gap in the literacy rate in the 2011 census which shows that 82% of males and 65% of females are literate. In

Asia, and particularly in South Asian countries, in many cases a girl child is seen as a burden on the family. Girls from disadvantaged families face both deprivation and discrimination. Because of the deeply patriarchal setting, boys are often given extra care and attention right from the childhood, whether it is giving them more freedom and importance, education, or food and nutrition. Often girls are not sent to school and are made to do housework from an early age. Thousands of girls are still married off when they should be in school, making them more vulnerable to violence and abuse. Child marriages occur more frequently in South Asia than in any other region of the world. Discrimination against girls begins even before birth and continues till old age. This low value given to girls' lives creates an environment where violence is often committed with impunity. Against this backdrop, the present paper deals with the issue of violence against girl child and women, analyses how patriarchal set up and unequal power relations are the root cause of violence against women, recent measure which have been taken to combat violence against women especially after Delhi December 2012 gang rape case and also looks for discourses and reasons for crimes especially in the context of rape cases. The paper also suggests some strategies to tackle the growing incidence of violence against women.

Defining Violence Against Women

Violence against women has been clearly defined as a form of discrimination in numerous documents. The World Human Rights Conference in Vienna, first recognised gender-based violence as a human rights violation in 1993. In the same year, United Nations declaration, 1993, defined violence against women as "any act of gender-based violence that results in, or is likely to result in, physical, sexual or psychological harm or suffering to a woman, including threats of such acts, coercion or arbitrary deprivations of liberty, whether occurring in public or private life" (Cited by Gomez, 1996 in Saravanan, 2000).

Radhika Coomaraswamy identifies different kinds of Violence Against Women, in the United Nation's Special Report, 1995, on *Violence Against Women;*

(a) Physical, sexual and psychological violence occurring in the family, including battering, sexual abuse of female children in the household, dowry related violence, marital rape, female genital mutilation and other traditional practices harmful to women, non spousal violence and violence related to exploitation.

(b) Physical sexual and psychological violence occurring within the general community, including rape, sexual abuse, sexual harassment and intimidation at work, in educational institutions and elsewhere, trafficking in women and forced prostitution.

(c) Physical, sexual and psychological violence perpetrated or condoned by the state, wherever it occurs.

This definition added 'violence perpetrated or condoned by the state', to the definition by United Nations in 1993(ibid).

The fourth conference of Women, 1995 has defined violence against women as a physical act of aggression of one individual or group against another or others. Violence Against Women is any act of gender –based violence which result in Physical, sexual or arbitrary deprivation of liberty in public or private life and violation of human rights of women in situations of armed conflicts.Violence against women is gender based, meaning that the acts of violence are committed against women because they are women, or as a result of patriarchal gender constructs. The UN Declaration on the Elimination of Violence Against Women States that:"Violence against women is a manifestation of historically unequal power relations between men and women" and that "Violence against women is one of the crucial social mechanisms by which women are forced into a subordinate position compared with men.

The United Nations General Assembly (UNGA), in its resolution on the declaration of the Elimination of Violence Against Women, defines "Violence against Women" as "any act of gender-based violence that results in, or is likely to result in, Physical, sexual or mental harm or suffering to women, including threats of such acts, coercion or arbitrary deprivation of liberty, whether occurring in public or in private life".

In addition, the term "gender –based violence' refers to" any acts or threats of acts intended to hurt or make women suffer physically, sexually or psychologically, and which affect women because they are women or affect women disproportionately".

Violence against girl child and women remains one of the most pervasive form of human rights violation.

Murders, harmful customary or traditional practices such as honour killings, rapes, dowry deaths, molestation cases, female foeticide, sexual harassment, Importation of girls/ Trafficking, kidnapping and abduction, Domestic Violence, acid attacks are the form of violence reported in India. Women face violence at every possible stage of their life right from infancy to old age. The World Health Organisation (WHO), in its research on Violence Against Women, Categorised it as occurring through five stages of the life cycle: (1) Pre-birth, (2) Infancy, (3) Girlhood, (4) adolescence and adulthood and (5) elderly.

Patriarchy, Unequal Power Relations: The Root Cause of Violence against Women

Gender is a multilevel system of social practices that produces distinctions between men and women. Gender is socially constructed through organisational arrangements, is embedded within the social structure and is a part of taken for granted reality in the form of Social Institutions such as family, school, marriage, religion etc. Gender Based roles, the existing power structures and gender system fosters power imbalances making women exposed to various forms of Violence. Violence grounded on sex based hierarchical order constitutes a breach of the fundamental rights to life, liberty, security, dignity, equality between women and men, non-discrimination and physical and mental integrity. The built-in gender discrimination, deprivation and discrimination provide necessary conditions for various forms of violence against women (Anand, 2014b).

Despite various provisions, constitutional guarantee of equality, laws and acts, gender discriminations exists which is reflected through varied kinds of institutionalised deprivations. Research has established that Violence against women is related to traditional gender role expectations and masculine ideologies (White and Chen, 2002-US). The underlying causes for such widespread violence and abuse within the family are attributed to patriarchy and the unequal power relations that exist between women and men. The attendant subordinate status of women and the discriminations they face, the perception of men being superior to women and socialisation make men and women internalise such attitudes and the gender role expectations that follow are considered to be the root causes of the violence that women have to endure. Physical Violence as well as explicit forms of aggression is used by the more powerful (men) in the household as methods to ensure obedience of the less powerful and therefore related to power dynamics in a household. At every stage in the life cycle, The female body is both the objects of desire and of control (Thapan, 1995).

The patriarchal set up is indeed all pervasive due to socialisation processes predominantly by the family and education system. Right from birth onwards as one passes through different phases of life-from infancy to childhood and then adulthood, different socialising agents reinforce gender specific stereotypic beliefs. Thus, all our social institutions reinforce the patriarchal beliefs and stereotypes through overt as well as covert means. Gender is transmitted through the very social context that produces gender distinctions and inequalities (Anand, 2014a).

One of the key challenges is dowry-a practice of bride's family giving gifts of cash and kind to groom and his family. In some cases the groom's family mistreats and harasses the bride if such demands are not met. To protect women against this threat the Indian government has enacted the dowry prohibition Act and the protection of Women from domestic violence Act and cruelty under Sec 498A of the Indian penal Code. In 2012, according to the National Crime Records Bureau (NCRB), dowry deaths-or murders of women by the groom or in laws because of unmet high dowry expectations- constituted 3.4% of all crimes against women (John, Ahmad, Schneider, 2013).

The NCRB report indicate that an Indian woman is most unsafe in her marital home with 43.6% of all crimes against women being "cruelty" inflicted by her husband and relatives. Of the 24,923 rape incidences in India in 2012, 98% of the offenders were known to the victim. This may also mean that –boys and girls-in India grow up in a situation where they see violence against women as the norm (ibid).

Crime Against Women in India- NCRB Report-2012-13

"Crime in India 2012" report of National Crime Records Bureau (NCRB) reveals the sorry state of affairs regarding crime trends and the criminal Justice system of our country, especially vis-à-vis the crime of rape. It is the most alarming that singular crime of rape is the fastest growing crime in India and has increased by

902% over 1971 to 2012. The incidents of rapes reported increased from 24,206 in 2011 to 24,923 in 2012. According to Shakil (2013), these figures for rape, however, should be taken with a pinch of salt because of the manner in which the NCRB collates data. Criminal incidents often involve more than one crime. As a result, FIRs often invoke multiple Indian penal Code (IPC) sections. The figures provided by the NCRB are segregated into very neat categories of rape, murder, kidnapping etc. This is because only the most serious charge mentioned in a FIR is taken into account. By this logic, an incidence of rape and murder is recorded as murder, because murder is more serious offence in law than rape. In view of the rising incidents of crimes against women in general, and rapes in particular, it is often claimed that the figures presented are a reflection of greater awareness and better reporting, rather than an increase in absolute numbers (Shakil, 2013).

A total of 3,09,546 cases of crime against women (both under various section of IPC and SLL) were reported in the country during the year 2013 as compared to 2,44,270 in the year 2012, thus showing an increase of 26.7% during the Year 2013.An increasing trend in the incidence of rape has been observed during the periods 2009-2013.

12.9% of rape cases were reported in Madhya Pradesh (4,335 out of 33,707 cases) followed by 9.8% in Rajasthan (3,285 cases), 9.1% in Maharashtra (3,063 cases) and 9.1% in Uttar Pradesh (3,050 cases). Delhi UT has reported the highest crime rate of 18.6 as compared to national average of 5.7. The rate of crime constituted against women was 52.2 in 2013. Delhi UT

Table 1

Crime Head-wise Incidents of Crime Against Women During 2009 - 2013 and Percentage Variation in 2013 over 2012

Sl.No.	*Crime Head*	*Year*					*Percentage Variation in 2013 over 2012*
		2009	*2010*	*2011*	*2012*	*2013*	
1	Rape (Sec. 376 IPC)	21,397	22,172	24,206	24,923	33,707	35.2
2	Kidnapping & abduction (Sec. 363 to 373 IPC)	25,741	29,795	35,565	38,262	51,881	35.6
3	Dowry death (Sec. 302/304 IPC)	8,383	8,391	8,618	8,233	8,083	-1.8
4	Cruelty by husband or his relatives (Sec. 498-A IPC)	89,546	94,041	99,135	1,06,527	1,18,866	11.6
5	Assault on women with intent to outrage her modesty (Sec. 354 IPC)	38,711	40,613	42,968	45,351	70,739	56.0
6	Insult to the modesty of women (Sec. 509 IPC)	11,009	9,961	8,570	9,173	12,589	37.2
7	Importation of girl from foreign Country (Sec. 366-B IPC)	48	36	80	59	31	-47.4

contd. table 1

Sl.No.	*Crime Head*	*Year*					*Percentage Variation in 2013 over 2012*
		2009	*2010*	*2011*	*2012*	*2013*	
A	**Total IPC Crime against Women**	**1,94,832**	**2,05,009**	**2,19,142**	**2,32,528**	**2,95,896**	**27.3**
8	Commission of Sati Prevention Act, 1987	0	0	0	0	0	0
9	Immoral Traffic (Prevention) Act, 1956	2,474	2,499	2,435	2,563	2,579	0.6
10	Indecent Representation of Women (P) Act, 1986	845	895	453	141	362	156.7
11	The Dowry Prohibition Act, 1961	5,650	5,182	6,619	9,038	10,709	17.9
B	**Total SLL Crime against Women**	**8,969**	**8,576**	**9,507**	**11,742**	**13,650**	**16.2**
	Total (A+B)	**2,03,804**	**2,13,585**	**2,28,649**	**2,44,270**	**3,09,546**	**26.7**

Source: Crime in India, 2013 Report, National Crime Records Bureau , Ministry of Home Affairs, GOI.

has reported the highest rate of crime against women at 146.8 during the year 2013 as compared to 52.2 crime rate at the national level.

Figure 1: Crime against Women Percentage Distribution during 2013

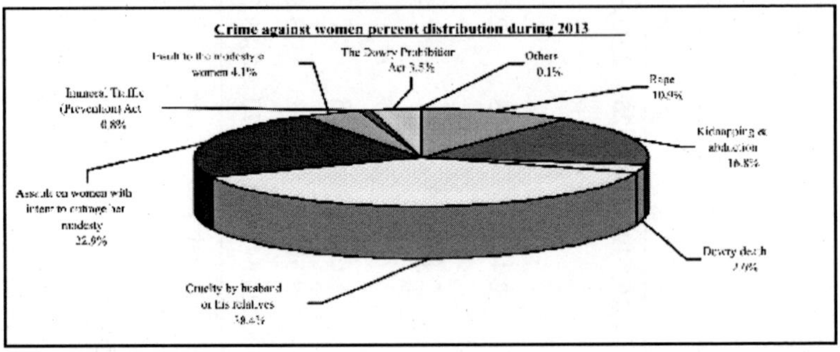

Source: Crime in India, 2013 Report, National Crime Records Bureau, Ministry of Home Affairs, GOI.

But still Rape and Violence against women are among the most under-reported crimes because in many cases culprits are known to the victim, the social and economic "costs" of reporting such crimes are high. General economic dependence on their families and fear of social ostracization act as significant disincentives for a woman to report any of sexual violence or abuse. Therefore the actual incidence of violence against women in India is probably much higher than the data suggests. Violence against girl child and women in India are rooted in societal norms and also to some extent in economic dependence.

December 2012 Delhi gang Rape, Public outrage and its Impact

Violence against Women, even in its most brutal forms, is not an uncommon event in India and , sadly stories of the most horrendous violations have seemingly inured the state and citizens to inaction. The Delhi case is unusual in that respect. The case appears to have generated, for no distinct reason, both publicness and personalisation of rape in a way that has not happened before. Thus, there have been earnest efforts to unearth a cause-or perhaps, a chain of them that might have helped to explain not just what happened that night on the bus but in the many, many instances before and since that day (Simon-Kumar, 2014). The December 2012 incident (gang-rape of a woman in Delhi on 16th December) drew attention and led to sudden outpouring of anger and frustration about the situation that allowed such attacks to take place. People took to the streets in large numbers and calling for change. Discourses on rape in response to the Delhi December rape case also impacted the justice discourses and remedial action. Short comings and public opinion were incorporated in the three member committee led by Justice Verma along with other eminent judges.

On December 23, 2012 the Government set up the Justice Verma Committee to propose amendments to criminal law dealing with sexual offences. The committee was constituted days after the incident to advice the government on the actions that needed to be taken to safeguard against other similar incidents. The committee deliberated for 29 days taking into account the views of a wide cross-section of society, including women's groups, intellectuals and jurists.

The Verma report recommended severe penalties for rape and sexual crimes (but they were strongly opposed to capital punishments), improvements in the criminal justice system, reforms within the armed forces and the police, broader definitions of sexual crimes (including stalking and trafficking as sexual crimes, clear protocols for victims of rape and the ban on the system of dowry paid by women to their husbands at the time of marriage (ibid). Thus, Justice Verma Committee in its report recommended wider inclusion of the definition of rape, changes in medico-legal examination procedures of the rape victim. In response, the parliament passed the Criminal Law (Amendment) Act 2013 which provides for amendment of the Indian penal Code, Indian Evidence Act and the Code of criminal procedure.

Criminal Law (Amendment) Act, 2013 With Special Reference to Violence Against Women

Lok Sabha on 19th March 2013 passed the Criminal Law (Amendment) Act, 2013 –an Indian legislation which provides for amendment of Indian Penal Code, Indian Evidence Act and Code of Criminal Procedure, 1973 on laws related to sexual offences. It was originally an ordinance promulgated by the President of India, Pranab Mukherjee, on 3 February 2013, in light of the protests in the 2012 Delhi gang rape case. The new Act has expressly recognised certain acts as offences which were dealt under related laws. These new offences like- acid attack, sexual harassment, voyeurism, stalking have been incorporated into Indian Penal Code: Acid Attack under Section 326A, Attempt to Acid Attack under section 326B, sexual Harassment under section 354A, Act with intent to disrobe women under section 354B, Voyeurism under section 354C and stalking under section 354D.

Further, changes have been made in law where section 370 of Indian Penal Code (IPC) has been constituted with new sections, 370 and 370 A which deals with trafficking of person for exploitation. If a person (i) recruits, (ii) transports, (iii) harbours, (iv) transfers, or (v) receives, a person, by using threats, or force, or coercion, or abduction, or fraud, or deception, or by abuse of power , or inducement fro exploitation including prostitution, slavery, forced organ removal etc. will be punished with imprisonment ranging from atleast 7 years to imprisonment from remainder of that person's natural life depending on the number or category of person trafficked. Employment of trafficked person will attract penal provision as well.

The most important change that has been made is the change in definition of rape under IPC. In the Act, the word 'rape' has been retained in section 375, and was extended to include acts in addition to vaginal penetration. Except in certain aggravated situation the punishment will be imprisonment not less than seven years but which may extend to imprisonment for life, and shall also be liable to fine. In aggravated situations, punishment will be rigorous imprisonment for a term which shall not be less than ten years but which may extend to imprisonment for life, and shall also be liable to fine.

A new section, 376A has been added which states that if a person committing the offence of sexual assault, "inflicts an injury which causes the death of the person or causes the person to be in a persistent vegetative state, shall be punished with rigorous imprisonment for a term which shall not be less than twenty years, but which may extend to imprisonment for life, which shall mean the remainder of that person's natural life, or with death" (Section 8, Criminal Law (Amendment) Ordinance, 2013). In case of "gang rape", persons involved regardless of their gender shall be punished with rigorous imprisonment for a term which shall not be less than twenty years, but which may extend to life and shall pay compensation to the victim which shall be reasonable to meet the medical expenses and rehabilitation of the victim. The age of consent in India has been increased to 18 years, which means any sexual activity irrespective of presence of consent with a woman below the age of 18 will constitute statutory rape. Certain changes has been introduced in the CrPC and Evidence Act, like the process of recording the statement of the victim has been made more victim friendly and easy but the two critical changes are: 1. the 'character of the victim' is now rendered totally irrelevant, and 2. there is now a presumption of 'no consent' in a case where sexual intercourse is proved and the victim states in the court that she did not consent.

Recent Discourses of Rape and Sexual Violence in India

It has been discussed earlier in this paper that violence and crime against women is a result of traditional patriarchal structures and gender relations which consider women subordinate to men.But there are other explanations also. Simon Kumar (2014) while analysing the discourses of Rape and the discourses of Justice especially after 2012 Delhi Rape incident highlighted that there has been intense public introspection into the nature of Indian society and the current structures of governance that have failed to keep women safe. Various discussions were made on causes of rape and sexual violence in India and measures to remedy them. The 'failure of Governance' is a foremost discourse that has emerged since the rape incident.In public commentary (especially from conversations) the discourse of blaming women, that they would have 'invited' this upon themselves either by their dress or mannerism is not uncommon.Discourse of socio-economic inequality in perpetuating gender violence and the possibilities of redistribution as the bases for gender justice also emerged.

Anand Soondas, blogging on Times of India newspaper's site, makes the following argument in his *Why Indian Men Rape*:

> *Strange theories are floated to explain the depravity of Indian men...but the truth is that at the root of all lies a culture built around hierarchies, of gender, faith, colour, caste, region.*
>
> *We are, quite simply, not used to people being equal.*

In accepting, Soondas's argument that rape is an outcome of societal transformation, the focus is on the movement from the traditional to the contemporary and on the tense relations that emanate from this transition (*ibid*). Here, he reflects on the transition from a hierarchical to an egalitarian system-facilitated, no doubt, by socio-economic development-that has had an effect on the emancipation of Indian women (their 'westernisation, as conservatives notes) which in turn has led to a crisis in the male identity and a rupture ingender relations precipitating violence (Doron and Broom in Simon-Kumar, 2014).

In this regard, Kabeer's (2013) assessment draws on poverty and socio-economic inequality as a possible explanation for the men's actions.

> *The six men in question came from one of the squalid slum neighbourhoods of Delhi and there is little question that, had this or something like this not happened , they would spend their lives in the same or similar slums. The youngest of them has been living on the streets since the age of 13.*

Kabeer's excerpt raises questions about poverty and violence-can conditions of deprivation instigate or create a culture which normalises sexual violence? At a simplistic level, there is a temptation to attribute violence among the poor as part of 'their culture'. No wonder in the days following the rape, other residents from the slums were keen to dissociate themselves from the rapists and establish that despite their poverty, they had decent values. 'We are good people', they insisted to the media (Burke, 2012). One resident told a news reporter, 'Do not think we are all like the accused…when you grind wheat to make flour, insects will come out with it too', suggesting that the same source can contain both the good and bad(Burke,2013 in Simon Kumar, 2014).

A more serious implication of Kabeer's statement (though she does not explicitly state it), and worth some reflection, is the possibility that economic hardship can be implicated in violence. The aim is not to suggest that only the poor rape; this is a simplistic conclusion amply sustained by evidence that show sexual violence occurring across all classes. Yet, it is not possible to rule out the role of economic institutions in sex crimes, given emerging contemporary research on the unanticipitated consequences of unregulated economic growth (Simon-Kumar, 2014).

Although set in the context of the global North, The spirit level written by Wilkinson and Pickett (2009) correlates inequality with social problems arguing that the wider the gap between the rich and the poor, the higher the incidence if a host of social ills, from crime to drug use to teenage pregnancies. Their analysis points not so much to poverty per se, but rather the degree of inequality prevalent in society. Is there, then, some coincidental relationship between the rise in reported rape by 20 per cent in India since 2007 and the rapid growth rate averaging 8 per cent alongside widening income inequalities in the Indian economy for most of the new millennium? (Bastagli, Coady and Gupta, 2012 in Simon-Kumar, 2014).

In this regard, Fernandes (2014) pointed out that while agreeing that crimes against women are a result of the strong patriarchal values of our society, one has to realise that they are conditioned by ethnic and caste attitudes too. The gender, class and caste attitudes that cause such abuses have to be tackled. Without change of social attitudes new laws can only give one peace of conscience but cannot solve the problem. One has also to look inwards and examine the social and cultural values that are behind such crimes.

The issues involved with regard to violence against women are deeply rooted and complex. One needs, therefore, to ask whether legal changes alone, even death sentence, can solve this problem. New Laws and police reforms are certainly needed. But they will not solve the problem because these and other crimes result from attitudes and values ingrained in our minds. If legal changes alone were to suffice, dowry, child labour, caste based discrimination and corruption should have disappeared from India some decades ago because they have been banned. That has not happened because no law can become effective without a social infrastructure to support it. Laws cannot be implemented as long as the attitudes that give birth to the abuses remain unchanged (Fernandes, 2014).

While laws need to be strengthened, and even more importantly, strictly enforced, what is equally important is education—both formal, and also within homes. The education system should be tailored to question the mindsets that perpetuate the gender bias in order to shatter gender roles and break out the vicious cycle (Thomas, 2014). The experiences of teaching faculty such as Rehana Ghadially (1988) provide not just an example of how sensitisation through classroom teaching helps but also as an example of why such teaching is required. Her account of teaching a class the psychology of sex roles at the prestigious IIT Bombay show the deep rooted biases which have been inculcated into even those considered the brightest of the nation (ibid).

Gender sensitisation in educational institutions, for police officials, at the level of family and community at large through various means is necessary. A mandatory training for auto rickshaw drivers in Delhi, provided by Delhi Government Transport Department in Collaboration with Manas Foundation (a mental Health organization) is new and good initiative in this regard. Mandatory training in women safety and gender sensitisation provides nuances of treating women with respect. The training was made mandatory in January, 2014 by the Delhi Government.

Kabeer (2013), in her article, quite rightly points out that the Millennium Development Goals when signed in 2000 did not include violence against women because it did not seem sufficiently important or perhaps it was thought that gendered development would iron out, at some future time, these acts. How we interlink system failures, dominant constructions of men and women as sexual beings, and economic parity may well pave the way for radical visions of gender justice.Parents need to treat boys and girls equally; boys need to be taught to treat girls equally. We must ensure that the issue of violence against women is not seen just as a "women's issue", but a societal issue.

References

Anand, M. (2014*a*), *Gender and School Education: Challenges and Strategies,* Regal Publishers, New Delhi.

Anand, M. (2014b), "The Gender of Violence: understanding the Metaphysics of Power and Identity", *Women's Link,* Vol. 20, No. 2.

Anderson. S. and D. Ray. (2012), "The Distribution of Missing Women in India", *Economic and Political Weekly,* XLVII, No. 47 & 48.

Bruke, J. (2012), In the Delhi Slum home of gang rape accused: We are good people, *The Guardian available at* http://www.guardian.com.co.uk/world/2012/dec/31/delhi-slum-home-rape-accused.

Criminal Law (Amendment) Act, 2013 available at *http://en.wikipedia.org/wiki/Criminal_Law_(Amendment)_Act_2013*

Das Gupta, M. (2005), "Explaining Asia's 'Missing Women':A New Look at The Data", *Population and Development Review, 31(3), 529-35.*

Fernandes Walter. (2014), The Delhi rape and the Social Challenge, *Women's Link*, Vol. 20, No. 2.

John Dona, Ahmad Omair & SchneiderMaria (2013), India: Violence Against Women-Current Challenges and Future Trends available at *http://www.freiheit.org/Aktuelle-Berichte/1804c27055i1p/index.html*

Kabeer, N. (2013), Grief and Rage in India: Making Violence Against Women history, Open Democracy, available at *http://www.opendemocracy.net/5050/naila-kabeer/grief-and-rage-in-india-making-violence-against-women-history.*

Ministry of Statistics and Programme Implementation (2012), Children in India, 2012-A Statistical Appraisal, *Social Statistics Division*, Central Statistics office, Ministry of Statistics and Programme Implementation, Government of India.

NCRB. (2012), *Crime in India, 2012*, NCRB, Ministry of Home Affairs, GOI.

NCRB. (2013), *Crime in India, 2013*,NCRB, Ministry of Home Affairs, GOI.

Saravanan, Sheela (2000), *Violence Against Women in India-A Literature Review*, Institute of Social Studies Trust (ISST), New Delhi.

Simon Kumar Rachel (2014), "Sexual Violence in India: The Discourses of Rape and the Discourses of Justice", *Indian Journal of Gender Studies*, Sage Publications, Vol. 21, No. 3.

Sen, A. (1990), "More Than 100 Million Women are Missing", *The New York Review of Books, 37(20), 20 December.*

Sen, A. (1992), "Missing Women", *British Medical Journal*, 304, March 587-88.

Shakil Albeena (2013), "Rape and Honour Crimes : The NCRB Report 2012". *Economic and Political Weekly*, Vol. XLVII No. 31.

Thapan, M. (1995), "Images of the Body and Sexuality in Women's Narratives on oppression in the Home", *Economic and Political Weekly*, Vol. 30, No. 43: WS72-WS80.

The Gazette of India. (2013), The Criminal Law (Amendment) Act, 2013, Ministry of Law and Justice, New Delhi.

Thomus, Anisha (2014), "Legal Institutions and Women: Need for a Sustained Women's Movement", *Women's Link*, Vol. 20, No. 2.

United Nations (1996), *Report of the Fourth World Conference on Women*, 1995, United Nations: Newyork.

United Nations General Assembly (1993), Declaration on the Elimination of Violence Against Women, United Nations General Assembly available at *www.un.org/documents/ga/res/48/a48r104.htm*

White, H. R. & Chen, P. H. (2002), "Problem of Drinking and Intimate Partner Violence", *Journal of Studies on Alcohol*, 63: 205-214.

WHO. (1997), Violence Against Women: Definition and Scope of the Problem available at *http://www.who.int/gender/violence/v4.pdf.*

Wilkinson, R. & Pickett, K. (2009), *The Spirit Level*, London: Penguin Books.

2

VIOLENCE AGAINST WOMEN : CAUSES AND CONCERN

ARADHANA AND MAHESH BHARGAVA

Violence against women is a global epidemic and a human rights violation occurring globally. It includes physical, sexual and psychological violence, and harmful practices such as rape, "honor killings" and human trafficking. In the Indian society, women were accorded the status of goddess but the present era of globalization has given rise to violence against women. Violence both inside and outside of their home has become a crucial issue in the contemporary Indian society. Violence against women destabilizes countries, impedes economic progress, and prevents women from contributing to their community, and creating better lives for themselves and their families.

Once the first Prime Minister of India, Jawaharlal Nehru said, "you can tell the condition of a nation by looking at the status of its women". It is a fact that the social condition of women of any nation is a pointer to the level of development of that nation.

In Indian society, woman occupies a vital position and venerable place. The Vedas glorified women as the mother, the creator, one who gives life and worshipped her as a 'Devi' or Goddess. A Sanskrit *sloka* about women says that *'Yatra Naryastu Pujyante, Ramante Tatra Devta'*– where woman are worshiped, God resides. So that was the social status of women in the Vedic era in India. But their glorification was rather mythical as women in India are suffering in the form of discrimination, oppression, exploitation, degradation, aggression, humiliation. In the era of globalization and modernization the present trends of crimes against women is on increase. Recently, the brutal gang rape against 23 year student in Delhi and a five year old girl again sparked the debate on Indian mental set up and the plight of women order in the Country. Today, fear of violence is an important factor in the lives of most women and is becoming the cause of lack of participation in every sphere of life.

The international community recognizes 'violence against women' as any act of gender-based violence that results in, or is likely to result in, physical, sexual or psychological harm or suffering to women. Gender-based violence is violence that is directed against a woman because she is a woman or affects women disproportionately. Examples include rape, domestic violence, trafficking, forced prostitution, sexual exploitation, sexual harassment and forced marriage. Violence against women includes threats of such acts, coercion or arbitrary deprivation of liberty. Violence against women can occur in private (such as in the home) or in public settings (including places of work and educational institutions).

The roots of gender-based violence lie in the pervasive systems of inequality that perpetrate the domination of men and the subordination of women. As recognized in the United Nations (UN) General Assembly's 1993 *Declaration on the Elimination of Violence against Women*, violence against women 'is a manifestation of historically unequal power relations between men and women, which have led to domination over and discrimination against women by men and to the prevention of the full advancement of women, and ... is one of the crucial social mechanisms by which women are forced into a subordinate position compared with men.'

Amnesty International defines violence against Women as: "any act of gender-based violence that results in, or is likely to result in, physical, sexual or psychological harm or suffering to women, including threats of such acts, coercion or arbitrary deprivation of liberty, whether occurring in public or in private life." Gender-based violence against women is violence "directed against a woman because she is a woman or that affects women disproportionately". In other words, not all acts which harm a woman are gender-based and not all victims of gender-based violence are female. More recent international legal instruments broaden the definition, in particular to include structural violence – that is, harm resulting from the impact of the organization of the economy on women's lives.

The statistics of violence against women reveal a worldwide human rights catastrophe.

- At least one out of every three women has been beaten, coerced into sex, or otherwise abused in her lifetime, according to a study based on 50 surveys from around the world. Usually, the abuser is a member of her own family or someone known to her (Heise, *et al.*, 1999)

- Domestic violence is the major cause of death and disability for women aged 16 to 44 and accounts for more death and ill-health than cancer or traffic accidents (Parliamentary Assembly of the Council of Europe, 2002).
- The World Health Organization has reported that up to 70 per cent of female murder victims are killed by their male partners (WHO, 2002).
- An estimated 5,000 women are burnt to death each year in 'kitchen accidents' because their dowry was seen as being too modest.
- The World Health Organisation estimates that globally one woman in five will be the victim of rape or attempted rape in her lifetime.
- The number of women forced or sold into prostitution is estimated at anywhere between 700,000 to 2 million per year.
- Over 60 per cent of HIV positive youth between the ages of 15 and 24 around the world are women.

In India, the report of National Crime Records Bureau (2012) has given the following figures of the Incidence rate of Crime against Women

2011 : 2,28,650 2011 : 18.9

2012 : 2,44,270 2012 : 41.74

- Assam reported the highest crime rate (89.5) as compared to the National average rate of 41.7.
- The total IPC crimes against women has increased during last 5 years from 8.9% in the year 2008 to 9.4% during the year 2012.
- The number of Rape cases, Assault on Women to outrage her Modesty and Importation of Girls from foreign country are 13.7%, 14.6% and 10.1% respectively which are reported in the country.
- Cases under Immoral Traffic (Prevention) Act increased by 5.2% (from 2,435 in 2011 to 2,563 in 2012).
- Offenders were known to the victims in 98.2% of Rape cases (24,470 out of 24,915).
- A total of 36,622 cases of crime against women were reported from 53 mega cities out of 2,44,270 cases reported in the country during 2012. The rate of crime in these cities at 47.76 was comparatively higher as compared to national rate at 41.74.

These are just an estimated statistics as actual figures can be much higher. Violence against women is characteristically under-reported because women are ashamed or fear skepticism, disbelief or further violence.

Violence against women is the greatest human rights scandal of our times. From birth to death, in times of peace as well as war, women face discrimination and violence at the hands of the state, the community and the family (Mazumdar, 2004). Female infanticide deprives countless women of life itself. Rape and sexual

Violence against Women Prevalence Data: Surveys by Country — *Compiled by UN Women (as of March 2011)*

Country	Survey	Coverage	Year	Intimate Partner Violence (%)						Intimate Partner and/or Non-Partner Violence (%)						Forced first sex (%)	Abuse during pregnancy (%)
				Physical		Sexual		Physical and/or Sexual		Physical		Sexual		Physical and/or sexual			
				Last 12 months	Life-time	Last 12 months	Life-time	Last 12 months	Life-time	Last 12 months	Life-time	Last 12 months	Life-time	Last 12 months	Life-time		
Ethiopia	WHO	Province	2002	29	48.7	44.4	58.6	53.7	70.9						55.9	16.6	7.5
Finland	Other	National	2005	6.3	17.6	2	4.3	7.9							43.5		
France	IVAWS	National	2002	2.5		0.9		10									
Georgia	CDC-RHS	National	2005	1.6	4.8	0.3	1.5	2	5								
Germany	IVAWS	National	2003		23		7		25		37		13		40		
Ghana	DHS	National	2008	18	20.6	5.2	8.2	20	22.9	17.2	36.6		18.8		44.5	14.9	5.2
Guatemala	CDC-RHS	National	2002	8.6		3.5											
Haiti	DHS	National	2005-2006	11.5	14.3	9.8	10.8	16.8	20	15.6	26.5						5.6
Honduras	DHS	National	2005-2006	6.3		4.4		8.6			14.7		8.7				
Hong Kong	IVAWS	National	2005	1	6	1	5	2	9	2	12	3	14		21		
India	DHS	National	2005-2006	21.4	35.1	7.2	10	23.9	37.2	18.9	33.5		8.5		35.4		
Indonesia	Other	National	2006												3.07		
Ireland	Other	National	2003	1.4	13	0.7	8	3.2	14.5								
Italy	IVAWS	National	2006	1.7	12.2	1	6.1	2.4	14.3	2.7	18.8	3.5	23.7	5.4	31.9		

abuse by relatives, other men, security officials or armed combatants are inflicted on millions of girls and women every year. Some forms of violence, such as forced pregnancies, forced abortions, bride-burning and dowry related abuses are unique to women. Others, such as domestic violence – also known as intimate partner abuse, wife beating and battering – are disproportionately suffered by women. During conflicts, violence against women is often used as a weapon of war, in order to dehumanize the women themselves, or to persecute the community to which they belong. Types of violence against women include:

Female Infanticide

Amartya Sen, the 1998 Nobel Laureate for Economics, estimates that more than 60 million women are demographically 'missing' from the world as a result of sex selective abortions and female infanticide in China, South Asia and North Africa. Infanticide has been practiced throughout human history in societies where boy children are valued, economically and socially, above girls. Technologies like amniocentesis and ultrasound used in most parts of the world, largely for detecting foetal abnormalities, has been used in large parts of the Indian subcontinent for determining the sex of the foetus so that it can be aborted, if it happens to be a female (Sheela Saravanan, 2000).Though sex determination tests are completely banned but still there are 917 females per thousand males in India according to the census of 2011, which is much below the world average of 990 females.

The 'Female Deficit'

In poor communities, little girls are often neglected and denied food, education and medical care. The women of India are prejudiced from birth itself. They are not breastfed for long whereas male members get adequate care and nutrition. Data from developing countries indicates that the mortality rate among girls aged one to four is higher than that among boys in the same age group. This is just the beginning of a lifetime pattern of discrimination against women in differential access to health care, education and leisure. This causes excess mortality among women and girls, and contributes to their lack of opportunities and powerlessness.

Table 1: Gender violence throughout the life cycle

Phase	Type of violence
Prenatal phase	Battering during pregnancy (emotional and physical effects on the woman; effects on birth); coerced pregnancy; deprivation of food and liquids; sex-selective abortion
Infancy	Female infanticide; emotional and physical abuse; differential access to food and medical care for girl infants
Childhood	Child marriage; genital mutilation; sexual abuse by family members and strangers; differential access to food and medical care; child prostitution
Adolescence	Rape and marital rape; sexual assault; forced prostitution; trafficking in women; courtship violence; economically coerced sex; sexual abuse in the workplace
Reproductive age	Abuse of women by intimate partners; marital rape; dowry abuse and murders; partner homicide; psychological abuse; sexual abuse in the workplace; sexual harassment; rape; abuse of women with disabilities; legal discrimination
Old-age	Abuse and exploitation of widows

Source: United Nations Development Programme, Regional Bureau for Latin America and the Caribbean, *A Life Free of Violence: It's our Right: United Nations Inter-Agency Campaign on Women's Human Rights in Latin America and the Caribbean* (1998)

The Feminisation of Poverty

Closely linked to the 'female deficit' is the increasing 'feminisation' of poverty. Women comprise more than two-thirds of the 2.5 billion people defined as 'poor': that is, living on less than US$2 a day. Women's economic vulnerability contributes to their vulnerability to violence - manifest when a woman cannot leave a violent partner because she has no other home or means of support. She cannot go to her parents home because of the stigma attached to it in the society.

Violence in the Family

Domestic Violence

For many women and girls, home is a place of violence. Domestic violence (or 'intimate partner violence') constitutes the most common form of violence against women worldwide, without regional exception. Other forms of violence in the family include sexual abuse of female children and dowry-related violence. Physical and sexual violence is commonly accompanied by emotional abuse, humiliation, intimidation and control (International Center for Research on Women, 2000).

Dowry Deaths

Domestic violence and murder may be related to so-called traditional practices. In India , thousands of women are victims of 'dowry deaths', killed because their bride-wealth is deemed insufficient by the groom's family. Courts are flooded with cases related to death due to dowry harassment by husband and in laws. In ancient times women were given 'Stridhan' when they departed from the house of their parents. This amount of money was given to her as a gift which she can use on her and her children but her in-laws did not have any right on that amount. This amount was supposed to help the girl in time of need. Slowly this tradition became obligatory and took the form of dowry. Nowadays parents have to give hefty amount in dowry, the in laws of their girl are not concerned whether they can afford it or not. If a girl brings large amount of dowry she is given respect and is treated well in her new home and if she does not bring dowry according to expectations of her in laws then she has to suffer harassment. Due to this evil practice many newlywed women of India have to lose their lives.

Psychological Abuse

Sometimes called mental violence, this type of abuse may include constant verbal abuse, harassment, stalking, excessive possessiveness, isolating the woman from friends and family, depriving her of physical and economic resources and destroying her personal property. Psychological abuse can lead to psychological consequences for the victim, including depression, low self esteem, fear of intimacy, inability to trust men, anxiety, antisocial behavior and, in some cases, attempted suicide.

Physical Abuse

Physical abuse may begin with grabbing, pinching or shoving and often results into more serious and more frequent attacks including kicking, punching, biting, throwing objects, holding down, and sexual assault.

Physical attacks and aggressive behavior, although they may not be life threatening at first, are not trivial and should not be excused or ignored. This abuse becomes life threatening when the attacks include choking, breaking bones or the use of weapon.

Sexual Abuse of Girls

A review of 25 studies worldwide indicates that 11 to 32 percent of women report having experienced childhood sexual abuse. Sexual abuse of girls, often by family members, is widespread but shrouded in taboo. Any time a woman is forced to take part in unwanted sexual activity, it is considered sexual violence. Physical abuse may be accompanied by sexual violence, but there is a clear and distinct line between physical domestic violence and sexual abuse. Perpetrators of sexual abuse sometimes physically harm their victims.

Prostitution

Women in prostitution suffer enormous physical and psychological health costs. The International Labour Organization has documented 'the rapes, beatings, imprisonments, sexual abuse, servitude, illness, and the permanent destruction of millions of women's souls' as a result of prostitution. Prostituted women have a high probability of acquiring sexually transmitted diseases. They commonly experience serious post-traumatic stress disorder. Many slide into drug and alcohol abuse. Suicide rates are high. Prostituted women are often maltreated by law enforcement authorities. In some cases, the police are part of the prostitution business, receiving bribe money or a sum for every transaction.

Trafficking

The volume of trafficking worldwide grew by almost 50 per cent from 1995 to 2000. The UNFPA estimates that 700,000 to two million women are trafficked across international borders annually. Women are trafficked for prostitution and other forms of sexual exploitation, for forced labour, for slavery and for the removal of their organs.

Roots of Violence

The underlying cause of violence against women lies in discrimination which denies women equality with men in all areas of life. Violence is both rooted in discrimination and serves to reinforce discrimination, preventing women from exercising their rights and freedoms on a basis of equality with men. Violence against women is an expression of historically and culturally specific values and standards. Although violence against women is universal, many women are targeted for specific forms of violence because of particular aspects of their identity. Race, ethnicity, culture, language, sexual identity, poverty and health are some of the many risk factors for violence against women. Poverty and marginalization are both causal factors leading to violence against women, and also consequences of violence.

The negative effects of globalization are leaving more and more women trapped on the margins of society. It is extremely difficult for women living in poverty to escape abusive situations, to obtain protection and to access the criminal justice system to seek redress. Illiteracy and poverty severely restrict women's ability to organize to fight for change. Young women are often subject to sexual assault not only because they are women, but also because they are young and vulnerable. Age provides no protection from violence against women. While some societies respect elderly women's wisdom and afford them greater status and autonomy, others abuse those who are frail and alone, particularly widows.

Long-term Damage and Harm to the Victim

The consequences of violence against women go far beyond immediate physical damage to the victim. Psychological damage, and the threat of further violence, erodes a woman's self-esteem, inhibiting her ability to defend herself or take action against her abuser. When the violence is unrecognized and unacknowledged, there are further psychological consequences and the woman is less likely to seek help. Some of the long-term effects of violence against women are abuse of alcohol and drugs, depression, other mental health disorders and suicide.

The repercussions of violence against women reverberate throughout the family and community (Buvinic *et al.*, 1999). Actual or threatened violence creates a pervasive atmosphere of fear that limits the lives of women, restricting their freedom of movement and their ability to participate in public decision-making and affecting their standard of living.

Violence against women impoverishes society economically, politically and culturally, by limiting the active role that women can make in the development of their community. While it is difficult to determine the full cost to society of violence against women, a growing number of studies point to the serious economic consequences, including loss of productive time, loss of earnings and medical costs. In the developing countries, an estimated five per cent of the working time lost by women because of disability or sickness results from gender-based violence.

The time has arrived for countries of the world to take action to remove the scourge of violence against women. Although legislation itself will not solve this multi-faceted problem, it can provide a platform from which women can launch a comprehensive attack on this monster. However, legal remedies alone are insufficient. There is a need to change our attitude to gender-specific violence. It is necessary to sensitize the young and the old, particularly males, that regardless of past attitudes and traditions women are not their property capable of ownership, but human beings with needs and emotions who must be respected and treated as equal partners in this complex world or ours. To eradicate gender-based violence, women must be empowered in all aspects of their lives. Women's participation is essential in decision-making, at family, community, national and international levels.

References

Buvinic, M., Morrison, A. and Shifter, M. (1999), "Violence in Latin America and the Caribbean: A Framework for Action:

Technical Study", *Sustainable Development Department*, Inter-American Development Bank, pp. 20-21.

Crime in India (2012), *National Crime Records Bureau Report*, Ministry of Home Affairs, India.

Domestic Violence in India (2000), "A Summary Report of a Multi-Site Household Survey", *International Center for Research on Women*, Washington, DC, p. 32.

Heise, L., Ellsberg, M. and Gottemoeller, M. (1999), "Ending Violence Against Women", *Population Reports*, Series L, No. 11. Baltimore, Johns Hopkins University School of Public Health, p. 1. (Hereafter Population Reports 11).

Mazumdar, Maya (2004), *Social Status of Women in India*, Delhi, Dominant Publishers and Distributors.

Parliamentary Assembly of the Council of Europe (2002), Domestic Violence against Women, Recommendation 1582.Adopted -27 September 2002.

Saravanan, Sheela. (2000), *Violence Against Women in India:A Literature Review*, Institute of Social Studies Trust (ISST) Report.

World Bank, (1994), A New Agenda for Women's Health and Nutrition, p. 14.

World Health Organization (WHO), Geneva, (2002), *World Report on Violence and Health*, p. 118. (Hereafter WHO 2002).

www.amnesty.org

3

VIOLENCE AGAINST WOMEN AND GIRLS THE IMPROVISED LIFE OF A GIRL CHILD: CASES FROM INITIATIVES OF AARAMBH-CHILDLINE

ARCHANA SAHAY

Girl child problem around the world has many dimensions but the root of all kind of discriminations and bias against the girl child lays in the customs, traditions and the typical mindset of the society which looks the girl child and women as inferior beings. Women and girls have been treated in the most inhuman ways if we look back at the last two thousand years of human civilization. This legacy is continuing even today in most parts of the world in one way or the other. Female foeticide, female infanticide, sexual abuse, marginalization in terms of nutrition, healthcare and education, violence against women and bias against women in all spheres of life including the social, political, economic and religious structures of society is a common norm even in today's world. Women and girls don't have decision making power of their own life. It is always somebody else who makes decisions for them.

Women in many parts of the world don't even have control of their own body and mind. Her reproductive and sexual rights are also compromised. Let me give some examples in this regard. Female Genital Mutilation is still practiced in many parts of the world. Half of the total sexual assaults are committed against girls age 15 or younger. An adolescent girl is married without her consent and becomes pregnant long before her body is ready. The leading cause of death for girls age 15-19 is complications from pregnancy and this is a glimpse of the girl child problem. Thus we can imagine the way women and girls are treated.

Girl Child Problem: The Improvised Life of a Girl Child

The girl child lives an improvised life. In Many places she does not get proper care in terms of food and nutrition, healthcare, security and education. For that matter she does not get love and protection from her own immediate family. She is forced into drudgery and house slavery from a very tender age. Whether at home, in factories or in the field, the little girls are always at work. She starts work at a very young age, and works from dawn to dusk, proving the adage. "A girl is never a child." She is not allowed to enjoy the beautiful days of her childhood when it is the ripe time to learn and grow. The girl child is abused sexually and violence against the girl child is a common phenomenon in many societies. In the name of customs, traditions and the typical mindset that exists in the society her body is mutilated and her reproductive and sexual rights are compromised. She is not sent to school. If she goes to school then most of the times she is forced to drop out of school by the age of puberty and she is forcefully married to someone to live a life of misery and slavery.

In India alone, more than 10,000 girl babies are victims of infanticide each year. If it doesn't kill her by infancy, violence is an ever present danger throughout her girlhood and throughout the rest of her life. Female foeticide, infanticide, rape, sexual abuse of the girl child and violence against girl child and women should be considered as the most heinous forms of crime against humanity and strictest forms of punishment should be reserved for the perpetuators. Further all round support should be extended to the victims including physical, psychological, legal and economic care. Apart from enforcement of strict laws it is also necessary to prevent crimes against the girl child through education and communication which promotes gender sensitization and gender based equality.

Many customs and traditions of our society propagate gender based bias, discrimination and violence. The real reason of the girl child problem stems from these highly deplorable customs and traditions that are practiced in the society. For example the custom of dowry is one of the main reasons for the practice of female foeticide and infanticide. Child marriage and early marriage curtails her chance for a decent education and in fact compromises her life with problems like premature pregnancy. Custom, culture and tradition are used as justifications for discriminatory and violent treatment against the girl child. This includes early and forced marriage, limited access to education, teenage pregnancy and the consequent impacts on health and education, and social acceptance of violent punishment of children. As a consequence, the situation of the girl child is characterized by a growing incidence of girl children in child labour, higher health risks, including exposure to HIV and AIDS, continued growing rates of teenage pregnancy, low self-esteem and psychological damage among girls. A little girl eats last and least and she is up to three times more likely than boys to suffer malnutrition. She is often not taken to the doctor when she is sick and she is less likely to be immunized. Girls are often kept out of school and put to work. If she does go to school, she's still at risk.

The Girl Child Problem: The Need to Change the Mindset

The mindset of looking at the girl child as a lesser being, a liability or a property needs to change if we want to address the girl child problem. All the discrimination and bias originate from this kind of regressive approach in the society and it eventually leads to heinous crimes like female foeticide and infanticide. The other side of the story is that even if the girl child comes into this world she faces a life full of dislike, marginalization and neglect in as many forms as possible. A small support if given timely can help them to fight for their own rights.

A few examples of cases which were successfully dealt by Childline Bhopal a Project run by AARAMBH an NGO Working for Child Rights.

Case Stories of Survivors from Violence against Girl Child With the support of Child Line 1098 -Bhopal A Project of AARAMBH Bhopal

Case -1

Ab Aur Nahi.....Minor rescued from Physical and Sexual Abuse

Rani aged 10years migrated from Chhattisgarh to Bhopal along with her elder sister aged 22 years and two more siblings last two years back. Her elder sister was lured by one lady with all promises of a better living for her and her two sisters aged 10 and 5,and one brother aged 13years.The lady arranged a job at a farm house and they got settled, until the day when the lady gave her Sister an offer to marry one man who belonged to a different caste. She got married to him, and thus the life started becoming hell for her and her siblings.

On 4th January , 2014 an unknown person gave the information to Childline Bhopal, that in Kanha Saiya village falling in the jurisdiction of Bilkheriya Thana, there is a 10 year old girl whose brother-in-law physical tortures her and has also tried to sexually abuse her many times. He has also forced her brother who is 14 years old to work in hotel as bonded labor and their younger sister aged 5-6 years is missing since last one year. Their brother-in-law beats them a lot. The girl has not gone to school since last 1 month. Kindly help them.

After receiving the information, the team did the social investigation at the village and reported the matter to the Police Station and informed the Child Welfare Committee. The TI took the case very seriously, and sent the Police team along with the Childline team to rescue the girl and her brother. The team rescued the girl from the farm and her brother from the hotel where he was working as bonded labor .They arrested the brother-in-law and brought him to the police station.

The children's custody was given to the Childline team and next day the FIR was lodged.

The story which the children revealed was horrified. The girl informed that after their sister married the man, for a few days everything went off well , but after sometime the brother-in-law started fighting and beating their sister and lately them also. One day the fight went so bad that their sister left him without informing and never returned till date. He then started beating the three of us and one day he took the brother to one hotel and made him work as bonded labor and also took Rs. 7500/- as advance money.

After that he started torturing the two girls and one fine day the younger one went missing. When she enquired about her sister he said that he has left her with his own sister. And thus she was left alone with him. One day the school teachers asked him to get her admitted to the school to which he disagreed, but after a lot of pressure on him he admitted her. She faced a lot of problem because of his physical abuse and his often attempts of molestation. She also stopped going to school .This went off for many days until somebody informed Childline.

The Police then made a search for the younger one and visited all the places mentioned by the man. After a search of three days and with the pressure of the Police he revealed on the fourth day that he has killed the younger on last one year back and threw her body in one of the Nallah near Baghsevenia. This was very shocking to all as well as the brother and sister. The police then charged him with murder case also and now he is behind the bar. The case is still going on and we all are hoping for serious punishment.

Case-2

The Menace.....for being a Girl.....

The day Akansha was born no one was happy ...because she was a girl. But she still survived with all the neglect and abuse, specially her grandmother and her own mother.

On 20th January,2013 Sub Inspector Sandhu from Habibganj Police Station called the Childline office and informed that they have found a 6 year old girl who was badly beaten by her mother and grandmother. The girl does not want to go home. Kindly help her.

After getting the information the team reached the police station. The girl was crying and she was very much scared . The little girl had many marks on her body of getting beaten up. SI Sandhu informed that they had found the girl during the night Police patrolling. The team took the girl under them and after looking at her wounds immediately took her to the hospital for treatment and informed the Child Welfare Committee. The story narrated by her was very sad. She at a tender age feels that if she was Boy she wouldn't faced such behavior from her family members. She revealed that her father does the work of painting and is out of the house most of the time. Till he is there at home the troubles are less, but once he is out her mother as well as her grandmother curses her and beats her for petty reasons.

For the current incidence she told that while she was playing she lost her gold nose ring which was gifted by her father on her birthday and thus she was beaten up badly by both mother and grandmother. She also informed that her grandmother had hit her 6 months back also so badly that she had fractured her hand. Now as it was unbearable she decided to run away never to return. Thus she was found by the Police .

The team took the girl to TT Nagar Police station where the case was filed under IPC Section 294/323 and Juvenile Justice (Care and Protection)Act 2000 under Section 23 ..

After this the team presented the girl in front of the CWC committee to get her shelter.

The mother and the grandmother of the girl were also presented before the CWC where they were scolded by the committee members and they gave the orders that the girl will be staying in the shelter home only. The case reached the court and as per her statement she was not handed over to her parents. She was sent to a girl's shelter home till the next order of the court.

Case -3

16 -Years old Afreen gets a chance at a new life....

Afreen's life became hell as soon as her mother died. Her life was so happy and cheerful with her mother, father also was so loving and caring. But everything got changed as soon as she lost her mother because of illness. On 8th June 2013 that one caller called up Childline and informed that she has found a 15-16 yr old girl in a very bad condition. She needs shelter. Kindly help.

The team immediately reached the spot and brought her safely. The team made her comfortable and next day spoke to the girl. She told that she is from Bhopal and since her mother's death when her father re-married, her life became hell. Her Step-Mother often beats her for petty reasons and the most horrified incident her step mother's brother often molested her and twice she was raped also. The first time when she was raped she gave the information about the same to Hanuman Ganj Thana with her neighbours. But her family members faked the report and told at the police station that she is mentally retarded and made the Police understand and thus they handed her over back to the to the family. She was beaten up again very badly by all including her father for reporting to the Police. After a month she was raped again and this time she decided to run away.

Somehow she met the lady and she came forward to help her and thus she called Childline. The matter was reported to the Police Station. Her step Uncle was booked under different sections of IPC and POCSO Act 2012.At present she is staying at the girls children's home. The Charge sheet has been produced at the Court and the hearing is on.

Case -4

A small help changed the life....

An unknown person from Baghseveniya area of Bhopal called up Childline and informed that there is a 12 year child (girl) in problem and her father is in jail after killing her mother. The Child, her brother and sister were handed over to her uncle (maternal uncle) by the court. Her uncle is very abusive and tortures the girl very badly .Kindly help. After getting the information Childline team immediately reached to the area and gave information to Thana In-charge. The team along with police reached the spot and met child. She had wounds on her head and back side, the child was totally frightened and she requested that her siblings also need support.

The children were brought to the Thana and the girl was taken for medical test and treatment. The case was registered under Sec 23 of J J Act 2000 and IPC Section 506,294 IPC.A search was made for her grandmother and other family members. Media also gave a good support.

Reading the news paper, the child's grandmother and Paternal uncle reached Bhopal and gave an application at SCPCR to take the custody of the children. Child protection commission asked Child line to take the children to the jail along with the family members and take the consent of the father .The three children were taken to the Central jail. The father gave the consent in front of the Commission members and thus they were handed over to their uncle and grandmother. The Child line team dropped them to their village at Raipur Baresiya road.

After two months the follow up was done and the children were found happy.

Case -5

Why? it happens to me only always.....is it because I am a girl?

Anushaka a 13 year old girl doesn't even know when she lost her own father. The person whom she knew from her tender age as her father was her step father, but she was happy because he loved her equally as her younger step sister who is around 6-7yrs younger to her. But one thing which troubled her always were the regular fights among her parents with each other.

Life was going on ... as well as the fights, until one day when her father was hit badly by some people and was seriously injured. After a few days her mother was caught by the police and was sent to jail. Lately she came to know that her father had informed the Police that her mother had hired some people to kill him and thus she has been charged with attempt to murder along with three more people who had beaten her father.

Since she was in jail their father put both of us in residential school .She lost one year of schooling because of all the issues.

Anushka was relieved for some months from the fights but kept on worrying for her mother. Their father used to visit them in the school with a promise that he will take them home during Durga Puja Holidays and will also take them to meet their mother. The day the holidays were beginning they were happy as they were going home. On 11th of October 13 their father brought both of them home and took them to enjoy Durga Puja. The same Night they slept well. Next day again ie. on 12th he took them around and returned at night. Her younger sister slept and she was watching TV when he called her and said that come we will watch TV in their grandfather's room. She agreed and at around 11pm he closed the door and started playing with her clothes and when she resisted he threatened her and took off all my clothes and raped me.

She cried a lot but he did not leave her. He went out and she was in pain, but after an hour he again came back and repeated the same. She almost fainted and she did not know when she slept or got unconscious. Next day morning ie. 13th with great difficulty she got up and as he had threatened her to be quite and that either he will kill her or will kick her out of the house she kept quite. He then asked both the girls to get ready as he was taking them to meet their mother in the jail. They went and met but she could not inform her mother regarding the happening. While returning he took them to meet one of her Uncle (maternal uncle) at Ayodhya Nagar. There they both had a big fight and they started fighting and hitting each other badly.

The matter reached the Police Station and we also reached there. While they were accusing each other her father told the Police that her Uncle tried to molest her and has also raped her, when he said this she started crying and then the SHO called her and asked why she was crying .She pulled up courage and told him that her father is speaking lies. He guessed something is wrong and called one lady Police. She took her inside and then she revealed everything and he immediately called Childline for Help. The team rushed to the Police Station and met the child. Mean while Police caught the father under Section 376, Section 506 of IPC along with

Section 5(n), Setion 10 of POSCO, 2012 and the investigations began.

SP then asked Childline Director to take the custody of the child and give the consent for Medical Examination. As there was no other option the Director took the custody, gave consent in writing and along with the police took her for Medical examination. By 3.30 am the medical got over and the sealed report and other evidences were handed over. She was also provided medicines for the external and internal injuries. The Case hearing is in the process and at present with the order of CWC the children are residing at the girls home. Childline Team is regularly meeting with the girls at the home and trying to bring her out of the trauma.

Towards the End ......

If we change our outlook and look at the other side then we can see the immense benefits and contributions that a girl child can make to the society. An empowered girl child becomes an educated, employed, confident, assertive and empowered woman in the future and a strong woman then becomes a supportive pillar for the nurturing and growth of the next generation of humanity. It creates a positive cycle which is beneficial for the individual, the family, the society, the nation and the world. We should also acknowledge the reality that girls cannot advance without the advancement of women and no improvement in women's lives will be sustained unless girls have education, good health and the opportunity to achieve their potential. So empowerment of women and girls are mutually inclusive and supportive phenomenon and it has the greatest overall positive effect on the health and well-being of a society. This happens because of various factors which include decreased population growth, faster economic growth, less corruption in governance, increased agricultural production, more children in school, reduced health hazards, lower childhood malnutrition and lower child mortality.

4

CYBER CRIMES AGAINST WOMEN

BHAMATHI BALASUBRAMANIAM

In the digital age, Information and Communication Technology (ICT) is benefiting billions across the world by bridging certain gaps and multiplying human potential in every walk of life. However, this growth has not been without negative influences in the social, political and economic realm. The ugly side of telecommunication technologies has reared its head globally in the form of cyber crimes.

Cyber crime is a fast growing, pernicious, global phenomenon enabled by the advent of and fast growing ICT. The Cambridge English Dictionary defines Cyber crimes as crimes committed with the expert use of computer technology or crime committed over the Internet, involving the use of computer as both tool and target. All these crimes are committed inside and outside cyber space. This could include a wide variety of criminal offences, including conventional crimes. Hence, those crimes that are committed against individuals and institutions, with an intention to harm a victim, directly or indirectly, using IT and telecommunication networks, such as, internet constitute cyber crimes. Cyber crimes could be sexual and non sexual in nature. The focus of this article is on sexual crimes in the cyber domain.

The types of Crime included in the above definition are

(i) Cyber crimes against property viz. financial crime, cheating online, illegal funds transfer, tampering computer source documents

(ii) Cyber crimes against persons viz. cyber pornography, obscene publication/ transmission in electronic form, cyber stalking, online harassment etc. and

(iii) Cyber crimes against nations viz. cyber terrorism, hacking, damaging critical information infrastructures, hate crimes

Global Scenario

Cyber crime is an uniquely gendered phenomenon as can be deduced from the above definition of cyber crime. However, globally, victimization of women in the cyber space has never been considered seriously or has been trivialised. Globally, the statistics of WHOA viz.halt online abuse, which documents statistics on cyber stalking, a more commonly recognized and reported crime, has clearly brought out that consistently high trend ratio of female victims and male harassers, demonstrating women's higher vulnerability. In India, the annual NCRB report, published by the Ministry of Home Affairs, has devoted a separate chapter on cyber crimes, but fails to show gender cum age disaggregated data.

Year	*Victims*	
	Women	*Men*
2000	87%	13%
2001	79.3%	16%
2002	71%	28
2003	70	27
2004	69	18
2010	73	27

Source: Crime in India Report, NCRB,2012 , Ministry of Home Affairs, GOI.

Differential Impact on Men and Women

Secondly, the differential impact on women has not been given due recognition. Cyber crimes against women results, for example, in considerable social stigma, loss of professional reputation, especially, when shown as sex. objects and when commodification of women takes place. Cyber Crime against women invokes women's sexuality and gender in ways that undermines women's agency, livelihoods, dignity and wellbeing. The subsequent harm experienced by women is specific to women, because men do not typically experience sexual threats and comments indicating their inferiority based on gender.

Based on the UN General Assembly Resolution 1997, India is one of the very few countries to enact IT Act 2000 to combat cyber crimes. The first step in this direction was taken to promote e -commerce. However, with increase in crimes on the internet viz. child pornography, cyber terrorism, video voyeurism, publishing sexually explicit content in electronic form, an amendment to IT Act was passed in 2008 and notified in 2009.

Typology of Crimes and Case Studies

The types of cyber crimes that are being committed and the relevant Indian case studies are as follows-

Cyber stalking is where adult men, stàlk vulnerable women or children, as paedophiles. They follow the victim stealthily in the virtual world using free mail and website space as also the anonymity provided by chat room forums to harass for love, revenge, hate etc. The Delhi Police has recently registered India's first case of cyber stalking. One Ms X complained to the police against a person, who was using her identity to chat over the Internet at the website *www.mirc.com.* She further complained that the person was chatting on the Net, using her name and giving her address and was using obscene language. The same person was also deliberately giving her telephone number to other chatters encouraging them to call her at odd hours. Consequently, she received almost 40 calls in three days mostly at odd hours from as far away as Kuwait, Cochin, Bombay and Ahmedabad. The said calls created havoc in the personal life and mental peace of Ms X who decided to report the matter. The IT Act could not be invoked as cyber stalking is not covered under the cyber laws in India. It is covered only under the ambit of Section 72 of the IT Act which states that perpetrator can be booked remotely for breach of confidentiality and privacy. The police filed a criminal case under section 509 IPC (outraging the modesty of women).

In another case, an engineering and management graduate, facing prosecution in a dowry harassment case, was arrested by Delhi police for sending obscene e-mails in his wife's name to several persons. In June 2000, a man was arrested by the Delhi police for assuming the identify of his ex-employer's wife in a chat channel an encouraging others to telephone net. The victim who was getting obscene telephone calls at night from stranger made a complaint to the police. The accused was then located "on line" in the chat room under the identity of the victim and later traced through the telephone number used by him to access the internet (Mishra, 2001).

A study[1] states that 12.5% of the respondents had intimate relationship with their cyber stalker before the stalking started. According to the research, 62.5% cases of harassment started through emails and online chats.

A case was registered under U/s 509 IPC r/w 66A, 66D IT Act,on a complaint received from one Ms Y residing in Delhi. It has been alleged in the complaint that she came to know that some unknown person had created a facebook profile and posted some vulgar and unparliamentarily comments about the complainant. She strongly suspected her estranged husband and her family members behind this. Details from facebook showed that alleged profile had been created and accessed from her in-laws' factory. It was also proved that the said account was accessed through a mobile registered in her husband's name but used by her uncle. Accordingly, her husband, brother in law and father in law were arrested after collecting necessary evidences from the concerned service providers.

Cyber Pornography includes sexually explicit pornographic sites, magazines produced/published using computers and Internet and then disseminated as pictures, writings, photos etc. In a recent case, of a male student of a well known public School In Delhi took revenge for being teased for his pock-marked face, by scanning pictures of teachers and classmates morphing them with nude photographs and uploading on to free web hosting service. When one of the girls of his class was detected on the website to be a victim, then a case was filed under sec 67 of the IT Act. The 16 year old boy was arrested and rusticated.

In another case of Delhi, a complaint was received by Delhi Police alleging therein that some unknown person had posted obscene pictures of her daughter and their residence telephone number on some pornographic websites, as a result of which she was getting unsolicited calls. On analyzing the logs received from the said websites, it was found that these images and information were uploaded from Holland. But due to no-availability of any treaty with Holland details of the user of the IP address could not be collected. In view of the cumbersome procedures involved, the complainants didn't want to pursue the matter as the said information was removed from the websites. Accordingly, the case had to be filed as untraced.

In another case of Delhi, the complainant reported that her daughter was working as junior engineer with an IT company in Mumbai. Prior to her present job, complainant's daughter posted her resume for a job to one company in Bangalore from where one Mr. X, an Indian, presently residing in USA started chatting with her on internet. Thereafter the victim got her present job in Mumbai and stopped chatting with the said MrX. On this he got enraged and started threatening her and in order to tarnish her image he uploaded lascivious material about the girl on the internet. The IP Logs activity revealed that all the uploading was done from USA. For details, a Letter Rogatory (LR) was sent but even after sending the LR the concerned website/ internet administrators in USA have not provided any details. So, in absence of required evidences, it has not been possible for the police to proceed further in the matter.

In 2009, Ms X, a Tamil cum Bollywood actress found her morphed photos being used in the adult entertainment sites. The tormentor, who had taken pictures without her consent during film shoots and used them to harass her, was later arrested by the police. Ms. SaniaMirza was another public personage who suffered, similarly.

Cyber Harassment is involved when offender calls either by his/her own name or by acquiring false identity by making landline calls/mobile calls, web based calls, VOIP calls, Skype, Yahoo messenger, Chat room calls, overseas calls etc.

In a case of Delhi, the complainant alleged that some unknown person has created a fake profile in her name on the social networking site www.facebook.com and posted morphed photographs depicting the complainant's face and nude female bodies of other women. The accused also sent SMSs on her phone to harass her. A case was filed under sec 67 of the IT Act. During investigation, the registrant and user IP log data was collected from Facebook. The IP logs so received were of ISP Airtel broadband and MTNL. The user details were collected from the ISPs MTNL and Airtel. The complainant was examined and she said that they suspected a boy in the opposite flat to be behind the crime. The log activity was traced to the computer and mobile phone of the same boy. In view of accused were seized and he was arrested.

In Mumbai, a complaint was lodged by a woman against the CEO of a Cricket Club stating that he had flooded her mail inbox with mails carrying obscene video clippings for over 2 years, before she finally reported to the cyber crime police.

Cyber Hacking

Recently, a software engineer who allegedly used fictitious email IDs and Facebook accounts to post defamatory messages about a woman, who spurned his marriage offer, was arrested by the cyber crime police officials in Hyderabad. The arrested techie, hacked the victim's email accounts, sent obscene content from those accounts about her. He had even created false profiles on Facebook and began chatting with her friends and relatives just to defame her. He had also tried to cover up his tracks by using proxy servers, but to no avail. Cyber sleuths gathered information from different service providers and traced the obscene content. The police waited for his return to India from United States and arrested him. He is facing charges under different sections of law including sections 66- A, 67 of IT Act 2000 and Sections 506 and 384 of the Indian Penal code. Quoting his confession statement police said, the arrested person had initially moved decently with the woman till he gained her confidence. He shared his family problems with her and details of his road accident and befriended her. Later he proposed to her, but she declined the request. Then on, he began harassing her initially by calling her on her mobile. Later he began to harass her with the fictitious emails and facebook posts.

Anecdotal references to incidence of Cyber Crimes against Women in India

Delhi

According to Pavan Duggal, advocate with the Supreme Court of India, While cyber crime cases continue to take place, only one out of 500 cases is reported (in M. Neela Malar,2012) and of the 40 cases of obscenity only 10 were registered. Following is the data on complaints received by Delhi Police since 2011..

Year	*2011*	*2012*	*2013 (up to July)*
Defamation/Impersonate	42	63	29
E-mail hacking	74	99	20
Fake profile	98	122	35
Harassment	24	31	19
Threatening	16	20	02
Miscellaneous	26	23	21
Total	280	358	126

However, compare the above data with published data of incidence of crimes registered in Delhi and reported by NCRB during 2011 and 2012, as shown below.

Incidence of Cases Registered Under Cyber Crimes in States/UTs During 2011 & 2012 and Percentage Variation

State/UT	*IT ACT*			*IPC Section*		
	2011	*2012*	*% Variation*	*2011*	*2012*	*% Variation*
Delhi	50	76	52.0	49	8	-83.7

The yawning gap between complaints filed and cases registered needs further exploration as to why women complaints do not get converted into registered cases.

Mumbai

While social networking and micro-blogging sites are great tools to stay connected, they are also easy to misuse. And mostly, it's women who are the victims, as per the Mumbai cyber crime police. An increasing number of women are approaching the cyber crime cell with complaints that their fake profiles with obscene content have been posted on sites such as Facebook, Orkut and Twitter.In 2009, the police received 268 applications of fake profiles, obscene content and defamation, but only nine cases were registered. Mumbai Police received 160 applications till June 30, 2012, but only six cases have been registered, so far. Though such incidents are on the rise, few victims are willing to register a case. Cyber security consultant Vijay Mukhi, who works with the police in such cases, explains that victims are afraid to proceed with complaints, as that could lead to exposure and social humiliation. Most victims want the obscene profiles deleted after which they are not interested in proceeding with complaints: Most complainants prefer with drawing their applications once the offender has been traced.

Pune

The increasing number of cyber crimes is a concern for the Pune police. Pune Police receive one or two complaints of cyber crime from women. But for Ms.Meera Borwankar, the city's first woman police commissioner, an even more serious issue is that of cyber crimes, especially against educated and professionally qualified young women in the city. She (2012) stated that many women victims want their problems to be solved, but are not willing to lodge a formal first information report (FIR), as they fear privacy issues, such as the possibility of their identity being revealed to the public..

Vishakapatnam

According to Inspector of Cyber Crimes Investigation Cell, Visakhapatnam, women and girls in Vizag are prime targets of cyber criminals either through abusive and filthy mails, uploading of objectionable pictures, online frauds, online threats or morphed profile pictures on Facebook and other social networks. There were more female victims than male in cyber crimes in Vizag in the last few years. According to statistics compiled by Cyber Crimes Investigation Cell in the city, a total of 153 cases were recorded under the IT Act in Vizag in 2012, around 100 cases out of 153 were lodged by women, including students, employees of private organisations and married women. Every month nearly 20 to 30 cases of cyber crimes are reported in the city and most of the victims are women and girl students. Rao said that the maximum number of complaints are related to lewd messages, uploading morphed images of girls on Facebook as also debit and credit card frauds. Police sources said that the majority of the accused in cyber crimes turn out to be friends or relatives of the victims. Differences with women or girls over petty issues lead to harassment of the women with abusive SMSes or phone calls.

Thiruvananthapuram

As many as 80,000 cyber crime-related complaints have been registered with police in Kerala in the last one year, of which 50,000 relate to harassment of women through new hi-tech devices as per the Home Minister, Kerala. Most victims of these crimes were teenage girls and women, he said, adding, there was a "nefarious attempt" to trap young girls to indulge in wrong doing. The increase in number of mobile phones has also led to an increase in the number of cyber crimes, he said, adding that Kerala now has three crore RPT and three crore mobile phones. Crimes were also reported by misusing social networking system and internet, he said.

Coimbatore

Though cyber crimes are on a steady rise in Coimbatore and the police cell dealing with it receives numerous complaints every week, a peculiar situation is emerging with petitioners refusing to proceed with the case after the person who sent the offensive data through email or mobile phone is identified and made to confess the crime. In most cases, the suspect is someone known to the petitioner and the petitioner is satisfied with an apology from the offender the criminal is traced. Petitioners are preventing us from registering FIRs and ensuring a closure to the case by moving the court," as per a senior police officer working with the Cyber Crime Cell.

Evidence from Studies and Surveys

- While a survey of literature shows that there are very few independent studies and surveys on cyber crimes against women in India, they are part of larger studies on crimes against women. The most researched among the cyber crimes against women is cyber stalking
- According to an Indian survey, both men and women are affected by cyberstalking, but a survey in India found that victims aged between 18-32 were predominantly females (Xu, Weiting- *www.genderit.org/es/node/2212*)
- Centre for cyber victim counseling an organization which works with victims of cyber crimes and involved in its prevention conducted a baseline survey in India. On cyber victimization of women and reporting behaviour, the following emerged-:
- 11.7%experienced bad incidences in the internet
- 85% received abusive mails with sexual images and dirty messages etc. from known /unknown senders in her email
- 16.7% received repeated mails from the same individual/asking to befriend him/them

- 50% received threatening mails from ex boyfriends /husbands
- 75.0% received sexually teasing remarks / images in her social networking profile / associated mail / message box
- 48.3% has been victim of hacking
- 40.0% has been victim of cyber stalking
- 61.7%has been victim of impersonation
- 71.7% were defamed in the cyber space / in the real space due to cyber activities of others
- 41.7% has received hate messages
- 45.0% has been targeted because of her sexuality/ feministic ideologies
- 33.3% were victims of morphing
- 33.3% has been bullied
- 40% were victimized by her virtual friend /s
- 50.0% has seen her cloned profile
- 76.7% feel that women are prone to victimization in the cyberspace
- 38.3% feel women's communities/groups etc are safe to discuss feminine issues
- 35.0% reported victimization
- 8.3% reported to police / lawyers

Court Observations/Rulings

1. Karan Girotravs State: The reported case on cyber stalking pertained to an application for granting bail. The petitioner was alleged to have blackmailed the complainant with nude and obscene pictures of her taken after the petitioner enticed her to visit his house before marrying her and after her first marriage failed. The petitioner had befriended her on internet. In this case, though the Court rejected the plea for anticipatory bail by the petitioner, it inter alia, observed that there was delay in lodging FIR by the complainant. The judiciary's bias to cases of cyber stalking was revealed.

2. *Dr.L.Prakash v. Superintendent:* In this case the accused was an orthopaedic surgeon forced women to perform sexual acts and later on uploaded and sold these videos as adult entertainment materials worldwide. He was*((2008) 3 MLJ (Crl) 578)* charged under section 506,whichprescribes punishment for criminal intimidation to cause death or grievous hurt), 367 (which deals with kidnapping or abduction for causing death or grievous hurt) and 120-B (criminal conspiracy) of the IPC and Section 67 of Information Technology Act, 2000 (which dealt with obscene publication in the internet). He was sentenced for life imprisonment and a pecuniary fine of Rupees 1, 25,000 under the Immoral Trafficking (Prevention) Act, 1956.

3. *State of Tamil Nadu v. SuhasKatti:* In this case the accused Katti posted obscene, defamatory messages about a divorced woman in the yahoo message group and advertised her as a solicit for sex. This case is considered as one of the first cases to be booked under the Information Technology Act, 2000 (IT Act). He was convicted under section 469, 509 of Indian Penal Code (IPC) and 67 of the IT Act 2000 and was punished with 2 years rigorous imprisonment and fine.

4. *Avinash Bajaj vs State of Delhi:* In the case of Avinash Bajaj, CEO of Bazee.com, an online auction website was arrested for distributing pornography. The criminal charge arose from the fact that video clips of sexual acts of two school going children was shot on their mobile phone. The pornographic CD was put on sale through bazee.com website. The CEO was prosecuted under section 292 IPC and sec 67 of the IT Act, although he claimed that he was only a service provider through his platform and in any case, the CD was withdrawn once he came to know of the content. The SC held that bazee.com had taken commission on the sale of CD to 8 buyers all over the country in no time after instantaneous copies were made i.e "published" and disseminated, which is prohibited under s/67 of the ACT. Till the amendment to the IT ACT came about, the existing Laws under IPC, The Indian Post office Act, 1898 and the Indecent Representation of Women (prohibition) Act 1986 made only obscene visual representation as focus of legislation. The amendment brought audio materials and simulated images under the purview of crime

5. ***PIL before SC Seeks to Block Child Porn*****:** Recently, a Bench of Supreme Court (SC) headed by the former Chief Justice Altamas Kabirin April 2013 sought response from the Union Government on a PIL plea to block and ban porn sites on the Web, mainly those which show child pornography. The SC described these sites as the major cause of crime against women. The Apex Court has issued notices to the ministries of Information and Broadcasting, Home Affairs, Information and Technology as well as Internet Service Providers Association of India. The notices were issued on the petition seeking to bring an anti-pornography law, as no law now exists against viewing pornography which is not an offence in India.

6. *MTNL case in Delhi High Court:* Personal viewing of obscenity is not mentioned as a crime in the IT Act. Recently, a female employee working as an assistant of state-controlled Mahanagar Telephone Nigam Limited (MTNL) accused her male colleagues of sexual harassment by 'forcing her to watch porn'. The matter came to light, after the aggrieved employee approached the Delhi High Court, as MTNL had failed to take any action against the woman's complaint. They used to surf porn websites from the office premises on a regular basis. On many occasions, they forced her inside the room to watch the sites with them. When she protested, they hurled abuses. The petition also stated that the colleagues of the victim extended threats and abuses to her after she objected to her male colleagues' acts. The victim stated that though MTNL had constituted an internal committee to probe the allegations against the four male employees, they had been 'let off with a mere warning'. The victim herself was transferred to another branch office when she protested against committee's decision of not punishing the accused. Admonishing MTNL for its insensitivity, Honble Justice Rajiv Shakdhar asked that on what basis was the victim, and not the accused, transferred to another location. MTNL has been ordered to file a reply to victim's charges

IT Act and Gender Sensitive Enforcement of Laws

1. It is clear from the above that the IT Act does not define cyber crime. Nor do all forms of cyber crimes come under the purview of the Act. Many of these

crimes come under the IPC. The Act is gender neutral and talks about security of persons, but makes no specific reference to crimes against women. While, the Act has termed certain offences, such as hacking (sec 66), publishing of obscene materials in the net (sec 67), tampering the data (sec 65) as punishable offences, it does not mention the crimes of cyber stalking, morphing and e mail spoofing as offences. Internet crime has outpaced the growth and evolution of internet laws.

2. While cases of cyber stalking are being booked under sec 509 IPC, it is clear that section 509 IPC does not cover cyber stalking. Sec 509 IPC stipulates that a word must be uttered or a sound or gesture must be made or any object must be exhibited. This is not applicable for chats on the Net to establish cyber stalking. Further, proving criminal intent in a case relating to insulting the modesty of any woman in cyberspace becomes difficult to establish in a court of law. It will be equally difficult to apply the other condition of sec 509 which talks about intruding upon the privacy of such woman. How would the courts adjudicate upon the intrusion of privacy of any woman in Cyberspace, which as a medium is free and unbounded. Hence, the police are booking cases under Section 441 of the IPC for criminal trespass.
3. Another cyber law issue concerning cyber stalking is something which court would have jurisdiction to try the offence of cyberstalking. There is a need to create more awareness amongst the legislature

and the law enforcing agencies regarding this new cyber crime in order to enable its early regulation.

4. Again, under no section in IT ACT 2000, Obscenity – personal viewing – Is an offence, in fact as in IPC sec 292 again if it is proved that you have published or transmitted or caused to be published in the electronic form only then under Section 67 it can be an offence.
5. The elementary problems, which are associated with cyber-crimes in general and those specifically relating to women, are jurisdiction, loss of evidence, lack of cyber forensics, lack of cyber army and cyber savvy judges who are the need of the day.
6. Judiciary plays a vital role in shaping the enactment according to the order of the day. One such stage, which needs appreciation, is the P.I.L., which the Kerala High Court has accepted through an email. Today with the growing arms of cyberspace, the territorial boundaries seem to vanish and thus the concept of territorial jurisdiction as envisaged under S.16 of C.P.C. and S.2.of the I.P.C. will have to give way to alternative method of dispute resolution.

Conclusion

Victimisation of women through cyber space is an extension of the pre internet era of offline crimes against women. The offline and online crimes have a symbiotic relationship and feed and build on one another. The Indian case studies quoted above show that victimization of women, especially single or divorced women, is focused on hitting women where it hurts most viz. through defamation, lowering the dignity, blackmailing, questioning and damaging the reputation and character and creating fear among women victims. The harassment and violations as in non-cyber, non-technological crime domains are carried out by either by individuals, or by a group. The motivational factors for online crimes against women are very much the same as offline crimes, revolving as they do around broken relationships, ex-partner harassments, professional rivalry, male dominance etc. However, it has become a more convenient mode of victimisation, as it gives anonymity to the perpetrators and the space to create and operate in crime hubs with impunity. The crime hubs or the platforms constitute a wide variety viz. social networking sites, chat rooms, blogs , message boards. The lack of expertise and capacity among the police, prosecutors and the judiciary over and above institutional and historical gender insensitivity to crimes against women, poor cyber forensics etc. have contributed to very low reporting, low registration of cases, poor investigations and low convictions.

Information and communications technologies (ICTs) like the internet and mobile phones are a double-edged sword – they can be used by abusers to deepen their control and by survivors of violence to connect to help and by women's rights defenders to inform, denounceand strategies to end violence. While the former is gaining unprecedented ground with the internet laws unable to keep pace with the vicious developments of the crime profile and the latter yet to be born in India, the stakeholders especially the government and in a great measure the private sector, the service providers need to sensitise their constituencies, especially the police, prosecutors and the judiciary on gender and crimes against women. Besides, trained personnel on cyber crimes should be a part of specialized units to be set up to investigate crimes, especially those against women.

There is no comprehensive, nationwide data on the magnitude, dimensions and extent of various forms of cyber crime in India. There is a need to reach out to some Internet Service Providers to compile statistics on the number and types of complaints of harassment and/ or threats involving their subscribers. There is also a need to conduct research on the profile of victims and perpetrators of all forms of cyber crime and the differential impact viz. Social, physical, emotional, psychological, economic, professional on men and women. While law enforcement agencies have compiled some helpful statistics, it is important to generate and publish gender cum age disaggregated data in the public domain.

Note

1. A Study conducted on 72 women by Megha Desai and K Jaishankar [1]

References

Debarati Halder and K. Jaishankar (2011), *Cyber crime and the Victimization of Women: Laws, Rights, and Regulations,.* Hershey, PA, USA:

Malar, M. Neela (2012), "Impact of Cyber Crimes on Social Networking Pattern of Girls", *International Journal of Internet of Things*, 2012; 1(1): 9-15.

Mishra R C. (2001), *Crime Trends and Criminal Justice, Author's Press: Delhi Delhi.*

National Crime Records Bureau.*Crime In India Report*, (2012), NCRB, Ministry of Home Affairs, GOI.

Xu, Weiting. (*www.genderit.org/es/node/2212*).

Note: Court cases discussed by the author of the paper are self written and are part of their experience as a senior Police Officer. Thus, references of the court cases have not been mentioned.

5

JURISPRUDENCE OF WOMEN EMPOWERMENT AND DOMESTIC VIOLENCE: THE LAWS AND FLAWS

BIR PAL SINGH

Introduction

The gender based division of labour has been the prime focus of many societies where it is generally considered and not assumed that women are created to do domestic works/or that is physically not hard labour and men are only for the hard labour outside the domestic arena. However, it is also known fact that depending on the nature of society, this division of labour also becomes vice-versa. The matrilineal societies like-Chamorros, Iroquois, Lycians, Kamchadales, Nicaraguans and Zambesis where women rule, the men mostly do the domestic occupations. In Egypt the men stay at the home and sit at the looms, whilst the women go abroad to seek the necessaries of life. Discrimination is the inherent character of every known human society. Discrimination as a form of social exclusion has various dimensions and directions leading to the inclusion and exclusion of the certain people in the mainstream of the society. Silver[1]notes:

> *The literature says people may be excluded from: a livelihood; secure, permanent employment; earnings; property, credit or land; housing; the minimal or prevailing consumption levels; education, skills and cultural capital; the benefits provided by the welfare state; citizenship and equality before the law; democratic participation in the decision making process; public goods; the nation or the dominant race; the family and sociability; humanity in relation to the notion of distributive justice, respect, fulfillment and understanding (emphasis mine).*

Gender has become the focal point of study in contemporary society. Society is gendered and gender is stratified depending the labeling and social boundary of a particular society. There are series and stages where women face discrimination in the name of gender identity. Female foeticide, infanticide, malnutrition, neglect in medical care, physical abuse, sexual abuse, early marriage, dowry harassment, and domestic violence, etc. have become the routine tasks to disturb the sanctity/ identity of women in the society. Tomasevski[2] has vividly highlighted this view in the followings words:

> *Gender has today become an integral part of global policies, not only in human rights, but also in development environment and housing, or with regard to combating violence or refugee protection. Towards the end of the 1980s, human rights were integrated into evolving global policies, and thus opened the way towards merging the previously dissociated women's and human rights approaches. No global*

conference is nowadays likely just to mention women as was customary during past decades, where women were added somewhere at the bottom of the agenda along with children and the disabled.

The picture of women empowerment is also not that much rosy in case of tribal India. Their participation in public affairs were not seen good. Even among the Khasi tribe, the dominance of women is not seen in public affairs. Nongbri [3]writes:

Although there are no formal laws which prevent Khasi women from holding public office, they are not allowed to attend traditional village and 'state' durbars (customary administrative and judicial councils). A woman who dares to voice her opinion on public affairs is regarded as a 'hen that crows'-a freak of nature. Men jealously guard their political prerogatives by defining politics as an arena for mature and physically fit persons.

Violence against women "is a form of dis-crimination that seriously inhibits women's ability to enjoy rights and freedoms on a basis of equality with men[4]". International Covenant on Civil and Political Rights, 1966 has categorically focused on the equality and non-discrimination. Article 26 enshrines the right to equality and non-discrimination more generally, irrespective of whether another Covenant right is involved or not:

All persons are equal before the law and are entitled without any discrimination to the equal protection of the law. In this respect, the law shall prohibit any discrimination and guarantee to all persons equal and effective protection against discrimination on any ground such as race, colour, sex, language, religion, political or other opinion, national or social origin, property, birth or other status[5].

Development vs. Empowerment

The plight of women has been given due consideration at the national as well as International level. It has been observed that no country can become the part of progressive social system by ignoring their women in the development process. Focusing its emphasis on the development of the women at the world level, the United Nations declared 1975 as the 'International Women's Year' and 1980 as the 'Year for development of Women'. The decade 1975-1985 was declared as the 'Women's Development Decade' by the member nations. Since then the demand for women's rights started gaining momentum and it is still continue. Generally there are three main areas where women all over the world, face the problem of discrimination. These are social, economic and political.

Taking inspiration from world organization, India has also ratified various international conventions and human rights instruments committing to secure equal rights of women. Key among them is the ratification of the Convention on Elimination of All Forms of Discrimination Against Women (CEDAW) in 1993. The Mexico Plan of Action (1975), the Nairobi Forward Looking Strategies (1985), the Beijing Declaration as well as the Platform for Action (1995) and the Outcome Document adopted by the UNGA Session on Gender Equality and Development & Peace for the 21st century, titled "Further actions and initiatives to implement the Beijing Declaration and the Platform for Action" have been unreservedly endorsed by India for appropriate follow up.

Empowerment is seen as a process by which the ones without power gain greater control over their lives. This means control over material assets, intellectual resources and ideology. It involves power to, power with and power within[6] . The National Policy for the Empowerment of Women, 2001 views empowerment as an enabling process that must lead to their economic as well as social transformation. Justice Iyer[7] has aptly remarked:

> *The fight is not for women's status but for human worth. The claim is not to end inequality of women but to restore universal justice. The bid is not for loaves and fishes for the forsaken gender but for cosmic harmony which never comes till woman comes.*

The survey, published by the Geneva-based World Economic Forum-better known for its annual business bash in Davos-shows that full economic and political empowerment remains a distant dream for million of women in much of the western world, let alone developing countries. Of the 58 countries covered by the survey,.....no country has yet managed to eliminate the gender gap but the Nordic states-Sweden, Norway, Iceland, Denmark and Finland-have 'succeeded best' in narrowing it. They are seemed to provide a 'workable model' for the rest of the world to follow. Other 'female friendly' countries include Britain, Germany, New Zealand, Australia and significantly, several East European countries where women still benefit from the support system built during the Communist era[8].The table 1 and table 2 present the sex ratio of few selected countries at the world level to understand the trend and Empowered Action Group States in India respectively.

Table 1
Sex Ratio of Selected Countries

Country	*Sex Ratio*
Russian Federation	1,165
France	1,056
Japan	1,054
Germany	1,038
United Kingdom	1,037
South Africa	1,028
USA	1,026
Australia	1,011
Indonesia	1,003
Nigeria	995
Malaysia	970
Iran	968
China	927
India*	940

*Provisional Population Totals, Census 2011, India:Source: World Population Prospects (Mid Year Estimates), 2010 Revision. Sex and Age, United Nations

The National Policy for the Empowerment of Women, 2001 views empowerment as an enabling process that must lead to their economic as well as social transformation. Government has sought to operationalise this approach through legislative and programmatic interventions as well as by mainstreaming gender into the development planning process. Numerous such initiatives were taken during the Eleventh Plan period. These initiatives need to be consolidated and built on during the Twelfth Five Year Plan to enable women to challenge and change the contexts in which they live[9]. Dr. Purnima Advani,

Table 2
Sex Ratio of India and EAG* States

Country/States	*1901*	*1911*	*1921*	*1931*	*1941*	*1951*	*1961*	*1971*	*1981*	*1991*	*2001*	*2011*
India	972	964	955	950	945	946	941	930	934	927	933	940
Chhattisgarh	1046	1039	1041	1043	1032	1024	1008	998	996	985	989	991
Orissa	1037	1056	1086	1067	1053	1022	1001	988	981	971	972	978
Uttarakhand	918	907	916	913	907	940	947	940	936	936	962	963
Jharkhand	1032	1021	1002	989	978	961	960	945	940	922	941	947
Madhya Pradesh	972	967	949	947	946	945	932	920	921	912	919	916
Rajasthan	905	908	896	907	906	921	908	911	919	910	921	926
Bihar	1061	1051	1020	995	1002	1000	1005	957	948	907	919	916
Uttar Pradesh	938	916	908	903	907	908	907	876	872	876	898	908

* Empowered Action Group. Source: Provisional Population Totals, Census 2011, India.

former Chairperson of the National Commission for Women, lamented the fact that inspite of good legislations the fight for women's rights is far from over. The implementation of the legislation leaves much to be desired. In matters of crime against women, the lackadaisical investigation, prosecution and adjudication prevents women from getting justice. Non-registration of crimes against women is also an important aspect in the whole criminal jurisprudence system, which needs to be tackled with urgency. Women have been weighed down by centuries of discrimination and negative socialization[10].

The measures taken by the planners of the country have brought some positive trends in the position of women in the country. Data on literacy rates, enrolment and drop rates in primary education, life expectancy, infant mortality, maternal mortality rates, etc has shown a progressive trend. However, other parameters that reflect the status and position of women in society such as work participation rates, sex ratio in the age group of 0-6 years and gender based violence continue to be heavily skewed against women (Table 3). New challenges such as increased intra-country migration, changing labour markets requiring new skill sets and rapidly changing technology have also emerged[11].

Violence and its Magnitude

The violence against women is multidimensional and multidirectional. Its magnitudes vary from society to society and from community to community. But most of the time, violence against women is done by the people who form close circle of social boundary. Major

Table 3
Selected Indicators on Status of Women

Indicators	*Male*	*Female*
Literacy Rate (%)Census 2011	82.14	65.46
Maternal mortality ratio (per100,000 live births) SRS 2009-10		212
Sex Ratio Census 2011	1000	940
Child Sex Ratio (0-6 years)Census 2011	1000	914
Worker Population ratios (Per1000)	819	336
MPs in Lok Sabha (%)	89.18	10.82

Source: XII Five Year Plan, Report of the Working Group on Women's Agency and Empowerment, Ministry of Women and Child Development, Government of India. P.5.

amongst these is violence against women- in the home and outside. Violence against a woman affects her sense of self esteem, demolishes her self confidence and is often used as a potent tool of subjugation and disempowerment. The 2005-06 National Family Health Survey (NFHS- III) reported that one-third of women aged 15 to 49 had experienced physical violence, and approximately one in 10 had been a victim of sexual violence. The survey also found that that only one in four abused women had ever sought help, and that 54% of women believed it was justified for a husband to beat his wife[12] .The table 4 shows the forms of violence against the women by their husbands.

The inclusion and mainstreaming of women have also received special attention under the programmes such as the MNREGA, the Right to Free & Compulsory Education, National Rural Health Mission, National Rural Livelihood Mission and National Skill Development Mission. Gender Budgeting initiatives

Table 4

Different forms of Spousal violence (Percentage of ever-married women age 15-49 by whether they have ever experienced emotional, physical, or sexual violence committed by their husband, 2005-06[13]

Background characteristics	*Emotional violence*	*Physical violence*	*Sexual violence*	*Physical or sexual violence*	*Emotional, Physical, or sexual violence*	*Number of women*
Caste/tribe						
Scheduled Caste	19	43.3	12.8	45.6	47.9	12701
Scheduled Tribe	20.9	41.8	11.4	43.7	47	5562
Other Backward Class	15.7	36	8.7	37.6	40.4	26438
Other	12.7	27.3	9.6	30	32.3	21393
Don't know	14.3	28.9	10.8	29.9	31.7	375
Total	15.8	35.1	10	37.2	39.7	66658

Note: Husband refers to the current husband for currently married women and the most recent husband for widowed, divorced separated or deserted women. Total includes women with missing information on education employment (past 12 months), religion, caste/tribe, and whether respondent's father beat her mother, who are not shown separately.

Source: NFHS-3, 2005-06, M/o H&FW, GOI

also led to development of new schemes in supposedly gender neutral sectors like Department of Telecommunications and Ministry of Petroleum and Natural Gas. Inspite of the efforts at government levels for the empowering the status of women with the help of economic supports in the form of schemes/plans, the incidents of physical violence are continue. The table 5 details the experience of physical violence among the women belonging to particular age groups.

Table 5
Experience of Physical Violence: Percentage of women age 15-49 who have ever experienced physical violence since age 15 and percentage who have experienced physical violence during the 12 months preceding the survey) India, 2005-06[14]

Background characteristics	*Percentage who have ever experienced physical violence since age 15*	*Percentage who have experienced physical violence in the past 12 months*			*Number of women*
		Often	*Some-times*	*Often or some-times*	
Caste/Tribe					
Scheduled Caste	41.7	4.9	19	23.9	15609
Scheduled Tribe	39.3	5.5	19	24.5	6866
Other backward Class	34.1	4	19	24.5	31938
Other	26.8	3.1	11.4	14.5	27582
Don't Know	28.5	1.6	15.5	17.2	466
Total	33.5	4	15	18.9	83703

Note: Total includes women with missing information on education, employment (past 12 months), religion, and caste/ tribe, who are not shown separately.

Source: NFHS-3, 2005-06, M/o H&FW, GOI

Legal Framework and Mechanisms

Discrimination and violence against women have become the inherent character of contemporary society. To reduce the disparity between men and women a series of successive legal enactments have taken place in the country from the colonial period to till date. Following the basic philosophy of protecting the basic rights of women what we now call the human rights of every person, legal initiatives have brought major shift in the position of women. The laws like-Sati Prohibition Act, 1829, Hindu Widow Remarriage Act, 1856, Child Marriage Restraint Act, 1929, Hindu Gains of Learning Act, 1930, Special Marriage Act, 1954, Hindu Marriage Act, 1955, Hindu Adoption and Maintenance Act, 1955, Hindu Succession Act, 1956, Hindu Minority and Guardianship Act,1956, Dowry Prohibition Act, 1961, Muslim Women's (Protection of Rights on Divorce) Act, 1986, Medical Termination of Pregnancy Act, 1974, Pre-Conception and Pre-natal Diagnostic Techniques (Prohibition of Sex Selection) Act, 2003, and Prohibition of Child Marriage Act, 2006, etc. have been instrumental in giving the equal rights to women at every arena of the society.

Despite the various legal enactments as mentioned above, the position of women has not faced desired change as expected by the planners of the country. Offence and crime against women are continuing due to improper implementation of laws in protecting the rights of the women. The most pervasive and widely spread violence against women has been the domestic violence. A major concern of human rights is the issue of domestic violence. **The Committee on the Elimination of Discrimination against Women, General Recommendation 19** also specifically addressed domestic violence as a form of discrimination against women, stating:

> *Family violence is one of the most insidious forms of violence against women. It is prevalent in all societies. Within family relationships women of all ages are subjected to violence of all kinds, including battering, rape, other forms of sexual assault, mental and other forms of violence, which are perpetuated by traditional attitudes. Lack of economic independence forces many women to stay in violent relationships. The abrogation of their family responsibilities by men can be a form of violence, and coercion. These forms of violence put women's health at risk and impair their ability to participate in family life and public life on a basis of equality*[15].

Crime against Women

Although women may be victims of any of the general crimes such as 'murder', 'robbery', 'cheating', etc, only the crimes which are directed specifically against women are characterized as 'crimes against women'. Various new legislations have been brought and amendments have been made in existing laws with a view to handle these crimes effectively. These are broadly classified under two categories[16].

(1) **The Crimes under the Indian Penal Code (IPC)**

- (i) Rape (Sec. 376 IPC)
- (ii) Kidnapping & abduction for specified purposes (Sec. 363 -373 IPC)
- (iii) Homicide for dowry, dowry deaths or their attempts (Sec.302/304-B IPC)

(iv) Torture - both mental and physical (Sec. 498-A IPC)

(v) Assault on women with intent to outrage her modesty (Sec. 354 IPC)

(vi) Insult to the modesty of women (Sec. 509 IPC)

(vii) Importation of girl from foreign country (upto 21 years of age) (Sec. 366-B IPC)

(2) **The Crimes under the Special & Local Laws (SLL)**

Although all laws are not gender specific, the provisions of law affecting women significantly have been reviewed periodically and amendments carried out to keep pace classified under two categories with the emerging requirements. The gender specific laws for which crime statistics are recorded throughout the country are -

(i) Immoral Traffic (Prevention) Act,1956

(ii) Dowry Prohibition Act, 1961

(iii) Indecent Representation of Women (Prohibition) Act, 1986

(iv) Commission of Sati Prevention Act, 1987

Reported Incidents of Crime

A total of 2,44,270 incidents of crime against women (both under IPC and SLL) were reported in the country during the year 2012 as compared to 2,28,650 in the year 2011, recording an increase of 6.4% during the year 2012. These crimes have continuously increased during 2008 -2012 with 1,95,856 cases in the year 2008, 2,03,804 cases in 2009 and 2,13,585 cases in 2010 and 2,28,650 cases in 2011 and 2,44,270 cases in the year 2012. West Bengal with 7.5% share of country's female population has accounted for nearly 12.7% of total crime against women by reporting 30,942 cases during the year 2012. Andhra Pradesh, country's female population, has accounted for 11.5% of total crimes against women in the country by reporting 28,171 cases in the year 2012[17].

Implementation of Protection of Women from Domestic Violence Act

The Protection of Women from Domestic Violence Act came into force on 26th October 2006. Under the provisions of the Act, the State Governments are required to appoint Protection Officers, register Service Providers and notify medical facilities. There is a provision in the Act under which the Magistrate may direct the respondent or the aggrieved person to undergo counseling with any member of a service provider who possesses prescribed qualifications and experience in counseling. There is no provision in the Act for providing financial assistance to the State Governments/UT Administration for implementation of the Act.

It is unfortunate that home, the sweet home, the abode of rich and complex feelings and a place of retreat for protective sphere of family life, could be a very dangerous place for women[18]. Bhat [19]has aptly remarked:

> *Domestic Violence in a wider sense includes all types of physical and mental cruelties, and use of force upon any members of family by its other members. In a limited or technical sense it means cruelty against female members of the family by other members. Undoubtedly, it involves human rights issue and is a serious obstruction to development.*

The Protection of Women from Domestic Violence Act, 2005[20]is a mile stone in the legislative history of laws related to women empowerment. According to Section 3 of this Act, any act, omission or commission or conduct of the respondent shall constitute domestic violence in case it:

(a) harms or injures or endangers the health, safety, life, limb or well-being, whether mental or physical, of the aggrieved person or tends to do so and includes causing physical abuse, sexual abuse, verbal and emotional abuse and economic abuse; or

(b) harasses, harms, Injures or endangers the aggrieved person with a view to coerce her or any other person related to her to meet any unlawful demand for any dowry or other property or valuable security; or . .

(c) has the effect of threatening the aggrieved person or any person related to her by any conduct mentioned in clause (a) or clause (b); or

(d) otherwise injures or causes harm, whether physical or mental, to the aggrieved person[21]. Section17 (1) Notwithstanding anything contained in any other law for the time being in force, every woman in a domestic relationship shall have the right to reside in the shared household, whether *or not* she has any right, title *or* beneficial interest in the same. (2) The aggrieved person shall *not* be evicted *or* excluded from the shared household *or* any part

> of it by the respondent save in accordance with the procedure established by law.

Giving a very wider meaning to the word 'shared household', the Supreme Court of the Country has categorically mentioned in the *S.R.Batra v. Smt. Tarun Batra*[22]. that the wife is only entitled to claim right to residence in a shared household, and "a shared household" would mean house belonging to or taken on rent by the husband or house which belongs to the joint family of which husband is a member. A very comprehensive Act in protecting the rights of women against domestic violence, the Sections 8, 9, and 10 of the Act further talk about its execution. It provides for appointment of Protection Officers and registration of non-governmental organizations as service providers for providing assistance to the aggrieved person with respect to her medical examination, obtaining legal aid, safe shelter, etc. By adopting the public verses private approach under the Act, the Government of India has made a very progressive effort for the mainstreaming of the women of the country.

Judiciary has always been very pro-active approach in protecting the rights of women. In *Pratibha Rani v.Suraj Kumar*[23] ,the Supreme Court held that a Hindu married woman was the absolute owner of her *stridhan* property and the husband who had ill-treated her and ultimately turned her out of the house without returning her dowry articles was guilty of the offence of criminal breach of trust as defined by section 406 of the IPC.

The new Act has very comprehensive meanings of various terms as used in the act related to the nature and relationship of the women with men in the family. Section 2(f) "domestic relationship" means a relationship between two persons who live or have, at any point of time, lived together in a shared household, when they are related by consanguinity, marriage, or through a relationship in the nature of marriage, adoption or are family members living together as a joint family. With the changing dimensions of marriage relations, the Act also protects the right of woman, who is live-in-relationship with a man. The Supreme Court has introduced new guidelines such as duration of relation, shared household and pooling of resources, with the intention of bringing live-in relationships under the Domestic Violence (DV) Act. Recently a bench of Justices K S Radhakrishnan and Pinaki Chandra Ghose said though the eight guidelines were not exhaustive, these will definitely give some insight to such relationships. The guidelines include the presence of a sexual relationship and bearing children which means a "marriage like relationship refers to sexual relationship, not just for pleasure, but for emotional and intimate relationship, for procreation of children, so as to give emotional support, companionship and also material affection, caring etc." The apex court passed the verdict while adjudicating dispute between a live-in couple where the woman had sought maintenance from the man after the relationship came to an end[24].

Conclusive Remarks

Law and society both go together. Law cannot work in vacuum. Laws applicability depend on their acceptance in the society at large. Though the laws related to women have brought major shift in minimizing the disparity between men and women, yet the statuses of women have not witnessed a secure position in the society. The crimes against women are continuing in the society. This shows the pathological conditions of the women in our society who are the producer of human beings. There is no doubt on the parts of legislature and judiciary but the way investigating agencies are showing their indifferent attitudes towards gender related issues in some cases that really negate the purpose of justice for the needy. The participatory approaches from the all corners of the society whoever so and whatever the positions people holding in the society may only helpful in giving a dignified life to our women in the society.

The issue of women empowerment is not mere a giving of equal rights to women but more about the keeping of space for their full personality development in a dignified way at each level of the society with their men. The crimes against women are more acute and complex which are happening inside the boundary of domestic arena. The responsibility of each stockholder as a father, brother, husband, and male relatives become here important to save the dignity of their sister, daughter, wife and female relatives. The protection of women from domestic violence act has far reaching effect in the country but the cultural barriers and the construction of fear phobia related to dignity (so called claim of family where a victim as woman never comes forward thinking that his family name would defame and thus further leading herself to face harassment and torture in the hands of male dominated social structure) need more sensitive approach in dealing. The approaches of prevention, protection, prosecution, and victim support will only enhance to combat violence against women in the society.

Notes and References

1. Silver, H., 'Social Exclusion and Social Solidarity: Three Paradigms' in *International Labour Review, no.* 133(1994) at pp. 531-78.
2. Tomasevski, Katarina, 2002.*Women's Rights.* In Janusz Symonides (ed.) *Human Rights: Concept and Standards.* New Delhi: Rawat Publications. PP.231-232.
3. Nongbri,Tilput.1993. *Gender and the Khasi Family Structure.* In Patricia Oberoi (ed.).*Family, Kinship and Marriage in India.* Delhi: OUP.
4. 64 (Committee on the Elimination of Discrimination against Women, *General Recommendation 19, "Violence against women"*, 1992, Para 1.).
5. 54 (UN International Covenant on Civil and Political Rights, 1966).
6. Statistical Profile of the Scheduled Tribes in India.2010, Ministry of Tribal Affairs, Govt. of India at *www.tribal.nic.in* visited on 16.08.2012, p. 55.
7. Iyer, V.K. Krishna, 1979. *Of Law and Life,*1979. New Delhi: Vikas Publishing House. P. 31.
8. Sinha, Mithilesh Kumar, *et al.*, 2008.*Gender Inequality: Some Issues* in Anil Kumar Thakur and Dalip Kumar (eds.), *Gender Empowerment and Development*, Deep & Deep Publications Pvt. Ltd., New Delhi. P 303.
9. XII Five Year Plan, Report of the Working Group on Women's Agency and Empowerment, Ministry of Women and Child Development, Government of India. P. 4.

10. *http://ncw.nic.in/pdfreports/All%20India%20Meeting%20of%20chief%20Justice.pdf*
11. XII Five Year Plan, Report of the Working Group on Women's Agency and Empowerment, Ministry of Women and Child Development, Government of India. P.5.
12. *Ibid.* P.6.
13. Statistical Profile of the Scheduled Tribes in India.2010, Ministry of Tribal Affairs, Govt. of India at *www.tribal.nic.in.* P. 171.
14. *Ibid.* P. 170.
15. Committee on the Elimination of Discrimination against Women, General Recommendation 19, Violence against women (Eleventh session, 1992), U.N. Doc. A/47/38 at 1 (1993), reprinted in Compilation of General Comments and General Recommendations Adopted by Human Rights Treaty Bodies, U.N. Doc. HRI/GEN/1/Rev.6 at 23 (2003), available at *http://www1.umn.edu/humanrts/gencomm/generl19.htm.*
16. National Crime Records Bureau (NCRB), Crime Statistics, 2012, Ch.5.P.79.
17. *Ibid.* PP. 79-81.
18. Michelle Adams, "Knowing your pace: Theorising Sexual Harassment in Workplace" (1998) 40 Arizona Law Review 23. P. 25.
19. Bhat, P. Ishwara . 2009. *Law & Social Transformation.* Lucknow: EBC. P. 556.
20. An Act to provide for more effective protection of the rights *of* women guaranteed under the Constitution who are victims of violence of any kind occurring within the family and for matters connected therewith or incidental thereto.
21. (i)"physical abuse" means any act or conduct which is of such a nature as to cause bodily pain, harm. or danger to life, limb, or health or impair the health or development of

the aggrieved person and includes assault criminal intimidation and criminal force;

(ii) "sexual abuse" include, any conduct of a sexual nature that abuses, humiliates, degrades or otherwise violates the dignity of woman;

(iii) "verbal and emotional abuse" includes-

(a) insults, ridicule, humiliation, name calling and insults or ridicule specially with regard to not having a child or a male child; and

(b) repeated threats to cause physical pain to any person in whom the aggrieved person is interested.

(iv) "economic abuse" includes-

(a) deprivation of all or any economic or financial resources to which the aggrieved person is entitled under any law or custom whether payable under an order of a court or otherwise or which the aggrieved person requires out of necessity including, but not limited to, household necessities for the aggrieved person and her children, if any, *stridhan*, property, jointly or separately owned by the aggrieved person, payment of rental related to the shared household and maintenance;

(b) disposal of household effects, any alienation of assets whether movable or immovable, valuables, shares, securities, bonds and the like or other property in which the aggrieved person has an interest or is entitled to use by virtue of the domestic relationship or which may be reasonably required by the aggrieved person or her children or her *stridhan* or any other property jointly or separately held by the aggrieved person; and (c) prohibition or restriction to continued access to resources or facilities which the aggrieved person is entitled to use or enjoy by virtue of the domestic relationship including access to the shared household.

22. 136 (2007) DLT 1 SC, see also *Amit Sundra v. Sheetal Khanna* [Delhi 2008 CriLJ66: I(2008)DMC5], *Nidhi Kumar Gandhi v. The State* [157 (2009) DLT 472 Del]
23. (1985) 2 SCC 370.
24. *http://www.firstpost.com/living/sc-brings-live-in-relationships-under-domestic-violence-act-1259715.html?utm_source=ref_article*

6

CRIME AGAINST WOMEN

KUSUM TRIPATHI

The world is changing rapidly. Civilizations have vanished, dynasties have disappeared, many races have gone extinct, rituals and customs have been reformed, but the fact is that the status of women has remained almost the same (Mahadevi Verma, 1933). Eighty years ago, what was said by the great lady Mahadevi Verma is still quiet relevant.

Over centuries, the world has been seeing social transformation and democracy has taken over dynasty, socialism has over-shadowed capitalism, castes and racism have been challenged, but the view of man towards women hasn't changed much. The world may be dreaming of settling on mars, but will the status of women be different there? No, certainly not. Looking at the present scenario, the mindset of men towards women won't change so easily. They will settle there but won't give up gender discrimination. Patriarchy will not vanish so easily from the world, as man will try best to protect it.

We all have read in history that after the death of husband, widows were burnt alive in the name of *sati* rituals. Throughout history, women have had to endure horrible things to appear beautiful. For example, the ancient tradition of foot binding in china and circumcision of the girl child in African countries. In Europe women were tortured and killed brutally by labeling them as witches, in America women were killed in the name of science and psychology. The brutality and hatred against women show the mindset of men of all over the world.

Of the various issues for discussion and analysis, violence against women is the primary issue raised by International women organizations. Violence is the most used tool to terrorize women and safeguard the patriarchal structure. Hence, all feminist scholars of the world believe that violence has a philosophical base. Also, all scholars agree that violence against women is well organized and well institutionalized. Maria Mies (1998) (Feminist scholar) says, 'Between genders, violence has played vital role in formalizing unequal division of labor. Violence has penetrated the family and government structure, supported by strong beliefs and ideology to justify the acts of violence. Religion has also played a pivotal role by believing that woman is part of nature and man has to have control and dominance over her.

Maria Mies (1998) has said, to validate the violence against women, to legitimate the crime, class society created the socio-philosophical structure. Court, law, state, missionaries, religion, caste, media, education, family, art and literature all these super structures, justifies the acts of violence against women.

In family, violence against girls begins much before they are born. As we know, today, with use of modern technology and illegal means, female foeticide has increased rapidly. Various other means of killings are also adopted if a girl child is born.

In patriarchy, to dominate and control women, various forms of violence are used and the bizarre part is that these acts of violence are easily justified by society. According to feminist scholars, violence is not only common, but it is quiet organized and structured. In India, laws, rules and regulations for women inscribed by *Manusmriti* are quiet discriminative, derogative and exploitative, which also justifies violence against women. *Manusmriti* is one of the world's ancient manuscripts which define social, legal and constitutional structure, on which our current constitution, judiciary and social organizations are based.

In ancient India there is evidence of girls having performed *'upnayan sanskar'* (**Upanayana** is the initiation ritual by which a person is invested with a sacred thread, to symbolize the transference of spiritual knowledge) but later *Manusmriti* objected to girls being part of it and advised them that rather than gaining spiritual knowledge they should serve their husband. Thus, women were made slaves of men.

There is clear evidence in ancient scriptures that girls used to remain unmarried till they were adolescent, whereas later, *Manusmiriti* propagates the marriage of girls at the age of 8, thereby advocating child marriage. Girls were also prohibited to study Vedic scriptures. *Manusmriti* recommended that in her childhood, a girl should stay under her father's shadow, in her young age under her husband and in her old age under her son and obey their dictats. Women at any stage of her life should never try to live independently; if she is refusing to do so then she is condemning her ancestors, whereas a woman who worships and serves their husband is worshiped in heaven by the demi-gods.

Even Aristotle had said, "Men are born to rule whereas women are born to obey." This proves that patriarchy was enforced by the men ages ago. Friedrich Engels (1981) in his book, "*Origin of the family, private property and state*" has said women began dependent after the origin of private property. According to him, along with the growth of state, patriarchy began dominating in marriages and women lost equal status in relationships, economically and as well as socially. Women became house-holder, show piece and lost the role in productivity whereas men grew considerably in power. Engels further elaborates, "loss of matriarchy was the historic defeat for women. Apart from workplace, men also begin dominating at home, making women their slaves. She becomes product of his sexual pleasure and machine for producing kids."

Radical feminist Susan Brownmiller pointed out that, "Men's power of raping women is the main cause of women being submissive According to her because of this power, men control women by creating fear in their mind. By creating this fear, men begin controlling and dominating them (in Walby, 1990).

Gerda Lerner (1986) explains that while taming animals, man realized his role in conceiving. Seeing the male species forcing themselves on their female counterparts, seeded, in man, the thought of raping women. She strongly believe that violence and aggression associated in the process of taming animals and element of animals manners towards its counterpart, made men more like animal and sexually dominating and hence violent acts of men became more legitimized in society.

"Over here I would like to discuss that in 60s and 70s all over the world, whichever protest and movement took place a great number of women and students took part in it. There was anger and resentment all over the world, which led to student movements, workers' movement, movement against racism, human rights protest, black panther movement of America, Latin Americans' protest, Vietnam revolt, China's cultural revolution. These movements bought many changes in the world. Women felt that although in capitalist society men and women both are suppressed equally, women have to face further exploitation from patriarchy (Mary Daly, 1978).

In a male dominated society, women don't have equal rights, hence they being fighting for their rights. They had sensed their power. They came under one roof, leaving behind their respective country, state, race, religion and caste. In 70s and 80s, slogans focusing on "bodies and ourselves, we are sisterhood; sisterhood will be a power," began blowing in the wind.

In 60s there was a massive unrest in workers community in India. During that period, all over the country, student and trade union workers protested against inflation, semi-colonialism, dictatorship human rights violations and great number of women from all over the country took part in it. From 1967-71 there was the Naxalite movement in West Bengal, Punjab and Andhra Pradesh. In 1974, there was uprising against inflation, corruption against Maharashtra, Gujarat, and Bihar government under the leadership of Jai Prakash Narayan. In the same year, tribals arise for their rights in Maharashtra, Bihar, Madhya Pradesh and in Andhra Pradesh. All over the country some protest or the other was happening and great number of women and students were participating in it. While protesting, as a political activist these students and women had to face various consequences, either personal, family or state.

While participating in the struggle, women activists sensed that even in progressive, socialist and revolutionary movements there is huge gender discrimination. The activists though on surface did speak about women's emancipation, beneath the heart they too were patriarchal. The male activists of these organizations though pro women's liberation and work, and wore the mask of a liberal man at home, they were typical pseudo male. This made women of the organization more agitated. They began addressing issues related to women emancipation, as they realized that they are not only exploited by the capitalist society, but were also victims of patriarchy at large.

Women face various kinds of violence: (1) Social violence (2) Sexual violence (3) Domestic violence (4) Violence at workplace (5) State violence (6) Violence on minority community.

Social Violence

Patriarchy is a social order as well as an ideology which propagates that men are supreme. Religious institutes have played an important role in reinforcing and propagating patriarchy. They conceived a story making all believe that Eve is made from Adam's rib hence she should follow him.

It's also very important to look at the role of media which is blatantly reinforcing patriarchy. Media plays an important role in manufacturing consent. They have been quiet successful in reinforcing the stereotype image of women which takes society backward.

Socially women are outcasts in many ways. For instance, apart from facing gender discrimination they are deprived of adequate nutrition. If there is a male child in the house, he will be given first preference with regard to education, food and caring. A girl child, on the other hand is brought up in a mal-nutritious condition, when grows up faces complexities at the time of pregnancy or dies because of ill health.

Even though on paper child marriage is abolished, the reality is different. Samiran Chakraborty in The Times of India (12 may 2005) has reported, "3 lakh girls below 15 years of age, gave birth."

Few factual figures to know the status of women of all over the world

(A) Out of total illiterates all over the world, 70% are women.

(B) 50% women are total illiterates.

(C) Kids who never went to school; out of them 60% are female.

(D) Every minute a woman dies due to pregnancy.

(E) All over the world, there are more women suffering from HIV than men.

(F) In most countries, women are underpaid.

Today tolerance level towards the women has declined considerably. It has been noticed that rejected boyfriends often attack girls with acid, burn them alive or kill them brutally. On 30th April 1990, a horrifying incident took place in Ulhasnanagar. Seema Patil (name changed), a 10th standard student, rejected the proposal of a boy who used to often eve tease her. In a fit of anger, he went to her class when she was appearing for her final exam and burnt her alive. In 1994, by mistake local goons threw acid on Priya Khanna's (name changed) face. Someone had hired goons to throw acid on his wife's face, but goons mistakenly threw acid on Priya's face, assuming her as the person's wife. Priya's lost her face and eyes forever. Many young girls burnt alive because they all rejected the so-called Romeos' proposals.

Acid is used as a weapon to shake up women's confidence and self-esteem. Such gruesome violent acts specify the growing phenomenon of feudal and patriarchal values in present society. In 1999 in Karnataka, 25 women were victims of acid attack. Out of this, 11 were sex workers from the city market area. Their faces were burnt by throwing acid on them. The attackers were either customers or their agents. Acid attack victims from all over Karnataka are protesting against acid attacks. They have asked the government to ban acid sale in retail market. Bangladesh government has banned acid sale in local market because of massive protests by the feminist movement in the year 2002. As men are aware that they won't be punished, they are using these new form of exploitation to dominate women.

The khaap fears are also quiet dominating. If a girl gets married by her choice or gets married in a different caste, Khaap Panchayat announces death sentence for them, or if couple gets married in the same 'gotra' and even if they have kids, they are made to live like brother and sister. Recently in a Sony television program, "Crime petrol" a case was broadcasted of an incident in Hosiyarpur Zilla district at Subhaanpur village in Punjab. The Incident took place on 10th of December. 25-year-old Jyoti Singh was in love with a lower caste boy. Her father Satyendra Singh and her mother killed her when they came to know about her affair, as for them society rituals, traditions and their outdated value system were more important than their daughter.

Khaap Panchayat's are least bothered about Indian constitution, as they make their own laws and use force to implement their orders against victims. Look at the horrifying well known case of Imraana. In June 2005,she was brutally raped by her father-in-law. Her case went to the local panchayat. In the panchayat, the masjid's Imaam and Ashraf-ul-ulmaa madarsa's ustaad (teacher) Maulvi Shamim Ahmed were present. Their crazy verdict stated that as Imraana has become illegitimate for her husband, she should accept her father-in-law as her husband. Imraana and her husband Noor Ilahi were shocked by the verdict. Imraana along with her husband and kid shifted to her maternal house. Her father-in-law even got arrested. But on 25th June, 2005, Devbund issued a fatwa that Imraana has become illegitimate for her husband and because of it Noor Illahi has to leave his in-laws house and come back home.

With regard to this Suhasasni Ali said in one of her interviews (Sahara Samay 2005), "Today, two things are very crucially needed. First and foremost government should take stern action against caste panchayat; the religious organization for issuing illegal fatwa's. People or organizations passing such statements must know that there is a law and constitution in our country. And secondly, personal law should be made women friendly." Surprisingly, Khaap panchayat sometimes ban girls for using mobile phones or for wearing jeans. Wonder, who give them the rights to impose such dictats? In the end, it is patriarchy which dominates the mindset of panchayat members. As they are men, they have the right to decide what is right and what is wrong for women. As women are docile and meek they should follow what men feel right for them; Khaap panchayat's mindset works this way."

Abandoned, widow, orphan, low caste and poor women are either victim of sexual crimes, physical violence or are killed and labeled as witches. Women who are staying independently, single mothers, not dependent on men, fearless are considered a threat to patriarchy; hence they are hated by men. They feel that women who are self made are not good women as they don't have to bow towards men. A society which is backward, superstitious and orthodox exploits women and doesn't want them to be independent. In Jharkhand alone between 1991 to 2008, 184 women were killed by labeling them as witches, even though there is an act against it (Prevention of Witch Practice Act added in

2001). Though there is a severe punishment if anyone is found guilty of harassing a woman by labeling her a witch, this inhuman custom is still practiced widely.

Sexual Violence

Sexual violence – rape -is a kind of political violence on women. It helps men to dominate women by constantly creating fear of violence in their mind. The fear of slander associated with rape is the biggest psychological violence against women. Rape is an act of violence rather than an act of sexual pleasure propagated by the patriarchal society. In our country, sexual violence primarily rape and molestation, is adopted by the ruling class to teach a lesson and to discipline the submissive class. Apparently, when farmers protest against the atrocities of zamindars, apart from trashing them and smashing their huts, zamindars along with their goons and police try to sexually abuse the farmers' wives and daughters. As per Maria Mies, "Class power and women's exploitation are closely interwoven. One who is the owner of land is also an owner of his wife. Hence, earlier marital rape was not considered a crime, but now after women's awakening and struggle it's considered rape as per the law. Eve-teasing, sexual harassment in workplace, slashing girls faces in public places, portraying women as a commodity, encouraging sex-tourism, child prostitution (highest in India), encouraging sexual harassment by the media etc are examples of the true colour of this patriarchal society.

The issue of rape has caught the attention of all international contemporary women's organizations. One of the main reasons for this is the inhuman and gruesome violence against women, which if nothing else, is an indication of male domination and chauvinistic ego. Secondly, a historical perspective imposed upon women with regard to rape and the way societies view women's dignity.

In independent India, communists and Naxalites have raised the issue of women's exploitation by the state and the ruling classes. There are two classes of rapists, one is the police, army, para-military forces and the other is the rich ruling class who believe that it is their god-given right to rape women. As women's organizations believed that both these sections of society are exploiters of working class women, hence there is a strong urge to bring consciousness among men from these sections with regard to women exploitation.

In 1978, in Hyderabad, a gruesome police gang rape incident came into focus. Ramza bi and her rickshaw driver husband were coming home after watching a late night show. Few policemen stopped them and gang raped Ramza bi. After abusing her the whole night, they went to drop Ramza bi at her house. When Ramza's husband protested, he was thrashed so badly that he died. There was uproar in the city. Around 22,000 rickshaw drivers took and kept Ramza bi's husband's body at the police station and protested. Roads were blocked. All vehicles at the police station were demolished and burnt. Electrical cables were destroyed and people stormed the police station with pebbles. Para-military intervened to control the situation. Various political parties supported the protest and joined them.

Next day, the chief minister was surrounded by the protesters. To clear the crowd, the police fired a few rounds, which created further chaos. A total bandh was called in protest of firing and the city came to a standstill. Eventually, curfew was imposed in 16 sensitive areas. Around Hyderabad and Secunderabad, 16 people were killed by the police firing and 80 were injured badly. The government was paralyzed and they had to take military help to control the situation, but even the military couldn't stop people's anger. The situation came into control when the President of India intervened. An inquiry committee was set up over the killing of Ramza bi's husband and her rape incident. The committee in their findings found out that all the police men were guilty, but the sessions court acquitted all of them. Stree Shakti Sangthana (Hyderabad), Vimochana and Mahila Adhivakta Association (Bangalore) protested against the order, and took the issue to the High Court.

The second biggest protest was over the Matura rape case. There was nationwide protest against the incident. This was seen as a turning point in the feminist movement. In 1979, Maharastra, Gadchirauli district, in Padirya village, two police constables arrested a 15/16 years old village girl, kept her in a lock up and raped her. A case was filed against Ganpat and Tukaram, the police men. The session court disagreed to accept Ganpat as a rapist and stated that the girl must have expressed a desire to get physical. Later, the High Court found Ganpat guilty and ordered five years imprisonment, but the Supreme Court challenged the High Court order and found both of them not guilty and they were freed.

In 1979, in relation to the Mathura rape case, four professors from the Delhi law college wrote an open letter to the Supreme Court of India, criticizing the verdict. In relation to this case "Forum against Rape" was formed in Mumbai. All over the country women came on the streets. Street plays, songs and street protests were organized. At the same time, the Maya Tyagi case came up. All the parties began protesting against the crippled law and the order system.

As per an *India Today* article, in India, every two hours, a rape takes place in some part or the other of the country.*The illustrated weekly of India* revealed in one of its articles that the Indian Army raped women in Assam, Mizoram and Nagaland. PUCL exposed in one of its findings that to suppress the Naxalite movement, rape is used as a weapon. It revealed that in Santhal Parganas to suppress peasants' struggle, the army raped peasant women.

In monsoon session of 1979, seeing the angry mood of protesters, government of India agreed to pass the bill in relation to rape. For the first time in Indian history, the government spoke to women organizations, opposition parties and with respected dignitaries with regard to the bill. The government had to bow down in front of the people's movements and agreed to open up and reinvestigate the Mathura rape case. This was the first victory of independent women's movement in India. On 8th March, various women organization from all over the country, came together and formed a National Coordination Committee. Massive protests were organized by women in Mumbai, Nagpur, Pune, Ahmedabad, Bangalore and Hyderabad. Socialists, communists, liberals and students also formed coordination committees. Thus, a rape protest movement pioneered a path for the feminist movement in India.

Domestic Violence

According to German philosopher Friedrich Engels, relation of property and issue of inheritance in the family arise along with the growth of desire for private property. In India, there is a strong relation between dowry and private property. In a marriage, the groom doesn't come free. One has to pay hefty amounts to get him. That money (dowry) is used by the groom's family for expansion of family business, for education or for marriage of the younger ones. Marriage is seen as sort of a business proportion, a source for acquiring asset or property and if these desires or demands are not fulfilled or partially fulfilled then the bride is harassed/ burnt/ killed/ humiliated / abandoned to settle the score. This is the gruesome act of feudal and patriarchal society.

Initial protests against dowry took place in 1975 in Hyderabad by Pragatisheel Mahila Sangathana. There were protests happening against bride killing and dowry in Punjab, Maharashtra, Karnataka, Gujarat, Madhya Pradesh, West Bengal and rest of the country. As the rate of killing in Delhi with regards to dowry was greater, in 1979 women's organizations organized massive protests against this ill of society. Mahila Dakshata Samiti was the first organization which raised its voice against dowry and dowry killing system in India. In Mumbai, against the Mathura rape case "Forum against operation of rape" organization and domestic violence "Forum against operation of women" was formed. It was common practice that when women went to police stations to complaint against physical or mental abuse/threat/assault by their in-laws, the police didn't file cases as they considered it a family problem. The women from Mumbai, Pune and Nagpur did surveys on these issues. Through the survey, we came to know that 78 percent women are victims of domestic violence. Thirty-one percent women are mentally harassed; often given threats of abandoning them, blackmailed, by not allowing them to participate in traditional rituals, not allowing them to move out of the house or not allowing them to go to their maternal house.

In 43 per cent cases, women are brutally assaulted. They are attacked by belts, knifes, rods, burnt with cigarette butts and are often threatened to be killed. The Maharastra government in 1983, under pressure from women's organizations, considered domestic violence as an act of crime and included it in section 498A. Later there was a massive uprise in feminist movements in India. Then Prime Minister, Chaudari Charan Singh promised Mahila Dakshata Samiti that he will bring new bills with regard to dowry. The bill was passed. Later on, the Supreme Court made a clear understanding of "Stree Dhan", since it quite often happens that the in-laws will throw the bride out of the house, keeping her jewellery, clothes, gifts given to her and other expensive items with them. Hence, a new law was introduced which defines that cash, jewellery, furniture and gifts which bride receives from her parental house, family and friends is considered as 'Stree dhan', which belongs to her.

In the meanwhile, in 1987 in Diwrala village of Rajasthan, Roop Kanwar performed/forced Sati. There were massive protests in all parts of the country. At the time of the reformist movement under the leadership of Raja Ram Mohan Rao, the gruesome ritual was banned on 4th Dec, 1829 by the British government. Unfortunately, even after 150 years, the mindset of people towards women didn't change much and such a bizarre incident took place in the 20th Century. Indian women were shocked. As "Sati Pratha" was banned ages ago, the government had not made any laws or provisions to punish the guilty for forcing women to perform 'Sati'. Women from all over the country came out on the streets to protest. Hence the government had to come out with a law to punish the guilty.

1988 in Patna, all women organization's held a seminar, where the issues discussed included the economical condition of women, sexuality and to understand the relation of violence in caste and class. The resolutions passed in the seminar were– Women have to face violence at various levels, for instance rape, different kinds of sexual harassment, infanticide, killing innocent women by declaring them as witches, dowry, sati and domestic violence. The fear and violence imposed on women makes them fearful and meek, and hence they shut themselves within four walls of the house because of which they become financially and socially dependent on men. In the struggle against violence at home, society or by the government, we believe that the government is the biggest source of violence against women, who hold the biggest hand in violence done by male members of the family, or at work places or by the society. Hence, women organizations have to focus their struggles and fight battles inside as well outside the house (Naari Mukti Sangarsh samellan Patna, 1988 report).

Violence at Workplace

Direct or indirect violence by male co-workers, officers and by bossès are of higher magnitude then what we had previously believed. This includes, zamindar's domination over workers and peasants, sexual exploitation of workers by contractors, domestic maids' physical beating and sexual harassment by the male members of the house, teachers, and sexual exploitation by staff members at educational institutions.

Though there is exploitation of women at various places, unfortunately they are not reported nor are they challenged. The financial insecurity, social fear, stigma, fear of losing jobs make women vulnerable and hence they remain mum towards exploitation. In Bhavri Devi case, the High Court labelled her as characterless and acquitted all people found guilty. To get justice for Bhavri Devi, an organization, Vishaakha came forward and challenged the high court order. Finally, in 1997 the Supreme Court order brought some relief when the rapists were given severe punishment and an order was passed that it's a company's responsibility to protect women from sexual harassment at their workplace.

Today, even after 16 years of the verdict, every day we read a headline in a newspaper, 'sexual exploitation of female government official by a politician' 'lure girl by assuring job', 'blackmailed female colleague by making their mms', 'uploaded vulgar images on computer screen saver by a male staff member in the office' 'Driver from call centre raped women employee' etc. After the Supreme Court verdict, organized sector, private sector, educational institution, Municipal Corporation, Central Government, factories etc came up with 'Mahila Vikas Cell' to protect the women employee's rights. In the last 14 years, the National Women Cell and State Women Cell held workshops and did around four amendments.

The Supreme Court defines, 'Sexual harassment as an act which a woman disapproves, which includes physical touch, or to put pressure for sexual relations, showing of a vulgar magazine or making sexual gestures.' The guilty has to resign from the post, should be suspended from work, to hold down his promotion, a written apology or transfers, are all various provisions for punishment. In 1990, a lady secretary of then chief minister of Goa alleged sexual harassment by him. In Kerala, two I.A.S lady officers complained that two ministers called them at their place and behaved indecently. Initially, both the ladies had to suffer obloquy, but later they became the shining example of bravery and continued their work with dignity.

In educational institutions, ragging is the biggest issue, which sometimes turns out to be dangerous. The government has made strict regulations in this regard. There are many myths associated with sexual exploitation in our society. Women are always blamed without any analysis or understanding. They say that if women now and then accuse men with sexual harassment, then how they will appreciate their beauty? There is also a belief that women who wear revealing clothes and apply make-up provoke men to behave indecently with them.

There is a strong myth associated that women who look smart, beautiful and young are eve-teased whereas fully-covered, simple looking girls are teased by none, but research has a different take on this. It has been proven that irrespective of their looks, age or clothing, girls are not spared. Today, women are playing an important role in nation building and economical growth. It is our duty to make a protective working environment for women. It's important to have a sexual-harassment-free environment for total empowerment of women.

Political Violence

Political violence is the biggest form of violence and the most organized violence. The ruling class has control over the state and hence it serves their interests. The state violence has a 'patriarchal' structure, it is 'politically fascist by nature and behavior', and it uses sexuality as a weapon to settle scores with women. It has been noticed that whenever and wherever people's uprising takes place, state, military and police illegally attack women to suppress the movement. They abuse, insult, humiliate and attack them. Police, military and para-military all have used rape as a tool to suppress people's movements. For example in Kashmir at Shopian, two women Aayasha and Nilofer were raped and killed. Similarly in the north-east, you have the Manorama case or the Singur Taapasi Malik case, in Chhattisgarh, the Soni Sodhi case where not only was she raped, but the rapist inserted pebbles in her uterus.

In whichever part of the country adivasi's protest against usurpation of their forests, they are tortured, their women are abused, raped and molested. State is the machinery which allows and silently approves men to exploit women. From the various types of exploitation of women, directly or indirectly, the state is responsible. Hence, while fighting and rising for rights like dignity of women one has to expose the patriarchal prejudice of state and its machinery.

Violence on Minority Class

It's a known fact that at the time of partition more than one lakh women were raped. At the time of communal violence, minority community women were the main targets. These kinds of attacks are done to teach a lesson to the rival community with the belief that women are property of men and by raping them they have humiliated the community. Recently, in Jhabua (M.P.) Christian nuns were raped because of communal tension. The Babri masjid demolition riots, Gujarat riots and Kherlangi are some of the other examples where violence has happened against women of minorities.

Analysis

In India, cases of rapes from the ages 6 to 75 years have been reported in our police stations. The sad part is that rapists and murderers of minor girls to adults are none other than their own fathers, cousins, uncles, father-in-laws, grandfathers, brothers-in-law, religious gurus, principals, teachers, friends etc. The question arises why our own people and relatives rape us? The answer is simple. They don't see us as daughters, mothers or sisters but instead see us as women. Hence, in our country, every 20 minutes, a rape takes place (*Times of India*, 23/12/2012), every 77 minutes a dowry death takes place, every year around 8,000 women are killed for dowry (2011-12 Report, *The Times of India*). Moreover, every 2 hours a girl dies because of abortion (20-12-12).

More recently, the Delhi rape case shook the country. The victim is known as Damini, Anamika or Nirbhaya. Women from all over the country could relate to her. The country was shocked! Though rapes do keep happening in the country, but the way the Delhi rapist violently raped a girl, insulted her and humiliated her, people thought that they were worse than any animal? No man does such act and nor does any animal behave this way, so how could they do such a disgusting act? How can any human be so violent, aggressive and egoistic? No mother would want to give birth to such kind of sons.

After the Delhi incident, the media began writing about them. Suddenly, various political parties began showing concern towards the condition of women. In Mumbai the Shiv Sena distributed knives to women. The police distributed chilly power to them, few gave them peppermint sprays and many began teaching them karate lessons. But the question is still being asked that can rape be stopped through all these measures? When will violence against women stop? By giving capital punishment, will rapes stop? Never?

Stringent laws, strong systems, severe punishments are all fine at one level but this can't be the only solution. Globalization portrays women as a product. In advertisements and films women are projected as 'Maal'. Men think that women are their property. These beliefs and mindsets of the society have to change. Mothers have to educate their sons about gender equality. Unequal behavior, discriminating mindset has to be challenged in the society. "You are the man of the house", mothers bring up their sons with such value system. When a kid grows up with such values he rapes women because according to him, this is how one shows his manhood.

It has been noticed that in most cases, the rapist/s get away without punishment. Why does it happen? Is it because the rapist is a man and the police, doctors, lawyers and judges are usually all men too? There is a strong need for correction. Rape laws should be amended. Women should raise their voice against rapist brothers, fathers, uncles etc, but this is possible only if women are financially independent. The patriarchy and class exploitation both are important issues and are interwoven and in many cases complement each other.

Women have to collectively fight against patriarchy, class and caste system. The power position in the family has to be changed. Man is the master and wife is a slave; the weaker is always exploited. In a family, a place of love there is violence, rather than equality; there is dominance, instead of support; there is a constant power game being played.

The desire for a male child in the house makes even a humble family person, killer of a girl child. The male child of the house is pampered by calling him 'raja beta' 'ghar ka chirag' and whereas a girl child is considered as 'paraya dhan' 'ghar ka bojh' etc. Such mindsets of the family have to change. It's an irony that in a country where goddesses are prayed, girls are discriminated, neglected, humiliated, burnt alive and raped. From now on, we should make the world a discrimination free society.

References

Friedrich Engels. (1981), *The Origin of the Family, Private Property and State,* International Publishers.

Lerner, Gerda (1986), *The Creation of Patriarchy,* Oxford University Press.

Mary Daly (1978), The Metaethics of Radical Feminism, Beacon Press.

Mies, Maria, Veronika Bennholdt-Thomsen and Claudia Von Werhof(eds). (1998), *The Women: The Last Colony,* New Delhi: Kali for Women.

Samiran Chakraborty in The Times of India (12 may 2005).

Verma, Mahadevi (1999), *Shrinkhala Ki Kariyan (Hindi),* Radhakrishna Prakashan.

Walby Sylvia (1990), *Theorizing Patriarchy,* Oxford: Basil Blackwell.

7

COMPETENCY OF LAWS FOR PROTECTION OF WOMEN AGAINST VIOLENCE: A NEED TO STRENGTHEN THE LAWS

NEELU RAWAT

Introduction

The important component of social development are basic health facilities, primary education and source of livelihood around which life of any person revolves, but besides these, as a human being life also requires dignity and respect which have been provided by Indian constitution in the form of fundamental rights. These fundamental rights are not partially for women and men in separate instead both have equal rights. India runs on the concept of 'Rule of Law' which refers that everyone is equal in front of law and there should be no discrimination on the basis of caste, creed, gender or sex. There are many acts and laws for protection of women which raise a question in mind to seek the reason behind the requirement of formulation and implementation of these acts or law, and at what extent these are successful as per the motive. From colonial period to contemporary India there are so many initiations for protection and promotion of women's freedom and right. Now, another queries which struck the mind is that against whom these protection and promotion of women's freedom and right and why so? With these objectives this is an attempt to explore relevancy of existing acts in the light of secondary sources of data and study already done in particular area. The status of women in India has been fluctuating; from vedic period to contemporary India, we can see the variations in status of women. With this fluctuating status, women also have to face the cruelty by men and in the era of technological development, the means of their victimization has been changed but their situation is the same. Violence against women in post-independence became a matter of concern which led a journey of Succession act 1954 to Domestic violence act 2005.

Violence Against Women

Violence against women refers to violent acts which are primarily or exclusively committed against women. This is gender based and committed against women because they are women or as a result of patriarchal gender constructs. It can fit under various categories which include violence carried out by individuals as well as states. The violence committed by individual are rape, domestic violence, sexual harassment, coercive use of contraceptives, foeticide, honor killing, dowry violence etc. and the violence condoned by the state are forced sterilization, forced abortion, violence by the police and authoritative personnel, stoning and flogging. Trafficking in women and forced prostitution are often perpetrated by organized criminal network. The World Health Organization in its research on violence against women categorized it as occurring through five stages of life cycle- 1. Pre-birth, 2. Infancy, 3. Childhood, 4. Adolescence and adulthood, and 5. Elderly. The UN Declaration on the Elimination of Violence Against Women states that "violence against women is a manifestation of historically unequal power relations between men and women" and that "violence against women is one of the crucial social mechanisms by which women are forced into a subordinate position compared with men."

In the country where the vedas glorified women as the mother, creator and worshipped as a 'Devi', in the same country they are suppressed and subjugated by men. Male violence against women is a worldwide phenomenon whether domestic or public, but in India at some sort it is legitimized on the basis of traditional law and culture which believes that men are superior to women, so they are subject to oppression, exploitation, degradation, aggression, humiliation etc. Women constitute nearly half of the India population and most of them are deprived of their right, freedom and dignity in name of socio-cultural and religious structures. In spite of these norms and values, initiations are there to improve the status of women and to protect and promote their right to equality, freedom and life. Since British period efforts were there to bring out women from the trap of suppression and subjugation, this effort is still going on in independent India which is reflected in provisions to safeguard the women.

Various Legislation for Safeguarding the Women

There are various legislation regarding the safeguarding of the women which can be classified under two categories:

The Crime under Indian Penal Code (IPC)

i. Rape (Section 376 IPC)
ii. Kidnapping and abduction for specified purpose (Section 363-373 IPC)
iii. Homicide for dowry, Dowry death or their attempts. (Sec. 302/304-B IPC)
iv. Torture both mental and physical (Sec.498-A –IPC)
v. Sexual Harassment (Sec. 509 IPC)
vi. Importation of girls (Up to 21 years of age) (Sec. 366-B IPC)

The Crimes under the Special and local Laws (SLL)-Gender specific laws

i. Immoral Traffic (Prevention) Act, 1956.
ii. Dowry Prohibition Act, 1961
iii. Indecent Representation of Women (Prohibition) Act, 1986.
iv. Commission of Sati (Prevention) Act, 1987.

Findings

In India, various safeguards are provided to women for protection and promotion of their rights and the above mentioned acts and laws are among those. Now, the matter of concern is to analyze the outcomes of these acts and laws. National Crime Records Bureau under

Ministry of Home Affairs publishes statistics on crime in India which depicts the real picture of violence or crime against women in India. Some of the data are extracted from Crime in India 2012. At national level, number of crimes against women are given below in which major six crime against women are taken i.e. rape, kidnapping & abduction, dowry deaths, assault on

Table 1
Incidence and Rate of Cognizable Crimes Against Women (IPC) Under Different Crime Heads

S. No.	*Crime Head*	*2002*	*2007*	*2008*	*2009*	*2010*	*2011*	*2012*
1	Rape (Sec. 376 IPC)	16373 (1.6)	20737 (1.8)	21467 (1.9)	21397 (1.8)	22172 (1.9)	24206 (2.0)	24923 (2.1)
2	Kidnapping & Abduction (Sec.371-373 IPC)	14506 (1.4)	20416 (1.8)	22939 (2.0)	25741 (2.2)	29795 (2.5)	35565 (2.9)	38262 (3.2)
3	Dowry Deaths (Sec.304B IPC)	6822 (0.6)	8093 (0.7)	8172 (0.7)	8383 (0.7)	8391 (0.7)	8618 (0.7)	8233 (0.7)
4	Assault on Women with Intent to Outrage Her Modesty(Sec. 354 IPC)	33943 (3.2)	38734 (3.4)	40413 (3.5)	38711 (3.3)	40613 (3.4)	42968 (3.6)	45351 (3.7)
5	Insult to the Modesty of Women (Sec. 509 IPC)	10155 (1.0)	10950 (1.0)	12214 (1.1)	11009 (0.9)	9961 (0.8)	8570 (0.7)	9173 (0.8)
6	Cruelty By Husband or His Relatives (Sec. 498A IPC)	49237 (4.7)	75930 (6.7)	81344 (7.1)	89546 (7.7)	94041 (7.9)	99135 (8.2)	106527 (8.8)

Source: Crime in India 2012, Statistics, National Crime Records Bureau, Ministry of Home Affairs.

women with intent to outrage her modesty, insult to the modesty of women and cruelty by husband or his relatives has been included.

Looking at the table 1, we can see that from 2002 to 2012 the number of cases of crime against women is more or less increasing, rape case only decreased from 2008 to 2009, the share of rape cases in total crime in India is nearly same in all those years. Kidnapping & abduction cases are increasing continuously. Dowry death was increasing from 2002 to 2011, it was only down in 2012 but by and large its share in total number of incidence is same in respective years. Cases of assault on women modesty and insult to her modesty are average but incidence of cruelty by husband or his relative is increasing continuously and its share in number of crimes is also increasing. Rape, kidnapping & abduction and cruelty against women are increasing instead of multi acts for protection of women and her rights. Factors responsible for this increasing crime rate can be analyzed in two ways- first, crime against women is really increasing, and second people have become more aware so there is an increase in reporting of crime. India is a country of villages and nearly 70 per cent population reside in villages, people of villages strictly adhere to old traditions and culture, these tradition and culture works on principle of dignity and disputes are solved out at local level and not reported to police station, some of the villages have traditional institutions to resolve such type of atrocities at village level. The metro cities of India show more number of crime against women but women exposure to modern culture in these cities are also high. It is a factor that reporting rate of crime here is high which shows higher incidence of violence against women. Unawareness towards reporting, inefficient administrator, improper implementation of laws etc. are the factor responsible for the violence against women. Government has passed police act but still it has neither been properly implemented by centre nor by states.

States not Implementing the Police Act

> *States like Uttar Pradesh, Maharashtra, Madhya Pradesh, Tamil Nadu, Odisha and West Bengal have been laggards. The apex court in its September, 2006, judgment had come out with seven key suggestions including prescribing minimum tenure of two years for state police chief and officers on operational duties, separating investigation and law and order functions of police and several other measures to insulate police personnel from political interference in discharging their day-to-day duties. Even the Model Police Act- submitted by an expert committee a month later could not be translated into legislation with the home ministry failing to put it before parliament. The Act, incorporate several suggestions including creation of state police board (for deciding on promotion and transfer of cops) ensure fixed tenure of police chief and other key functionaries earmarking dedicated personnel for crime investigation and improved service condition of policemen.*

This is one of the factors responsible for insignificant effectiveness of acts and laws formulated for protection of women and so many another are there which should be focused. Now look at the incidence of crime against women in the year 2012 and variation between 2011-12.

Table 2
Incidence of Cognizable Crime (IPC) in Madhya Pradesh 2012

S.No.	*Crime Head*	*2011*	*2012*	*Variation in %*
1	Rape(Sec.376 IPC)	3406	3425	0.6
2	Kidnapping & Abduction (Sec.371-373 IPC)	1088	1127	3.6
3	Dowry Deaths (Sec.304B IPC)	811	743	-8.4
4	Assault on Women with Intent to Outrage Her Modesty (Sec.354 IPC)	6665	6655	-0.2
5	Insult to the Modesty of Women (Sec. 509 IPC)	762	774	1.6
6	Cruelty By Husband or His Relatives (Sec. 498A IPC)	3732	3988	6.9

Source: Crime in India 2012, Statistics, National Crime Records Bureau, Ministry of Home Affairs.

Madhya Pradesh has the highest rape cases amongst the states of India, from the above table we can see that there is some decrease in variation in one year but the motive of the protection acts is to reduce the crime rate to the negligible but the reality at grassroot level is different.

The cities having higher population are also having higher number of incidence but it can also be noticeable that higher the literacy rate, higher the reported case which indicates level of awareness. There is insignificant improvement in crime rate instead of so many years of enacting the provisions of protection. India is a traditional society where traditional norms and value, respect in the society and dignity are being given importance which can also be a hindering factor for not reporting about cases of violence against women

Table 3
Incidence of Cognizable Crime (IPC) in Madhya Pradesh 2012 District Wise

S. No	District	Rape (Sec. 376 IPC)	Kidnapping & Abduction (Sec. 371-373 IPC)	Dowry Deaths (Sec. 304B IPC)	Assault on Women with Intent to Outrage Her Modesty (Sec.354 IPC)	Insult to The Modesty of Women (Sec. 509 IPC)	Cruelty By Husband or His Relatives (Sec. 498A IPC)
1	Alirajpur	22	12	0	31	1	2
2	Anuppur	62	8	12	80	6	53
3	Ashok Nagar	50	5	10	62	1	21
4	Balaghat	78	7	6	113	11	63
5	Barwani	50	8	2	72	5	13
6	Betul	118	10	11	151	15	57
7	Bhind	49	25	40	83	7	50
8	Bhopal	143	49	19	244	52	254
9	Bhopal Rly.	4	1	0	14	1	3
10	Burhanpur	23	5	2	42	22	47
11	Chhatarpur	62	39	26	172	0	68
12	Chhindwara	122	19	18	202	41	108
13	Damoh	50	27	20	165	0	108
14	Datiya	23	20	8	61	0	25
15	Dewas	70	29	19	146	31	130
16	Dhar	81	45	39	173	16	69
17	Dindori	40	6	5	80	6	39
18	Guna	60	25	8	131	11	34
19	Gwalior	85	75	35	158	13	202
20	Harda	26	10	7	51	4	16

contd. table

21	Hoshanga-bad	69	27	12	129	21	57
22	Indore	173	42	24	405	114	448
23	Indore Rly.	3	3	0	3	1	0
24	Jabalpur	127	45	33	253	43	219
25	Jabalpur Rly.	3	0	0	13	1	0
26	Jhabua	62	17	0	92	0	24
27	Katni	58	14	12	146	14	46
28	Khandwa	66	5	6	136	6	34
29	Khargon	67	20	30	133	22	45
30	Mandla	75	8	3	94	12	40
31	Mandsaur	49	28	6	100	6	78
32	Morena	32	29	29	107	3	94
33	Narsinghpur	71	14	16	158	31	79
34	Neemuch	25	10	4	43	13	42
35	Panna	34	4	18	72	10	31
36	Raisen	92	16	22	158	0	72
37	Rajgarh	90	47	6	181	25	50
38	Ratlam	72	25	13	128	11	85
39	Rewa	92	35	39	115	7	101
40	Sagar	125	61	34	441	22	145
41	Satna	89	25	17	138	7	121
42	Seoni	65	8	11	100	7	24
43	Shahdol	81	27	13	133	7	141
44	Shajapur	67	17	7	102	15	42
45	Sheopur	17	4	5	40	0	29
46	Shivpuri	104	22	9	148	19	67
47	Sidhi	48	38	18	84	5	59
48	Sihore	69	14	10	100	13	47
49	Singrauli	32	33	13	87	6	63
50	Tikamgarh	61	8	16	124	7	27
51	Ujjain	73	31	11	180	53	202
52	Umariya	22	2	0	68	7	17
53	Vidisha	94	23	19	213	23	97

Source: Crime in India 2012, Statistics, National Crime Records Bureau, Ministry of Home Affairs.

because these are solved out at regional and local level through traditional institution and so many cases are not reported due to fear of losing respect in the society with highlighting the case. Whatever the situation is, the question is that what are the reason behind ineffectivness of rule for protection of women and how these can be strengthened and hindering factors should be tackled.

Conclusively, it can be said that complexities of laws, people unawareness, ineffective policies etc are the factors responsible for the incompetency of the acts. Participatory approach should be there for the fruitful effort of government to remove an evil named violence against women in the society. The acts should be in hindi or in regional dialect so that people can easily understand the provisions and can be benefitted. The prolonged period of resolving matter in the court is also a factor that people are not reporting to court because it is a process of time and money wastage in view of common people. One who is authorized to deal with the matter doesn't interested in such kind of matter, he formally perform his job without actively participation. The increasing violence against women indicate that there is a need to strengthen the acts and law to make them more competent.

Recommendations

- Promote gender equality and women's human rights.
- Establish, implement and monitor multi-sectoral action plans to address violence against women.

- Enlist social, political, religious, and other leaders in speaking out against violence against women.
- Enhance capacity and establish systems for data collection to monitor violence against women, and the attitudes and beliefs that perpetuate it.
- Develop, implement and evaluate programme aimed at primary prevention of intimate-partner violence and sexual violence.
- Prioritize the prevention of child sexual abuse.
- Integrate responses to violence against women in existing programme for the prevention of HIV and AIDS, and for the promotion of adolescent health.
- Make physical environments safer for women.
- Make schools safe for girls.
- Develop a comprehensive health sector response to the various impacts of violence against women.
- Use reproductive health services as entry points for identifying and supporting women in abusive relationships, and for delivering referral or support services.
- Strengthen formal and informal support systems for women living with violence.
- Sensitize legal and justice systems to the particular needs of women victims of violence.
- Support research on the causes, consequences, and costs of violence against women and on effective prevention measures.
- Increase support to programme to reduce and respond to violence against women.

References

Division for the Advancement of Women. (2005), *Violence against Women: A Statistical Overview, Challenges and Gaps in Data Collection and Methodology and Approaches for Overcoming Them,* Expert Group Meeting, DAW, ECE and WHO. Geneva, 11–14 April, 2005.

National Crime Records Bureau (2012), *Crime in India, 2012 Report,* National Crime Records Bureau, Ministry of Home Affairs, GOI.

World Health Organization (1996), *Violence against Women: WHO Consultation,* Geneva, 5–7 February 1996. Geneva, World Health Organization.

8

MANAGEMENT OF DATA ON CRIME AGAINST WOMEN (CAW): A SOCIOLOGICAL ANALYSIS

P. M. NAIR

Introduction

Data management is an integral part of the Management Information System (MIS). No less significant it is, when managing the affairs of Crimes Against Women and Children. This chapter focuses on the dimensions of this management, its implications and identifies ways and means of professional management of data, from the perspective of good governance.

Data Manipulation Vs Data Management

Data on Crime Against Women (CAW) are often quoted, highlighted, discussed in different parlance including the hallowed portals of the Legislative Assemblies and the Parliament. This shows the importance of the data on CAW. Often, the data on CAW is utilized by 'X' party to criticize 'Y' party quoting that the crime numbers have gone up during the regime of the latter. The 'Y' party is made to struggle to find ways and means of explaining the number. When the political scenario leads to change of places for 'X' and 'Y' parties, in true sense following the philosophy of 'circulation of elites' by Vilfredo Pareto, the eminent sociologist. Accordingly, when 'Y' comes to power, the roles are reversed and 'X' makes it a point to criticize 'Y' on the perceived increase in the numbers of CAW. Therefore, the data on the increase in the number of crimes often assume the role of a demon. At times, it can even shake up the very existence of governments. The parties in the opposition use it as a safe tool to disgrace the party in power, to defame and even bring them down.

No less is the importance given to the data by certain sections of the media. Electronic journalism has transformed the crime reporting and crime perception scenario. In the process of sensationalization and in the mad race for fathoming out 'breaking news' especially after ghastly incidents, wherein 'experts' are called upon to debate and discuss the crime scenario, inevitably crime data assumes centrality in the deliberations. Microscopes are used for finding faults. Reading between the lines becomes an art. The number of crimes per year, drilled down to number of crimes per week, then per day and even per hour, become pertinent issues for discussion. Tact lies in interpolating and manipulating the data and presenting a view that one would like to project. If the data for three years does not satisfy the appetite, one would go for the data for three more years or even further to bring out, establish or substantiate one's theory. In the whole process, truth becomes, and unfortunately so, the casualty.

How Does Crime Data Manipulation Impact?

It does not require rocket-science to understand the negative impacts of crime data manipulation. The following illustration will exemplify the commonly known aspects.

- In the law and order review in a particular region, the chief political personality, who was in chair, wanted to know the comparative data of CAW for the five months after the person's assuming the charge. The data showed constant increase of CAW, almost on all aspects of crime. The chairperson was prompt to admonish the law enforcement officials for their "ineptness, inefficiency, lack of concern, incapability" and what not. They were told in no uncertain terms that during the ensuing months, the number of crimes" shall be less", in comparison to previous months.
- The question was how does one ensure that the number of crimes is less in a particular period in comparison to the previous period? Expectedly, certain senior officials got back to their subordinates and conveyed the message from the political chief "demanding strict compliance of the orders". Compliance was possible only when crimes were either not reported or suppressed, the commonly known field of burking.
- If an upright law enforcement official wants to perform his duties with sincerity and commitment, he would ensure that the crimes

are not suppressed. Naturally the crime data will go up in leaps and bounds. The officer may be able to sustain for some times and convince his bosses, executive and political, but one is not sure as to how long one can sustain. If ever the data becomes a point of dispute or debate, the officer is likely to be thrown out. However, if the officer invites the wrath of the bosses, the data will be used to substantiate his "mishandling, ineptitude and lack of concern". No wonder, at times, the data is manipulated to disgrace and break the bones of such competent officials. The onlookers and fence-sitters may choose the path of least resistance "by not involving oneself in adventures", the commonly used phrase in such parlance. Obviously, they fall into the trap of manipulating crime data. Many times, the officials simply succumbs to the dictats and "ensures" that the reporting of crimes is drastically reduced in the ensuing months! Be as it is, this is not the rule of the game. There is no dearth of good officers and good political leaders who believe in good governance and rule of law. They do not indulge in crime data manipulation. Such persons welcome timely reporting and registration of crimes and focus attention on proper law enforcement and prevention.

Tool in Crime Prevention: Crime data is an important tool in crime prevention. Even in the simplest terms, when the incidents are plotted on a GIS map, the hot spots and the cold-spots emerge during the plotting. A conscientious and capable police officer would focus his attention at appropriate places, based on the picture that emerges from the crime map. Certain officials might go for studying the hot-spots on priority, whereas others may go for studying 'smaller' crimes first, in consonance with the 'broken windows' theory. All these efforts and acts of management are designed, planned and executed based on the data emerging from the ground. Obviously when the data is manipulated, the entire crime map becomes a joke. Planning gets distorted and meaningless. Hotspots will never be known, attention gets diverted, energy gets drifted and criminals have the last laugh.

Prevention of Crime is one of the two essential tasks every police officer in India, mandated under the Indian Police Act. Prevention pre-supposes thoughtful planning and action which requires understanding the crime scenario. This is not possible if the data is manipulated. Therefore, preventive strategies seldom come up in a stage-managed data system. Crimes indeed go up as criminals have a free run. Eventually the situation would erupt like a volcano. It will be too late, by the time , for positive action. Fire fighting will start. Had data management been done properly, it would have been an effective tool in crime prevention.

Good Governance Indicator: Crime Data Manipulation is a major issue impeding good governance. Governance is a comprehensive aspect of management including crime prevention and control. Indeed it is much more. In a place where the crimes were under-reported and no initiative was taken to combat the crimes, criminals had the upper-hand in taking away the contracts for developmental activities and welfare activities. They use to stage-manage the contracts, usurping all the contractual works to themselves, sometimes in their names and sometimes *benamis*. The developmental works were completely put into disarray, many of the schemes never implemented, most of the schemes half implemented and only very few completely implemented. The development of the area and, consequently good governance was a complete casualty. Therefore, good governance gets properly reflected by the real data on the security scenario. Security index is directly proportional to good governance.

Rule of Law: Manipulation of crime data is the enemy of rule of law. The victims suffer, the criminals rule the roost and ensure that the victim's grievances are never redressed. The frustration level of the victims and the vulnerable persons increases. A situation would emerge where they have no option but to succumb to the designs of the criminals or those in collusion with them, which may include even government officials, law enforcement officials and political bosses. A systemic disaster, indeed! Rule of law becomes a complete casualty. A few individuals take over the reigns of the system. Institutions collapse, conflict level increases and anomie becomes the norm.

Crime Data Manipulation affects the quality of life too. Those with criminal records and those who perpetrate crimes gain the upper-hand. The law-abiding citizens, despite being in majority in numbers, get reduced to a minority in strength. They are silenced due to fear, coercion and compulsion from the criminals and their ilk. It is indeed an irony that he silent majority succumbs to the criminal minority. The gangsters, though may be few in number, take over the reigns of governance, and thereby the quality of life hits rock bottom. Sometimes, such criminals-run polity continues for years with no respite to those who contribute and adhere to genuine democratic values.

- **Fear Psychosis**: Data manipulation of CAW has no positive value at all, whereas it has endless negative outcomes, one of them being the fear factor in the society. In certain places, women, especially girls and more so young girls, dare not move out when they are alone or during evening hours, let alone during night. More often, even for vocational calls, they would excuse themselves or try to bargain for a day-time job so that they are back home before dusk. The parents become paranoid about their daughter's safety. Business establishments find difficulty in getting lady staff for shift duties, especially after evening hours. Some of the business houses which have collaborative work with countries across the globe like US, necessarily have to work during night hours as their clients in US will be working at that point of time. Despite the fact that there is an urgent and genuine need for women staff besides male staff to attend to various activities, many corporate houses shudder to employ women due to the fear factor. Many of them have to make extra provisions to pick up and drop them. Even then, one is not sure about the credentials, antecedents and mindset of the transport agent or the drivers who are dropping them. The fear factor eats into the vitals of the economy, polity, psychology and the entire socio-economic system.

Ensuring Good Governance and Rule of Law

The discussion on the impact of data manipulation of CAW brings home the imperativeness and urgency to ensure that the "business of data manipulation" of CAW is stopped at the very beginning itself. Law enforcement agencies must record all crimes and undertake investigation, taking all crimes to their logical end. Adequate trained and capable staff need to be provided by the administration and polity for undertaking this task. The police-public ratio has to be improved. The professional capacity and capability of the investigators has to be strengthened periodically. Good systems of reward and accountability need to be brought in. Executives and political bosses should stop questioning the grass-root functionaries on the data *perse*.

Questions should be addressed to the promptness of response, quality of delivery as well as preventive steps. There is a need for a paradigm shift from the crime data manipulation which is usually given a façade title as 'crime data management' to a positive system of 'crime prevention' and 'crime detection'. Once emphasis is on investigation and prompt response, the criminals will be brought to book. Effective deterrence will do wonders. Public response will improve, information and intelligence on criminals will pour-in, community policing will improve; good governance and rule of law will come to stay. The 'crime-criminal perspective' will give way to the 'rights perspective'. The "Crime Against Women" cell, i.e. CAW, should be substituted by "Women's Rights Cell". So is the case with Child Rights Cell. The rights approach entails a "duty holder assignment" to the responders. They have to transform themselves from 'stakeholders' to 'duty holders'. The transformation will bring in a paradigm shift in the security scenario. It is not rocket science, nor is it insurmountable. It starts with a rights oriented leadership. The case-study below will substantiate the point.

Human trafficking is a crime where the victim, male or female, is violated in different ways by different perpetrators at different times, at different places. It is an organized crime beyond boundaries. It is a crime where the offenders make big business out of sale of human life and dignity. It is an offence where the victim's life and dignity are deprived and demolished. Despite such serious dimensions of human trafficking, the issue was never given importance in the law enforcement scenario in India till the beginning of this century. In fact, the response systems were quite vicious, victimizing the victims and distorting the scenario. In the case of trafficking for sexual exploitation, the trafficked women and girls were being considered as 'prostitutes' and therefore, arrested and treated as offenders. They were prosecuted and even convicted. The vicious cycle continued for years. After the UN Convention on Trans National Organized Crime and its protocol on human trafficking came into existence in 2000, the national scenario also improved drastically. A paradigm shift in the enforcement scenario was brought about by two major aspects. The first one was the Action Research by the National Human Rights Commission[1].

This research demystified many myths and exposed the inefficiencies, inaccuracies and distortions in the law enforcement scenario and the complete lack of rehabilitative systems. The research report, looking into the organized crime, did not remain as a coffee table book. Surprisingly, it was a bible for action. Accordingly, Govt. of India and the State Governments undertook several initiatives to improve the existing response system. One of the major initiatives was that of MHA, along with UNODC, supported by US government to implement the project on capacity building of the law enforcement agencies in five States in India[2].

This project ensured focused capacity building of almost 50,000 law enforcement officials including police officers, prosecutors, executive magistrates and judicial magistrates and brought about effective tools, set up comprehensive Anti Human Trafficking Units (AHTU) as well as a national network of Nodal Officers in the States and competent NGOs across the country and outside.

In this process, through positive action, the era of data manipulation was exposed. For example, during the year 2004, the average number of crimes on trafficking in India was more than 9,500, whereas, after the initiative, the number of trafficking cases came down to less than half in 2006. One may think that there was complete burking of crime but it was not so. To understand the situation, one needs to have a closer look. Earlier, Section 8 ITPA was liberally used to arrest and prosecute trafficked victims declaring them as 'soliciting persons'. The police officers who were trained during this period realized their folly and improved their functioning. They stopped mass raids and arrests of trafficked persons. Naturally the number of crimes u/s 8 dropped. Crime figures had an overall drop. The victimization of victims was brought down effectively and, consequently, the crime numbers got rationalized. Rule of law and good governance were ensured. Some of the States even came up with administrative orders not to arrest any victim under this section of law. Government of India brought about an advisory on this very same issue. The activism at the various levels in the government and non-government sector sparked off by several initiatives, facilitated and promoted by the two landmark developments mentioned above, viz. Action Research by NHRC and the UNODC project, made a tremendous impact in exposing the data and accordingly brought about positive changes in the system. Much more to go, but qualitative improvement which has come into the system is bound to stay and improve in the days to come. Good initiatives also have a snowballing or cascading effect. The stakeholders in the process have become duty-holders and, therefore, the data on crime on trafficking on women and children in India in 2011-12 and the data on related issues like missing women and children in 2011-12, is qualitatively of a high level vis-à-vis the data of these issues 10 years before. It proves the impact of the commendable initiatives in the country in preventing and combating human trafficking. The crime data speaks. It is a testament to the hard work and effective delivery by all the responders. Therefore, those in power and authority can and should utilize it in the best positive manner to ensure good governance and rule of law. Data never lets one down, data managers can and may. What is required is that the managers need to be truthful as the data itself.

Notes

1. Where P M Nair was the Principal Researcher and Investigator. The report of the Action Research submitted to the NHRC, was eventually published by Orient Longman as 'Trafficking in Women and Children in India, 2005.
2. The project of the MHA-UNODC-US Government, under a tripartite agreement, was run by UNODC South Asia Office at Delhi during 2006-2008, where P M Nair was the Project Coordinator.

9

DNA FINGERPRINTING IN SOLVING CRIME AGAINST GIRL CHILD AND WOMEN

PANKAJ SHRIVASTAVA, TOSHI JAIN AND S. K. TIWARI

National Crime Records Bureau's, Crime in India report 2012 alarms that the number of reported crimes against women has increased at an annual clip of 4.7% between 2001 and 2012. Safety and security of women in India remains questionable as overall crime graph against women has witnessed 6.8% rise in 2012. In 2012, 28,206 rape cases were registered in India although experts agree that the unreported cases of sexual assault is much higher. Madhya Pradesh reported the highest number of rape cases (3,406) accounting for 14.1% and Incidents of molestation (6,665) amounting to 15.5% of total such cases reported in the country. There has been a drastic increase in the cases of sexual violence against girl child as well which has increased by 15.33 percent in 2012 over the previous year. Now on one side is the rise in figures of rape and overall crime against women and children and on the other side more vulnerable scenario is, the low conviction rate in sexual assault cases. The conviction rate in MP is around 25%, i.e. only one of every four suspects gets convicted. The issues which should be taken care are proper sensitization of investigating officials, proper investigation of crime involving forensic scientist at crime scene and then very importantly a proper and updated forensic analysis to prove incidence in court of law. With a technology like DNA profiling now it is possible to prove identity of rapist with 100% certainty. Besides focusing the present status of crime against women and child in this paper we present a few real case variants to show how DNA technology has resulted in the increased ability of forensic scientist to conclusively link the suspect with the crime beyond any doubt.

Introduction

"A society that is unable to respect, protect and nurture its women and children loses its moral moorings and runs adrift." (The Hindu- Opinion Sept 15, 2012).

The present study felt the need that in the era of globalization and modernization the present trends of crimes against women is on increase and the proper investigation and use of modern technology is needed to combat the situation. "The Semantic meaning of "crime against women" is direct or indirect physical or mental cruelty to women. Crimes which are 'directed specifically against women' and in which 'only women are victims' are characterized as 'Crime against Women'. Centuries have come, and centuries have gone, but the plight of women is not likely to change. Time has helplessly watched women suffering in the form of discrimination, oppression, exploitation, degradation, aggression, humiliation. In Indian society, woman occupies a vital position and vulnerable place. The Vedas glorified women as the mother, the creator, one who gives life and worshipped her as a 'Devi' or Goddess. But their glorification was rather mythical for at the same time, in India women found herself totally suppressed and subjugated in a patriarchal society. There are various forms of crime against women. Sometimes it is even before birth, some times in the adulthood and other phrases of life. In the Indian society, position of women is always perceived in relation to the man. No matter how much we Indians step forward, we cannot get higher on the cost of our moral and social values.

In spite of numerous law enforcements, India remains one of the most violent nations to live in that has been further reinforced by NCRB's crime in India report-2012. Madhya Pradesh has been recording highest number of rape cases (3425) in comparison to other states. Rajasthan and West Bengal with 2049 and 2046 cases are way behind the state in this context. The state has been topping the chart of rape cases since last several years now. The data exposed herein will clear our myths that we are breathing in a protected country.

Alarming Facts from Madhya Pradesh (Source: NCRB, June 2013)

- Madhya Pradesh has been recording an alarming number of rape cases in comparison to other states. Madhya Pradesh still continues to be worst off in country having recorded 3425 rape cases – 13.74% of all rape cases in year 2012.

- There were 3,404 rapes committed in 2011 and the number rose to 3,425 in 2012.
- An average nine rapes were committed every day in Madhya Pradesh in 2012.
- Of the 3,425 cases in 2012, in 1,779 cases, the accused were neighbours of victims, in 255 the culprits were relatives and in 36 cases family members, including father of victim, it said.
- Women between ages of 18-30 were most vulnerable target as 1,385 women in this group were raped in 2012.
- Followed by this was the age group of 14-18 years, which accounted for 1,210 victims.
- The total number of rape incidents against children in year 2012 stands at 1632 in state, compared to 1262 in year 2011 – a rise of 29.31%.
- MP was ahead of others in the juvenile offenders' category in the country.
- A total of 1,175 children were booked on charges of rape in the country in 2012, of which 249 were from Madhya Pradesh.
- Madhya Pradesh has achieved another shocking low as incidents of rape of children have risen by as much as 30% in a single year.

Crimes Against Women in Cities: Crimes rates are much higher in big cities than in either small cities or rural areas. As far as cities within the state (MP) in concerned, Indore has shown the worst record with 922 cases of crime against women and 270 cases of rape child rapes in year 2012. Bhopal follows Indore in matter of crime against women (641) while Gwalior has second highest incidents of crime against children.

The Problem

While the rise in figures of rapes and overall crime against women and children on one hand shows the increasing sensitivity of the police department to such cases, on the other hand it strongly highlights the need for preventive action, especially in context of the children.But cases would be reported only when they happen and thus the focus now has to be on prevention with help of society, NGOs and different government departments. The major problem which needs to be addressed and the aim of this paper is to present the very low conviction rate in sexual assault cases. Poor coordination cause low conviction rate in cases of sexual offence means "Lack of coordination among police and prosecution, advocates and the court is the key reason for delay as well as in disposing of atrocity cases against women. Sometimes cases of sexual assault are underreported. Stigma is still a problem adding that rape survivors prefer not to go to the police and is usually discouraged from pursuing a case by even their families. Another very important reason of low conviction rate is improper sample collection, preservation and not choosing the right and updated analysis technique can conclusively link your suspect with the scene of crime as well as with the complainant. Legal experts blame poor investigation for this problem. The number of sexual offences against women is on the rise, the rate of conviction for rape, molestation and sexual harassment is too slow and low. The conviction rate in MP is around 25%, i.e only one of every suspect gets convicted. The reason behind may be still in most of the cases, the investigation is opting comparatively older investigation techniques of like serology and blood typing.

Just Take one Example of Rape Case

A girl child is sexually violated. There is enough blood present on the clothing of victim, on the scene of occurrence and also on the undergarment and other clothing of suspect.

Results which can be obtained from Biological and serological examination:

In case of Blood Analysis

Presence of blood on the different articles can either be found positive or negative. And also the origin of the species can be determined. But many times the group can not be determined. The reasons are many which may include:

- Disintegrated stain
- Non availability of control sample, and
- Insufficient quantity of sample.

Because of these limitations, the results remain inconclusive.

Limitations: If Blood group is determined, what purpose it solves?

- Even if blood group is determined, it is useful for exclusion only. It can be used as screening or to exclude.

- The important point is to prove the crime beyond any doubt in court of law, the investigation is required to prove the conclusive matching with accused which is not possible.
- IInd important aspect is conclusive matching with crime scene which is also not possible with this examination.

In case of Semen analysis

With biological examination, only the following aspects can be concluded:

- Presence of semen positive or negative, and
- Whether the human spermatozoa present or not.

But the Source of Human Spermatozoa and its matching with accused is possible only with the biological examination.

This needs to be improved and for this its time, to believe on to the technology like DNA fingerprinting for the analysis to prove the case without any doubt. Besides this, it requires coordinated multi-disciplinary approach among victims, police and prosecutors to deal with crimes against women. Law enforcement agencies should get specialized training to enable them to investigate such cases and the government should try such cases only in fast-track courts. The committee, which tabled its report in the assembly earlier this year, pointed to the abysmally low conviction while recommending amendments in criminal law to speed up investigation and trial. In our report, we recommended some solutions to bring about better coordination.

The issues which should be taken care are-

1. Proper sensitization of investigating officials,
2. Proper investigation of crime involving forensic scientist at crime scene investigation.
3. A proper and updated forensic analysis to prove the factual state.

Use of Advance Technology like DNA Profiling

Every individual in the world have unique DNA profile which can be identified at the molecular level on the basis of an extremely high level of polymorphism in the sequence of his or her DNA, which he or she inherit from his or her biological parents and is identical in every cell of the body.DNA fingerprinting as a technique of identification is called, can confirm with certainty the parentage of an individual. In the field of investigation, we can consider forensic science as a queen of investigation process so as the king criminology that we know. DNA profiling demonstrates the amazing potential of this technology, not only to guilty but also to exonerate the innocent. In this paper we present the scenario of crime against women in MP where low conviction rate and remedies like DNA profiling are discussed by taking example of a real case which finally resulted in to conviction that too in a record time of 15 days.

A Real Case

The case from Madhya Pradesh, which is a very good example of team work, dedication and fast processing and analysis by forensic laboratory of MP. A girl was found murdered with crushed head and head was cut and body was identified by the frock of the girl. The incidence took place just near the bungalow of the then Home Minister. The quick sensitized action of police, involvement of crime scene expert, quick preliminary tests at Regional Forensic laboratory, Bhopal and final conclusive and fast report within 24 hours DNA Fingerprinting unit, State Forensic Science Laboratory, Sagar resulted in death sentence in the record time within 15 days.

Exhibits Received for DNA Analysis

Sr. No.	*Marking*	*Sample*	*Source of Sample*
1	1	Blood sample	Accused
2	2	Blood sample	Father of the Girl
3	3	Blood sample	Mother of the Girl
4	4	Vaginal smear slide	Deceased
5	5	Vaginal swab	Deceased
1	A	Not opened	
2	B	Not opened	
3	C	stone	Spot
4	D	Underwear	Accused
5	E	Underwear	Spot
6	F	Not opened	
7	G	Not opened	
8	H	Piece of bone, teeth	Spot
9	I	Cloths	Deceased
10	J	Pant	Accused
11	K	Shirt	Accused
12	L	Kanni	Accused
13	O	Swab	Accused
14	P	Swab	Accused
15	Q	Nails	Accused
16	R	Bone with muscle	Unknown Skeleton
17	S	Liquid paste	Unknown Skeleton
18	T	Skull piece with muscle	Unknown Skeleton

The clothes of suspect

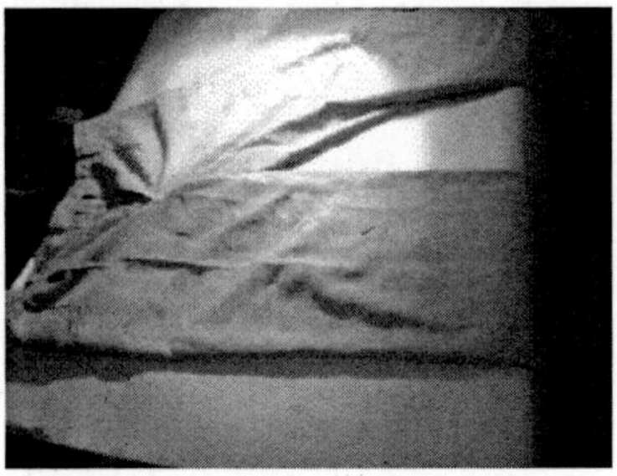

The clothes of deceased girl

Other articles used in murder

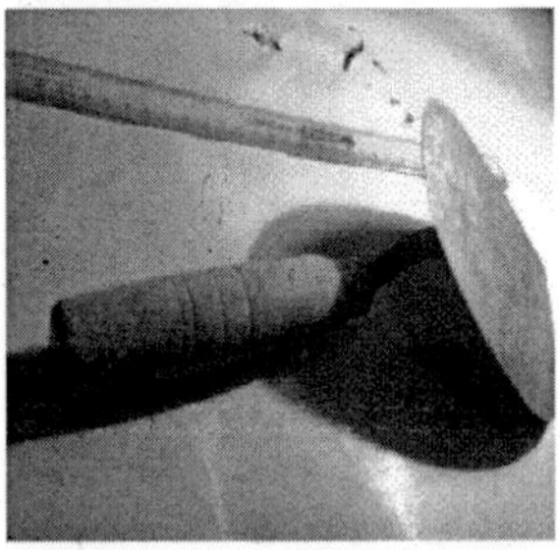

Material and Methods

The stain on stone and suspected weapon was scrapped and taken in a presterile 1.5 mL tube in 200 ìL forensic buffer (100mM Tris, pH 8.0; 5mM EDTA,.50mM NaCl). The tube was kept at 560C for two hours and was squeezed using a 2mL syringe without needle to get the elute in a fresh 1.5 mL tube. This was then added with 20 mg/mL proteinase K and 2% SDS and was incubated at 560C for 2 hours. After incubation 200 ìL of this was loaded with prefilled cartridges on Automated DNA extraction system 12 GC (Make PSS) and 50 ìL DNA was obtained using manufacturer's protocol.

DNA from all the cloth materials was obtained by the method described elsewhere (Shrivastava,2012; Shrivastava and Trivedi,2012). Root of 2 teeth were exposed in 50 mL presterile tube and it was incubated in appropriate quantity of forensic buffer, SDS and proteinase k at 560 C and after incubation isolation was done by phenol chloroform extraction procedure. DNA from referral blood samples was isolated by loading 200 ìL of blood with prefilled cartridges on Automated DNA extraction system 12 GC (Make PSS) .

DNA Quantification - Real Time PCR ABI 7000 was used for quantification of the isolated DNA using Quantifiller Kit of Applied Biosystems using manufacturer's recommended protocol.

PCR - PCR was performed using the ½ reaction volume of the manufacturer's recommended protocol using AmpflSTR plus Identifiler multiplex Kit. The PCR mix comprised of the reaction Buffer 5.0 µL, Primers 2.5 ìL, MQ water 4.0 µL, and DNA 1.0 µL., made up to a final volume 12.5 µL)Genotyping - The samples were run on Genetic Analyzer (ABI,3100) using the G5 matrix set using matrix standards DS-33 (ABI). These have included 6 FAM (blue), VIC (green), NED (yellow), PET (red) and LIZ (orange) size standard. The samples were prepared using 12 µL of Hi-Di formamide, 0.2 µL of Gene ScanTM 500 LIZ size standard (both from ABI), and 0.3 ìL of the PCR product. The samples were denatured for 3 min at 950C, and snap cooled on ice before loading on to the instrument. The 3100 were equipped with 36 cm arrays, with separation of fragments using POP-4 polymer. The analysis was done by using Genemapper software v3.5.

Results and Discussion

Deceased girl was found to be the biological daughter of couple. This proved the identity of child with certainty as a year back there was acquittal in a case of murder because the identity of murdered person was not proved. In this case as the body of the girl was found in pieces with crushed head, also the identity of the girl was established by the clothes during investigation, therefore to prove the guilt in court of law proving identity was a must. Male DNA was not detected on vaginal slide of deceased girl, this is obvious as the small vagina of a girl child is not ready to bear this type of act, so most of the time as it gets ruptured as because of resultant high bleeding most of the time in this type of cases presence of male DNA is not detected in vaginal smear slide, however presence of male ejaculate may be detected on the clothes of victim. And in the similar manner the presence of female DNA (blood transfer due to vagina rupture) may be detected on the clothes of suspect as well as on the penile swab of suspect. Presence of body fluid of deceased girl was confirmed on Stone which was suspected to be used to crush the head of girl. Presence of body fluid of deceased girl was confirmed on *Kanni* which was supposed to be used to cut the neck of the girl by the suspect. As it often happens in the justice delivery system, conventional evidence can be tempered with, witnesses turn hostile, but DNA evidence remains the same. The Passage of time does not affect it and neither does is change. DNA evidence thus unravels the truth-it never lies.

Suggested Readings

Gill P, DNA as Evidence — The Technology of Identification Engl. J Med. 352; 26 *www.nejm.org* June 30, 2005.

M K Verma and Pankaj Shrivastava. (2014), *Advances in Forensic Investigation*, Shiv Shakti Publications Pvt Ltd, Delhi.

Shrivastava Pankaj. (2012), "STR as Confirmation of Rape When no Spermatozoa or Semen is Detected in a Case of Sexual Assault", *Journal of Advance Biotech, Advanced BioTech*, Volume: 12: 6.

Shrivastava Pankaj & Veena Ben Trivedi (2012), "Customized differential extraction method for excess female DNA in sexual assault case: A case study", *Journal of Advance Biotech, Advanced BioTech*, Volume:12 : 05 : 10.

Crime against women data *http://ncrb.nic.in/*.

10

"VIOLENCE AGAINST UNBORN GIRL CHILD: FEMALE FOETICIDE-A CRIME AGAINST SOCIETY"

PARUL GAUR AND LALIT MOHAN SHARMA

Even after 66th year of Independence, age old traditional beliefs are still prevalent in India. We are evidencing an extreme form of discrimination which resulted in the rise of violence against girl child and women. One British official, James Thomason, while speaking to a group of landowners in Uttar Pradesh in 1835 referred to one of them as a son-in-law of another. His remark "raised a sarcastic laugh among them and a bystander briefly explained that he could not be a son-in-law since there were no daughters in the village. Thomason was told that the birth of a daughter was considered a most serious calamity and she was seldom allowed to live[1]"

The root cause of this violence is gender inequality and the belief that boys are more valuable than girls. This discrimination and violence starts even before birth, with an alarming rise in female foeticide since last decade[2]. Female foeticide has been in practice for hundreds of years. Declining girls' population is a matter of great concern to us. To eradicate this evil practice, the Pre-Conception and Pre-Natal Diagnostic Techniques (Prohibition of Sex Selection) Act, 1994(PNDT Act) has been enacted by the Parliament, with an object to provide for the prohibition of sex selection, before or after conception, and for regulation of prenatal diagnostic techniques for the purposes of detecting genetic abnormalities or metabolic disorders or chromosomal abnormalities or certain congenital malformations or sex-linked disorders and for the prevention of their misuse for sex determination leading to female foeticide; and, for matters connected therewith or incidental thereto[3]. Under the provisions of the Indian penal code, 1860 causing miscarriage or injuries to the unborn child of exposure to the infants and concealment of birth is an offence[4].

If a woman sentenced to death penalty is found to be pregnant, the High Court shall commute the sentence to imprisonment for life[5]meaning thereby that law also indirectly recognizes the right to life of unborn in the foetus. Under various provisions of the Transfer of Property Act, 1882, Unborn has the right to enjoy certain interest in the property[6].

Female Foeticide is a serious crime against women in society which is a total violation of their right to born and live with dignity in the men dominated society. Socio-economic causes like arranging huge amounts of dowry at the time of her marriage and craze for a male child, people are murdering their unborn daughters. Even cases of female infanticides are growing in India since last decades. Before we proceed further we have to understand female foeticide and female infanticides.

Female Foeticide is killing of unborn female in the mother's womb while a female infanticide is killing of a newly born female baby. Infanticide is also defined as *"Killing of an entirely dependent child under "one year of age" who is killed by mother, parents or others in whose care the child is entrusted*[7]*"* .It can be rightly said that Female Foeticide & female infanticide is a slow poison given which are killing our society at large.

Srivastava (2001) states that, *"the spectre of domestic violence chocks their voices and silences their opposition to attitudes and practices derogatory to their dignity. This social reality does not allow women to protest against any suggestion or coercion to get the female child aborted. It is unthinkable that any woman would readily agree to be a party to the crime. They do so under male pressure, coercion and domination*[8]*"* .

Many women are compelled to undergo tests and seek abortion on acceptable as well as unacceptable grounds under compulsion. A new spirit has to be imbibed propagating that a female child is not a curse. It is not a liability. It is not a drain on economy. It is not an instrument through which dowry has to be given. A feeling has to be nurtured that she is the daughter, she is the mother and she is the life partner[9].

Sushma Swaraj speaking as chief guest at a function organized by the All India Marwari Yuva Manch to launch the Orissa chapter of its campaign *"Jago Maa Jago"*, a national drive to save female foetus said rituals like offering "shradh", "peend dan", and performing the last rites of a person have made the people believe that their soul would not rest in peace if a male child is not born to a family. She said these false and obsolete notions are to be removed from the society in order to treat the girl child at par with her male counterpart.[10]

A PIL petition was filed in the Supreme Court by the Centre for Enquiry into Health and Allied Themes (CEHAT), Mahila Sarvangeena Utkarsh Mandal (MASUM) and Dr. Sabu M. George in which the Hon'ble Supreme Court passed an order which aims at ensuring the effective implementation of the PNDT Act[11] and to include pre-and during conception techniques, like X and Y chromosome separation Pre-implantational Genetic Diagnosis (PGD). The order largely concerns only the implementation of the Act and putting the required infrastructure in place. However, the order entrusts the responsibility of examining the necessity to amend the Act to the Central Supervisory Boards, keeping in mind emerging technologies and the difficulties encountered in the implementation of the Act and to make recommendations to the Central Government[12].

Technology Advancement

The traditional method of getting rid of the unwanted girl child was female infanticide, where the female baby was done away with after birth in various ways – either by poisoning the baby or letting her choke on husk or simply by crushing her skull under a charpoy. With the advancement of medical technology sophisticated techniques can now be used or rather misused, to get rid of her before birth. Through ultrasound scans and amniocentesis, the sex of the foetus can be determined during the pregnancy of the woman and then the foetus is aborted if found to be female[13].

Sex selective abortion, also called female foeticide, is a two-step process. The first step involves determination of the sex of the foetus in one of three ways: amniocentesis, chorionic villus sampling, or ultrasound. The second step consists of the therapeutic abortion which, in India, was legalized in 1971 under the Medical Termination of Pregnancy Act and is readily available and free of charge in government hospitals and clinics throughout the country[14].

Advancement in medical technology viz. Ultrasound and other medical tests help millions of our population to detect serious diseases at an early stage like Amniocentesis, Cancer, Cardiac diseases, *Haemolytic disease of the newborn*(*HDN*) and various gynaecological disorders. Misuse of medical technology and other activities of social perception of having a male child as a heir of a family led to rampant practice of sex selection followed by pre birth elimination of females in the country leading to decline in child sex ratio. Hence, advanced medical technologies are misused for aborting a female child.

It is rightly stated "*w*ith the advent of privatization and commercialization, the use of pre-natal diagnostic technologies is growing into a thriving business in India. This is primarily for the purpose of sex determination selective abortion of the female foetus. The misuse of technology simply reinforces the secondary status given to girl children in such a way that they are culled out even before they are born"[15].

Sex Ratio (females per 1000 males), India[16]

Group	*2001*	*2011*
Rural	946	949
Urban	900	929
Total Average	933	943

As per population census 2011, in comparison to 2001 census there is a marginal increase of females per 1000 males from 933 to 943. The main reason is being the awareness in the society and increase of literacy rate from 64.84 in 2001 to 74.04[17] in 2011 at all India level. Haryana has the lowest sex ratio among the states while Kerala remains at the top with the highest sex ratio. In the national capital Delhi, the statistics stand at 821 girls against 1000 boys in 2001 compared to 866 in 2011. Sex-selective abortions have increased among the more educated and economically better-off Indians in relatively wealthy states like as Delhi, Punjab, Maharashtra and Haryana[18] .But in comparison to 1901, child sex ratio in the country has declined sharply from 972[19]girls per 1000 boys in 1901 to 943[20] in 2011.

No doubt, if this practice continues it will disturb the social balance and it may lead to serious problems like increase in sexual offences, sharing of women within and outside wedlock and greater insecurity to women[21].

Various programmes has to be launched to aware our Medical practitioners and public at large so that the objectives of the PNDT Act can be achieved. It has to be ensured that no one from medical profession will indulges in unethical and unlawful practices. No person including a relative or husband of a woman shall seek or encourage the conduct of any sex-selection technique on her or him or both[22].Female Foeticide can be eradicated from the society only with the efforts of common man and cooperation of medical fraternity. It is evidenced that medical fraternity has the potential to play a major role in eradicating malpractices for sex selection.

In State[through District Appropriate Authority-cum-Civil Surgeon, Faridabad], the Complainant] filed a case against Dr. Anil Sabhani, Prop. M/s Dr. Anil's Ultrasound Opp. G.H. Palwal, Faridabad, Sh. Kartar Singh son of Sh. Lakhi Singh, Technician M/s Dr. Anil Ultrasound, Opp. G.H. Palwal, Faridabad Resident of V.P.O. Maheshpur, District Faridabad, and Ms. Dr. Anil Ultrasound, Opp. G.H. Palwal, Faridabad (H) through Dr. Anil Sabhani) [CASE NO. 295/2 OF 2001] In the present case, the convicts orally conveyed the sex of foetus to the patients, but due to the check of such illegal acts the persons like the convicts have worked out their own sex determination code. It was reported in the news paper[23] as follows:-

> *"If the doctor tells us to come and get the report on Monday, we know it's a boy. Friday means a girl, "says Sarla a proud mother of three strapping boys in Karnal's Chonchda village. Her neighbour's doctor adopted a slightly different modus operandi signature in red ink to indicate a girls and blue for a boy. "no words are exchanged. Its an unspoken thing and one doesn't even have to ask." she says. If the doctor doesn't oblige, some tout does".*

The Court held that the convicts together have been indulging in a very serious crime. To kill a person who may have the opportunity to defend himself is a very serious offence, but even more serious is the offence where a person kills someone who is not even in a stage to defend himself. The determination of sex by persons like the convicts lead to the above reality where on determining sex of the foetus as female, the same is killed in a cruel manner. The act of the convicts is to be condemned and in view the punishment to be awarded to the convict should act as a deterrent to and other persons, so that no one indulged in such heinous crime. The court convicted the accused to undergo simple imprisonment for a period of two years and to pay a fine of Rs. 5,000/- each for the offence mentioned in section 6 (a), 6(b), section 5(1), 5(2), section 4(1), 4(2), 4(3) and section 29 read with Rule 9 of the Act and all the offence are punishable under section 23 of the Act.

In ***Vinod Soni and Another Vs. Respondent: Union of India (UOI)***[24] [Criminal Writ Petition No. 945 of 2005 and Criminal Application No. 3647 of 2005], the petitioners who are married couple, seek to challenge the constitutional validity of Preconception and Prenatal Diagnostic Techniques (Prohibition of Sex Selection) Act of 1994 (hereinafter referred to Sex Selection Act of 1994). The petition contains basically two challenges to the enactment: First, it violates Article 14[25] of the Constitution and second, that it violates Article 21[26]of the Constitution of India. At the time of argument, the learned counsel appearing for the petitioners submitted that he does not press his petition in so far as the challenge via Article 14 of the Constitution of India is concerned. It was observed by the Hon'ble Bombay High Court that the enactment proposes to control and ban the use of this selection technique both prior to conception as well as its misuse after conception and it does not totally ban these procedures or tests. If we notice provisions of section 4 of the Act it gives permission in when any of these tests can be administered. Sub section 2 says that no prenatal diagnostic techniques can be conducted except for the purposes of detection of any of the (1) chromosomal abnormalities, (2) genetic metabolic diseases, (3) heamoglobinopathies, (4) sex-linked genetic diseases, (5) congenital anomalies and (6) any other abnormalities or diseases as may be specified by the Central Supervisory Board. Thus, the enactment permits such tests if they are necessary to avoid abnormal child coming into existence. Apart from that such cases are permitted as mentioned in sub clause 3 of section 4 where certain dangers to the pregnant woman are noticed. A perusal of those conditions which are five and which can be added to the four, existence on which is provided by the Act. It will therefore be seen that the enactment does not bring about total prohibition of any such tests. It intends to thus prohibit user and indiscriminate user of such tests to determine the sex at preconception stage or post conception stage. The right to life or personal liberty cannot be expanded to mean that the right of personal liberty includes the personal liberty to determine the sex of a child which may come into existence. The conception is a physical phenomenon. It need not take place on copulation of every capable male and female. Even if both are competent and healthy to give birth to a child, conception need not necessarily follow. The right to personal liberty cannot expand by any stretch of imagination, to liberty to prohibit coming into existence of a female foetus or male foetus which shall be for the Nature to decide. To claim a right to determine the existence of such foetus or possibility of such foetus come into existence, is a claim of right which may never exist. ***Right to bring into existence a life in future with a choice to determine the sex of that life cannot in itself to be a right. In our opinion, therefore, the petition does not make even a prima facie case for violation of Article 21 of the Constitution of India.*** Hence it is dismissed by Hon'ble High Court of Bombay. In view of the fact that the petition itself is rejected, the application for intervention is also rejected.

Implementation of the PNDT Act at the outmost and the Supreme Court directives issued in 2002 help States to take actions but there is enough scope in taking responsibility to eradicate this crime from the society.

There are various views to stop and eradicate these crimes at the outmost level, some are elaborated below[27]:

> Hon'ble Former President of India, Smt. Pratibha Devisingh Patil, at the 17th convocation of Mother Teresa Women's University said: *'The worst manifestation in our country of gender discrimination is female foeticide. Unfortunately, female foeticide is committed not only by the illiterate and the impoverished, it is being committed in cities and among the educated and well-to-do. It is shocking that there are higher incidents of female foeticide in the more developed districts and regions of our country. Society has to be made aware that a girl child is a boon and a gift."*

Pre-Conception and Pre-Natal Diagnostic Techniques (Prohibition Of Sex Selection) Act, 1994 (PNDT Act)

- PNDT Act came in force from 1st January, 1996 as notified by the Central Government. It is divided into eight chapters comprising of 34 sections. It prohibits sex selection even before or after conception. "***Conceptus***[28]" means any product of conception at any stage of development from fertilization until birth including extra embryonic membranes as well as the embryo or foetus.
- PNDT Act allows restricted use of medical technology only for the following abnormalities[29]:
  - Chromosomal abnormalities;
  - Genetic metabolic diseases;
  - Haemoglobinopathies;
  - Sex-linked genetic diseases;
  - Congenital anomalies;
  - Any other abnormalities or diseases as may be specified by the Central Supervisory Board;

Important definitions prescribed under the PNDT Act, 1994 are enumerated as follows:

- **"Pre-natal diagnostic procedures**[30]" means all gynaecological or obstetrical or medical procedures such as ultrasonography, foetoscopy, taking or removing samples of amniotic fluid, chorionic villi, blood or any other tissue or fluid of a man, or of a woman for being sent to a Genetic Laboratory or Genetic Clinic for conducting any type of analysis or pre-natal diagnostic tests for selection of sex before or after conception;

- **"Pre-natal diagnostic techniques[31]"** includes all pre-natal diagnostic procedures and pre-natal diagnostic tests;
- **"Pre-natal diagnostic test[32]"** means ultrasonography or any test or analysis of amniotic fluid, chorionic villi, blood or any tissue or fluid of a pregnant woman or conceptus conducted to detect genetic or metabolic disorders or chromosomal abnormalities or congenital anomalies or haemoglobinopathies or sex-linked diseases;
- **"Sex selection[33]"** includes any procedure, technique, test or administration or prescription or provision of anything for the purpose of ensuring or increasing the probability that an embryo will be of a particular sex;

Genetic Counselling Centres, Genetic Laboratories and Genetic Clinics

Only those Genetic Counselling Centre, Genetic Laboratory or Genetic Clinic registered under this Act, shall conduct or associate with, or help in, conducting activities relating to prenatal diagnostic techniques as well as employ or cause to be employed or take services of any person who possess necessary qualifications as may be prescribed, whether on honorary basis or on payment[34].

Any pre-natal diagnostic techniques shall be conducted or cause to be conducted or aid in conducting at a place registered under this Act by only medical geneticist, gynaecologist, paediatrician, registered medical practitioner or any other person[35].

No person[36] shall be allowed to conduct or cause to be conducted or aid in conducting by himself or by any other person, sex selection on a woman or a man or on both or on any tissue, embryo, conceptus, fluid or gametes derived from either or both of them.[37] Sell of any ultrasound machine or imaging machine or scanner or any other equipment capable of detecting sex of foetus to any Genetic Counselling Centre, Genetic Laboratory, Genetic Clinic or any other person not registered under the Act has been prohibited[38].

Conditions for Pre-natal Diagnostic Techniques[39]

Pre-natal diagnostic techniques shall be used or conducted by qualified person unless he is satisfied for reasons to be recorded in writing that any of the following conditions are fulfilled, namely:—

- (i) age of the pregnant woman is above thirty-five years;
- (ii) the pregnant woman has undergone of two or more spontaneous abortions or foetal loss;
- (iii) the pregnant woman had been exposed to potentially teratogenic agents such as drugs, radiation, infection or chemicals;
- (iv) the pregnant woman or her spouse has a family history of mental retardation or physical deformities such as, spasticity or any other genetic disease;

(v) any other condition as may be specified by the Central Supervisory Board;

Provided that the person conducting ultrasonography on a pregnant woman shall keep complete record thereof in the clinic in such manner, as may be prescribed, and any deficiency or inaccuracy found therein shall amount to contravention of provisions of section 5 or section 6 unless contrary is proved by the person conducting such ultrasonography;

Pre-natal diagnostic procedures shall be followed only with the written consent in the prescribed form of the pregnant women explaining all known side and after effects of such procedures in such language which she understands and also prohibiting the communication of sex of foetus[40].

Constitution of Central Supervisory Board

Central Government has the power to constitute Central Supervisory Board [41]having following members:

(a) the Minister in charge of the Ministry or Department of Family Welfare, who shall be the Chairman, *ex-officio*;

(b) the Secretary to the Government of India in charge of the Department of Family Welfare, who shall be the Vice-Chairman, *ex-officio*;

(c) three members to be appointed by the Central Government to represent the Ministries of Central Government in charge of Women and Child Development, Department of Legal Affairs or Legislative Department in the Ministry of Law and Justice, and Indian System of Medicine and Homoeopathy, *ex-officio*;

(d) The Director General of Health Services of the Central Government, *ex-officio;*

(e) Ten members to be appointed by the Central Government, two each from amongst[42]—

(i) eminent medical geneticists;

(ii) eminent gynaecologist and obstetrician or expert of *stri-roga or prasuti-tantra;*

(iii) eminent paediatricians;

(iv) eminent social scientists; and

(v) representatives of women welfare organisations;

(f) three women Members of Parliament, of whom two shall be elected by the House of the People and one by the Council of States[43];

(g) four members to be appointed by the Central Government by rotation to represent the States and the Union territories, two in the alphabetical order and two in the reverse alphabetical order[44]:

Provided that no appointment under this clause shall be made except on the recommendation of the State Government or, as the case may be, the Union territory;

(h) an officer, not below the rank of a Joint Secretary or equivalent of the Central Government, in charge of Family Welfare, who shall be the Member-Secretary, ex-officio.

The Central Supervisory Board so constituted shall meet at least once in six months having following functions[45]:

(i) to advise the Central Government on policy matters relating to use of pre-natal diagnostic techniques, sex selection techniques and against their misuse;

(ii) to review and monitor implementation of the Act and rules made there under and recommend to the Central Government changes in the said Act and rules;

(iii) to create public awareness against the practice of pre-conception sex selection and prenatal determination of sex of foetus leading to female foeticide;

(iv) to lay down code of conduct to be observed by persons working at Genetic Counselling Centres, Genetic Laboratories and Genetic Clinics;

(v) to oversee the performance of various bodies constituted under the Act and take appropriate steps to ensure its proper and effective implementation;

(vi) Any other functions as may be prescribed under the Act.

Likewise Central Supervisory Board, State Supervisory Board or the Union territory Supervisory Board is constituted in every state or Union territory as the case may be having following functions:

(i) to create public awareness against the practice of pre-conception sex selection and pre-natal determination of sex of foetus leading to female foeticide in the State;

(ii) to review the activities of the Appropriate Authorities functioning in the State and recommend appropriate action against them;

(iii) to monitor the implementation of provisions of the Act and the rules and make suitable recommendations relating thereto, to the Board;

(iv) to send such consolidated reports as may be prescribed in respect of the various activities undertaken in the State under the Act to the Board and the Central Government; and

(v) any other functions as may be prescribed under the Act.

Appropriate Authority and Advisory Committee

The Central Government shall appoint, by notification in the Official Gazette, one or more Appropriate Authorities for each of the Union territories for the purposes of this Act. The State Government shall also appoint, by notification in the Official Gazette, one or more Appropriate Authorities for the whole or part of the State for the purposes of this Act having regard to the intensity of the problem of pre-natal sex determination leading to female foeticide.

The Appropriate Authority grant, suspend or cancel registration of a Genetic Counselling Centre, Genetic Laboratory or Genetic Clinic; enforce standards prescribed for the Genetic Counselling Centre, Genetic Laboratory and Genetic Clinic; investigate complaints of breach of the provisions of this Act or the rules made there under and take immediate action; seek and consider the advice of the Advisory Committee, on application for registration and on complaints for suspension or cancellation of registration; take appropriate legal action against the use of any sex selection technique by any person at any place, *suo motu* or brought to its notice and also to initiate independent investigations in such matter; to create public awareness against the practice of sex selection or pre-natal determination of sex; to supervise the implementation of the provisions of the Act and rules; recommend to the CSB and State Boards modifications required in the rules in accordance with changes in technology or social conditions; take action on the recommendations of the Advisory Committee made after investigation of complaint for suspension or cancellation of registration[46].

The Central Government or the State Government, as the case may be, shall constitute an Advisory Committee for each Appropriate Authority to aid and advise the Appropriate Authority in the discharge of its functions as enumerated above.

The Appropriate Authority shall have the powers to summon any person who is in possession of any information relating to violation of the provisions of this Act or the rules made there under; compel production of any document or material object; issue search warrant for any place suspected to be indulging in sex selection techniques or pre-natal sex determination[47].

Offences and Penalties

***General Rule*:** No person, organization, Genetic Counselling Centre, Genetic Laboratory or Genetic Clinic, including clinic, laboratory or centre having ultrasound machine or imaging machine or scanner or any other technology capable of undertaking determination of sex of foetus or sex selection shall issue, publish, distribute, communicate or cause to be issued, published, distributed or communicated any advertisement, in any form, including internet, regarding facilities of pre-natal determination of sex or sex selection before conception available at such centre, laboratory, clinic or at any other place[48] .Any advertisement in any manner regarding pre-natal determination or preconception selection of sex by any means whatsoever, scientific or otherwise is prohibited[49] ."**Advertisement"** includes any notice, circular, label, wrapper or any other document including advertisement through internet or any other media in electronic or print form and also includes any visible representation made by means of any hoarding, wall-painting, signal, light, sound, smoke or gas.

Penalties

Any medical geneticist, gynaecologist, registered medical practitioner or any person who owns a Genetic Counselling Centre, a Genetic Laboratory or a Genetic Clinic or is employed in such a Centre, Laboratory or Clinic and renders his professional or technical services to or at such a Centre, Laboratory or Clinic, whether on an honorary basis or otherwise, and who contravenes any of the provisions of this Act or rules made thereunder ***shall be punishable with imprisonment for a term which may extend to three years and with fine which may extend to ten thousand rupees and on any subsequent conviction, with imprisonment which may***

extend to five years and with fine which may extend to fifty thousand rupees[50].

The name of the registered medical practitioner shall be reported by the Appropriate Authority to the State Medical Council concerned for taking necessary action including suspension of the registration if the charges are framed by the court and till the case is disposed of and on conviction for ***removal of his name from the register of the Council for a period of five years for the first offence and permanently for the subsequent offence***[51].

Any person who seeks the aid of a Genetic Counselling Centre, Genetic Laboratory, Genetic Clinic or ultrasound clinic or imaging clinic or of a medical geneticist, gynaecologist, sonologist or imaging specialist or registered medical practitioner or any other person for sex selection or for conducting pre- natal diagnostic techniques on any pregnant women for the purposes other than those specified in sub-section (2) of section 4, he shall, ***be punishable with imprisonment for a term which may extend to three years and with fine which may extend to fifty thousand rupees for the first offence and for any subsequent offence with imprisonment which may extend to five years and with fine which may extend to one lakh rupees***[52]. This provision shall not apply to the woman who was compelled to undergo such diagnostic techniques or such selection[53].

Looking into the gravity of the offence committed, it is to be noted that every offence under this Act shall be ***cognizable, non-bailable and non-compoundable***[54].

Offences By Companies

Where any offence, punishable under this Act has been committed by a company, every person who, at the time the offence was committed was in charge of, and was responsible to the company for the conduct of the business of the company, as well as the company, shall be deemed to be guilty of the offence and shall be liable to be proceeded against and punished accordingly.

If any such person proves that the offence was committed without his knowledge or that he had exercised all due diligence to prevent the commission of such offence, such person shall not be liable to any punishment.

Where any offence punishable under this Act has been committed by a company and it is proved that the offence has been committed with the consent or connivance of, or is attributable to any neglect on the part of, any director, manager, secretary or other officer of the company, such director, manager, secretary or other officer shall also be deemed to be guilty of that offence and shall be liable to be proceeded against and punished accordingly. ***"Company"*** for this purpose means any body-corporate and includes a firm or other association of individuals, and ***"Director"***, in relation to a firm, means a partner in the firm.

Court of a Metropolitan Magistrate or a Judicial Magistrate of the first class shall take cognizance of an offence under this Act except on a complaint made by[55]—

(a) the Appropriate Authority concerned, or any officer authorised in this behalf by the Central

Government or State Government, as the case may be, or the Appropriate Authority; or

(b) A person including a social organisation who has given notice of not less than fifteen days in the manner prescribed, to the Appropriate Authority, of the alleged offence and of his intention to make a complaint to the court.

Suggestions & Conclusion

We have a very good statute but a need is felt to monitor and evaluate implementation of PNDT Act through community participations including identifying violators of the Act by various means including conducting thorough audits of form 'F' filled in for the pregnant women in the clinics and test audit under any conditions is allowed in these cases.

A compact plan shall be designed at a National, State and District level showing full coordination among them to attain the objectives of the PNDT Act, 1994. ***While laws like PNDT need to be strengthened, and even more importantly, strictly enforced, what is equally important is education—both formal, and also within homes. Parents need to treat boys and girls equally; boys need to be taught to treat girls equally. We must ensure that the issue of violence against women is not seen just as a "women's issue", but a societal issue***[56]***.***

Regular inspection is to be done by making a team which has the power to take action immediately on receipt of any complaint or suo-moto. Registrations as well as their renewal of PNDT clinics shall be taken on the basis of track record in terms of record keeping, impartiality in doing an act for the mankind etc. Our Judiciary shall be provided an advanced training as well as qualitative legal professional shall be hired at district, state & national level fight against this crime to eradicate it from the society.

Meetings of State Supervisory Board, State Appropriate Authority, State Advisory Committee and District Advisory Committee shall be conducted at regular intervals to review the progress of implementation at different levels.

Seminars, workshops and awareness programmes are conducted at District, State and National level on regular basis to aware our society in fighting against this crime.

There is also a need to utilise the proper use of funds given to the States by the Centre in Centrally Sponsored Schemes/ Projects like MP scheme, Grant in aid to NGOs, Medical audit as well as funds routed through State Health Society and District Health Society shall be scrutinised at every level so that the objectives be attained. Responsibility shall be framed to stop misuse of the funds.

Our media especially print media can also play a major role to fight against female foeticide and female infanticides. Even though our law is strong enough to bring change but to address this social problem, need is also felt to form a network of NGOS, Social Organisation, women and child development department/ or social welfare departments, Medical professionals, educational institutes including schools, colleges, professional colleges, Universities and society at large to understand their responsibilities and duties to **eradicate completely female foeticide and female infanticides from the society.**

Notes and References

1. Miller B. 1981. *The Endangered Sex: Neglect of Female Children in Rural North India*, Ithaca, N.Y.: Cornell University Press.
2. Manuscript/brochure of National Seminar on "Violence Against Girl Child and Women: Issues and Concern" conducted on 3-4th March.2014 by Women's Studies Department, Barkatullah University, Bhopal.
3. Preamble PNDT Act, 1994.
4. Chapter 18 of the Indian Penal Code, 1860 under Section 312 to 318.
5. Section 416 of the Criminal Procedure Code, 1974.
6. Section 20.
7. Kolloor, T.M. 1990. " Female Infanticide: A Psychological Analysis", *Grass Roots Action, Special Issue on Girl Child,* 3 April 1990.
8. Srivastava, S.P. 2001. "The Perils of Pre-Birth Murder – A Sociological Analysis of Female Foeticide.", *Journal of Social Welfare,* Vol.47, No. 10 January 2001. pp. 7-12.
9. *Mishra Dipak .2007.* " Female Foeticide – A Social Menace", *Nyaya Deep, Official Journal of NALSA,* Vol.VIII Issue-2, April 2007.
10. National Daily" The Hindu" dated 02.09.2007.
11. *Supreme Court of India Civil Original Jurisdiction Writ Petition (Civil) No. 301 of 2000.*
12. *Shanmugavelayutham K.2003.,* "The Pre-Conception and Pre-Natal Diagnostic Techniques (prohibition of Sex Selection) Act 2002 – A Bold step", *Legal News & Views,* Vol. 17, No. 5, May, 2003.
13. *Swati Mehta & Jayna Kothari. 2001.* " It's A Girl ! Pre-Natal Sex Selection and the Law", *Lawyers Collective, Nov, 2001.*

14. Solapurkar ML, Sangam RN. 1992. "Has the MTP act in India proven beneficial?" , *Journal of Family Welfare.* 38 (2): 46-52.

15. *Anand,Meenu .2005.*"Indian Legal Framework to Arrest Female Foeticide", *Legal News & Views, September 2005.*

16. As per Population Census 2011.

17. As per Population Census 2011.

18. Manuscript/brochure of National Seminar on "Violence Against Girl Child and Women: Issues and Concern" conducted on 3-4th March 2014 by Women's Studies Department, Barkatullah University, Bhopal.

19. PROVISIONAL POPULATION TOTALS Chapter 6 Census of India 2001 Series 1, India, Paper 1 of 2001 pg.3 downloaded from *http://censusindia.gov.in/Data_Products/Library/Provisional_Population_Total_link/PDF_Links/chapter6.pdf*

20. As per Population Census 2011.

21. *Srivastava Alka, 2002.* "Declining Sex Ratio: The Marginalized Girl Child", *Women's Link, Vol. 8, No. 1, January March -2002.*

22. Section-4(5) of the PNDT Act, 1994.

23. Times of India, Delhi Edition dated 25.03.2006.

24. 2005 CriLJ 3408 Bombay High Court.

25. Equality before law : The State shall not deny to any person equality before the law or the equal protection of the laws within the territory of India Prohibition of discrimination on grounds of religion, race, caste, sex or place of birth

26. Protection of life and personal liberty - No person shall be deprived of his life or personal liberty except according to procedure established by law.

27. 'Speaking up for girl child' at *http://pndt.gov.in/* maintained by Ministry of Health and Family Welfare, New Delhi.

28. Section-2(ba) of the PNDT Act, 1994.

29. Section-4(2) of the PNDT Act, 1994.
30. Section-2(i) of the PNDT Act, 1994.
31. Section-2(j) of the PNDT Act, 1994.
32. Section-2(k) of the PNDT Act, 1994.
33. Section-2(o) of the PNDT Act, 1994.
34. Section-3(clause 1 & 2) of the PNDT Act, 1994.
35. Section-3(clause 3) of the PNDT Act, 1994.
36. Including a specialist or a team of specialists in the field of infertility.
37. Section-3A of the PNDT Act, 1994.
38. Section-3B of the PNDT Act, 1994.
39. Section-4(3) of the PNDT Act, 1994.
40. Section-5 of the PNDT Act, 1994.
41. Section-7(2) of the PNDT Act, 1994.
42. *Terms of office of members=03 yrs*
43. *Terms of office of members=03 yrs*
44. *Terms of office of members=01 yrs*
45. Section-16 of the PNDT Act, 1994.
46. Section-17(4) of the PNDT Act, 1994.
47. *Powers of Appropriate Authorities under* Section17A of the PNDT Act, 1994.
48. Section-22(1) of the PNDT Act, 1994.
49. Section-22(2) of the PNDT Act, 1994.
50. Section-23(1) of the PNDT Act, 1994.
51. Section-23(2) of the PNDT Act, 1994.
52. Section-23(3) of the PNDT Act, 1994.
53. Section-23(4) of the PNDT Act, 1994.
54. Section-27of the PNDT Act, 1994.
55. *Cognizance of offences* under Section 28 of the PNDT Act, 1994.

56. Manuscript/brochure of National Seminar on "Violence Against Girl Child and Women: Issues and Concern" conducted on 4-5th March 2014 by Women's Studies Department, Barkatullah University, Bhopal.

11

CRIME AGAINST WOMEN- WAKE UP CALL

Renu Sharma

"Violence against women is a manifestation of historically unequal power relations between men and women, which have led to domination over and discrimination against women by men and to the prevention of the full advancement of women..." The United Nations Declaration on the Elimination of Violence against Women, General Assembly Resolution, December 1993.

Violence against women is any violence that targets a woman because she is a woman. It includes physical, sexual or psychological harm such as domestic violence, sexual assault, forced marriage, stalking, 'honor' attacks, human trafficking and female genital mutilation. It also includes threats of violence and kidnapping.

Violence against women and girls continues unabated in every continent, country and culture. It takes a devastating toll on women's lives, on their families, and on society as a whole. Most societies prohibit such violence yet the reality is that too often it is covered up or tacitly condoned.A quick look through the daily newspapers will give us an idea of the epic proportions the phenomenon has taken. Sample some of these facts from around the world:

- One woman in four has been abused during pregnancy.
- More than 60 million women worldwide are considered 'missing' as a result of sex-selective abortions and female infanticide, according to an estimate by Nobel Laureate Amartya Sen.
- The World Health Organization has reported that up to 70% of female murder victims are killed by their male partners.
- Interpersonal violence was the 10th leading cause of death among women between the ages of 15 and 44, in 1998.
- Population-based studies report that between 12 and 25% of women have experienced attempted or completed forced sex by an intimate partner or ex-partner at some point in their lives.
- Nearly one in three women have experienced domestic violence.
- Nearly one in four women have experienced some form of sexual assault.
- 39% of women saying fear of crime had impacts on their quality of life.
- 53% of all serious sexual assaults are committed by a partner or ex-partner.

- Nearly one in ten women say that they have been stalked.
- Children who have witnessed domestic violence are 2 times more likely to have serious behavioral problems than other children.
- A survey by Sugar Magazine and the NSPCC in 2005 found that one in five teenage girls who responded said they'd been hit by a boyfriend.
- 40% of victims of serious sexual assault tell nobody.

Afghanistan, Congo and Pakistan are the world's most dangerous countries for women due to a barrage of threats ranging from violence and rape to dismal health care and "honour killings", a Thomson Reuters Foundation expert poll showed India and Somalia ranked fourth and fifth, respectively, in the global perceptions survey by Trust Law, the Foundation's legal news service..

Indian Situation: As of 2011, the Speaker of the LokSabha and the Leader of the Opposition in the LokSabha (Lower House of the parliament) were women. The status of Women in India, both historically and socially has been one of the respect and reverence. The Constitution of India not only grants equality to Women but also empowers the State to adopt measures of positive discrimination in favor of Women for neutralizing the cumulative socio-economic educational and political disadvantages faced by them. Article 15 forbids discrimination on grounds of Caste, religion, sex, race and place of birth, whereas, Article 16 ensures equal opportunities of employment.

Despite the ostensible acceptance of women being equal to men, and a plethora of laws and human rights guarantees, violence against women which is also referred to as gender-based violence is a reality that has assumed huge proportions. Women in India continue to face atrocities such as rape, acid throwing and dowry killings while young girls are forced into prostitution; as of late rape has seen a sharp increase following several high profile cases of young girls brutally raped in public areas. Not only does violence against women exist, in our vocabulary of progress it has taken on insidious forms that are justified in the name of faith, community, even development.

A secure environment for women appears to be a far cry in India. Crime against women traditionally includes rape, kidnapping and abduction, dowry death, torture, molestation, sexual harassment, importation of girls, cases under the Immoral Traffic (Prevention) Act, Sati Prevention Act, Dowry Prohibition Act, and Indecent Representation of Women (Prevention) Act. Crime against the fairer sex is steadily increasing and less and less number of the accused is getting convicted. Among the crimes listed by the National Crime Records Bureau rape, molestation, sexual harassment, murder and dowry deaths are reported more frequently than dacoity, arson or counterfeiting.

Thomson Reuters Foundation poll results showed that Female feticide, child marriage and high levels of trafficking and domestic servitude make the world's largest democracy India, the fourth most dangerous place for women.100 million people, mostly women and girls, are involved in trafficking in one way or another, according to former Indian Home Secretary Madhukar Gupta.Up to 50 million girls are "missing" over the past century due to female infanticide and feticide.44.5% of girls are married before the age of 18.

One bride was murdered every hour over dowry demands in 2010, says the National Crime Records Bureau. "The courts are flooded with cases of gender-related crimes," said retired Supreme Court judge MarkandeyKatju. He said honor and dowry murders should be punished with death."These are not normal crimes. These are social crimes because they disrupt the entire social fabric of the community. When you commit crimes against women, it has a lasting impact.

Almost 45 percent of Indian girls are married before they turn 18, says the International Center for Research on Women."The inheritance law was reformed in 2005, bringing women's legal equality in agricultural land. In reality, however, less than 10 percent women own some kind of land," said GovindKelkar from land rights group, Landesa India. "This is starker as 84 percent of rural women are engaged in agricultural production. There is policy silence on the implementation of laws for women's rights."

According to the National Crime Records Bureau 2005 Crime Clock, there was:

- 1 crime committed against women every three minutes.
- 1 molestation case every 15 minutes.
- 1 sexual harassment case every 53 minutes.
- 1 kidnapping and abduction case every 23 minutes.

- And every 77 minutes an incidence related to dowry took place.

In 2005, a whopping 1.55 lakh cases of crime against women were registered across India, but convictions were recorded in only 30,826 cases, a mere 19.8%.In 2006, case registration jumped to 1.64 lakh, but convictions declined to 28,998, or 17.5%. . Over 32000 murders, 19,000 rapes, 7500 dowry deaths and 36500 molestation cases are the violent crimes reported in India in 2006 against women.Continuing the trend, more than 1.85 lakh cases were registered in 2007, but the trial courts found the charge sustainable only in 27,612 cases, a meager 14.9%.

That India remains one of the most violent nations to live in has been further reinforced by NCRB's 'Crime in India' report - 2012.

- The total incidence of violent crimes has increased by 65 percent in 2012 over the previous year.
- Safety and security of women in India remains questionable as overall crime graph against women has witnessed 6.8 per cent rise in 2012.
- Madhya Pradesh with 3425 cases in 2012 is the new rape capital of India. Overall at the country level, incidence of rape has risen by 2.96 per cent in 2012 over the previous year.
- Kidnapping& abduction of girls and women continues unabated. A 7.5 percent rise in cases of kidnapping & abduction of girls and women has been reported in 2012.

- Good news for women as number of women police stations have increased from 455 in 2011 to 510 in 2012.
- A major relief to Indian brides,dowry deaths have fallen by four per cent in 2012.
- Crime against children has increased by 15.33 percent in 2012 over the previous year.
- Incidence of murder and rape committed against children increased by 13 per cent and 55 per cent respectively in 2012 over the previous year.
- The involvement of girls in juvenile crime has increased from 5.8 per cent in 2011 to 5.9 per cent in 2012.

Rapes alone accounted for nearly 25,000 of the cases (about 1,000 more than in 2011), with a conviction rate standing at a miserable 24 per cent. A poor conviction rate promotes crime and encourages the predator. However, these statistics are misleading and only reveal tip of the iceberg. A very large number of cases are either not reported to the police, or if reported, not registered. Further because of the attached stigma and shame, rape remains one of the most misunderstood and unregistered crimes. But the mismatch between cases registered and conviction does not only casts an ominous shadow on functioning of the justice delivery system at the lower levels, but importantly, it also raises a serious question about the ability of the police to conduct proper investigation and prepare a watertight case.

India has robust gender laws, but they are hardly enforced, partly because a feudal mindset is still prevalent among bureaucrats, magistrates and the police. Politicians are also unwilling to crack down on customary biases against women for fear of losing conservative votes. Amid empty talk of 'empowerment of women'rapes have become a routine affair with girl-children or teenagers being regularly targeted in every city, town or rural area. It is as if wolves have been set on the second-sex, feticide to outright killing.

Most of the violence against women is related to and grows out of their position in society. If a female fetus is destroyed it is because a girl child is unwanted as she is seen as a burden.If a wife is beaten, at least partly it is because women are seen as property to be treated as the husband, her owner, desires. On a broader level, it is also because a woman is perceived as the "weaker" sex, dependent on man, so he can bully her.

Rape is not just about sex. It is not just the act of an individual man against an individual woman, a manifestation of psychological aberration. It is more about power and dominance, asserting total control over a helpless woman. Violence against women is further complicated by other factors in society. Caste, religious, communal and class factors also play a role in the violence against women.

Religious fundamentalism imposes restriction on women and they are the ones penalized for trying to break out of blatantly unfair and unrealistic codes of behavior that have no relevance in the life of today.

The systemic brutality against the girl-child has, over a period, led to an imbalance in the sex ratio, with Haryana the citadel of public lynching of women having the highest skewed ratio (877 women against 1,000 men). It is no better in Punjab, Delhi, Maharashtra and other states the northern India.

Haryana's infamous 'khap panchayat' which order 'honor killings' of young couples marrying against the wishes of their elders, has the blessings of the political class, playing regressive politics of vote bank even after 63 years of independence and in spite of the Supreme Court's scathing remarks on 'khaps.'

The so called 'liberated classes or educated parents give dowry to their daughters as a matter of false prestige and the fear of societal stigma. There are thousands of instances where parents of daughters have paid lakhs of rupees succumbing to the 'black mail' of in-laws or that of the husband but did not have the courage to bring their daughters back home. The end result in a majority of such cases is daughters are done to death by in-laws lusting for more money or the women takes her life.

The rising incidence of violent crimes against women like rape is affecting the self-confidence and sense of security of millions of girls and women. Legal experts point out that many rapes go unreported. Due to "family honor" many complaint files are withdrawn and in many cases the police do not give a fair hearing. Medical evidence is often unrecorded making it easy for offenders to pass scot free under prevailing laws. The police reaction to such cases has compounded the issue of low acquittal rate. It is from this same sense of insensitivity that the police do not file complaints when children from underprivileged households go missing, and allow male policemen to grill rape victims when cases are reported, often asking humiliating questions.

Such behavior is not only ruining the image of the police but also creating a sense of indignation among the public.

Outside of formal Criminal Justice System, it is not uncommon in India's interior villages and hamlets for local kangaroo courts to advise the woman to marry her rapist to "preserve her honor". In some cases, rape can be used to settle caste issues and local disputes.

A lot of lip service is paid to the women's liberties, their rights and empowerment. The promises of protection galore, but when it comes to creating a space for women in society, where they can live and work with respect, crime is unleashed against them. The irony is that there is not even a semblance of a pro-active step from governments, human rights organizations, women's organizations or women politicians to bring a visible major policy shift in respect of administration of justice, law and order and change in the functioning of police which has a mindset tilted against women specially working or 'liberated women. The rising number of women parliamentarians and the presence of many high profile women in India's political parties and public offices will remain only cosmetic until effective laws and mindsets are not properly implemented to safeguard ordinary women.

So often there is reported a crime, so heinous that it makes one and all sit up. But, as is expected, the pace of investigation and the action to follow slackens and it becomes another of those unfortunate incidents that would be soon forgotten. This is especially true in the case of crime against women, where, the extent of horror keeps extending the threshold of mental acceptance and after a while the repeat incidents are reported, often for sheer titillation. Even today, it is not only the repressed and the uneducated woman or the unsuspecting children that become targets of the sick machinations of the human mind, but it is also the emancipated women who are not safe.

There are number of Acts and legal provisions to protect and safeguard women and punish those who commit crime against them. But due to ineffective enforcement, women are exploited by the male dominated society. There are very strict guidelines on how a case (crime against women) should be investigated and prosecuted. Guidelines have been passed keeping in mind the sensibilities and sensitivities of the victim and to reduce the 'agony and sufferings' of the victim.

The higher judiciary has shown concern for women's right in recent times. The Supreme Court in number of land mark judgments has expanded the scope of fundamental rights.

In Delhi Domestic Women's Forum Vs Union of India 1995 SCC 14, the court asserted that "speedy trial is one of the essential requisites of law" and that expeditious investigation and speedy trial only could give meaning to the "guarantee of "equal protection of law", under Article 21 of the Constitution. The Supreme Court suggested the formulation of a segment for awarding compensation to rape victims at the time of convicting the person found guilty of rape.

In Vishaka and others Vs State of Rajasthan and others 1997 6SCC 241, case the Supreme Court held, "gender equality includes protection from sexual harassment and right to work with dignity, which is universally recognized basic human right. The common minimum requirement of this right has international acceptance.

In Municipal Corporation of Delhi v. Female Workers (Muster Roll) (AIR 2000 SC 1274), the Supreme Court extended the benefits of the Maternity Benefit Act, 1961 to the Muster Roll (Daily Wagers) female employees of Delhi Municipal Corporation. In this case, the Court directly incorporated the provisions of Article 11 of CEDAW, 1979 into the Indian Law. Supreme Court also held that a just social order could be achieved only when inequalities are obliterated and women, which constitute almost half of the segment of our society, are honored and treated with dignity.

In Chairman, Railway Board v. Chandrima Doss (AIR 2000 SC 988), the Supreme Court awarded compensation of 10 lakhs to an alien woman under Article 21 of Constitution, who has been a victim of rape.

In Githa Hariharan v. Reserve Bank of India (AIR 1999 SC 1149), the Supreme Court interpreted Section 6(a) of Hindu Minority and Guardianship Act, 1956 and Section 19(b) of the Guardians and Wards Act, 1890 in such a way that father and mother get equal status as guardians of a minor.

In Mohammed Ahmed Khan v. Shah Bano (AIR 1985 SC 945), the Supreme Court granted equal right of maintenance under Section 125 of Cr. P.C. 1973 to a divorced married woman notwithstanding the personal law. The Supreme Court also held that "large segments of society which have been traditionally subjected to unjust treatment, women are one such segment."

In Charansingh v. Union of India (1979 Lab IC 633), the Delhi High Court expressed that women are a backward class as compared to men. In Government of Andhra Pradesh v. P. B. Vijay Kumar (AIR 1995 SC 1648), the Supreme Court has held that the issue of reservation for women in State services was upheld under Article 15(3) of the Indian Constitution. In Uttarakhand MahilaKalyan Parishad v. State of Uttar Pradesh (AIR 1992 SC 1695), the Supreme Court struck down the discriminatory rules of Education Department of Government of Uttar Pradesh.

In Air India v. Nargis Mirza (AIR 1981 SC 1829), the Supreme Court struck down the discriminatory Rules of Indian Airlines. In Bodhisattwa v. Ms. Subhra Chakraborty (AIR 1996 SC 922), the Supreme Court held that rape is a crime against basic human rights. The Supreme Court observed that rape was not only an offence under the criminal law, but it was a violation of the fundamental right to life and liberty guaranteed by Article 21 of Indian Constitution.

In Apparel Export Promotion Council v. A. K. Chopra (AIR 1999 SC 625), the Supreme Court found all facets of gender equality including prevention of sexual harassment in the fundamental rights granted by the Constitution. In C. B. Muthamma v. Union of India (AIR 1979 SC 1868) : 1979 Lab IC 1307, a service rule whereby marriage was a disability for appointment to foreign service was declared unconstitutional by the Supreme Court.

In case of State of Maharashtra Vs. Madhukar N Mardikar (1991) I SCC 57, Supreme court held that even a prostitute has a right to privacy and no person can rape her just because she is a woman of easy virtue.

In Shobha Rani v. Madhukar (AIR 1988 SC 121), the Supreme Court held that dowry demand was held enough to amount to cruelty.

In Prathibha Rani v. Suraj Kumar (AIR 1985 SC 628), the Supreme Court upheld women's right to the Stridhana. In State of Punjab v. Gurmit Singh (AIR 1996 SC 1393), the Supreme Court held that rape was held to be violative of the right of privacy.

In Saveetha Samvedhi case ((1996) 1 SCR 1046), the Supreme Court held that a married daughter was allowed accommodation in parental house. In Gourav Jain v. Union of India (AIR 1997 SC 3012), the Supreme Court laid down guidelines including the necessity of counseling, cajoling, and coercing the women to retrieve from prostitution and rehabilitate them.

In Rupen Deo Bajaj v. Kanwar Pal Singh Gill,1996 AIR 309, 1995 SCC (6) 194, the Supreme Court said that the offence under section 354 IPC should not be treated lightly as it is quite a grave offence. In certain western countries privacy to person and even privacy to procreation are regarded as very sacrosanct rights and if this offence is studied in that prospect the offence would clearly show that it affects the dignity of women and, therefore, the accused of this offence, when proved, should be appropriately dealt with.

People's Union for Democratic Rights v. Police Commissioner, Delhi, Police Headquarter and another: 1990 ACJ 192, (1989) 4 SCC 730, the supreme court after holding that the accused was guilty of offence under section 354 of IPC, awarded, to the victim, compensation which is to be recovered from the salary of the guilty officers.

The Supreme Court has forged new tools, devised new methods and adopted new strategies for the purpose of making fundamental rights meaningful even to the victims of crime.

Bachpan Bachao Andolan Petitioner(s) vs Union of India & others, 2011 STPL(Web) 400 SC S.C directed "in case a complaint with regard to any missing children is made in a police station, the same should be reduced into a First Information Report and appropriate steps should be taken to see that follow up investigation is taken up immediately thereafter".

State of A.P. v. GanulaSatya Murthy, the Supreme Court judgment dated19.11.1996, made an observation that it is an irony that while we are celebrating women's rights in all spheres we show little or no concern for their honor. Their lordships further observed that the courts must deal with rape cases with utmost sensitivity and appreciate the evidence of the totality on the background of the entire case and not in isolation.

An aspect which needs to be stated here is that a woman who has been raped is not an accomplice. She is the victim of a carnal desire. In a case of rape, corroboration need not be searched for by the judge if in the particular circumstances of the cases before him he is satisfied that it is safe to rely on the evidence of the prosecutrix. If the prosecutrix is able to give a vivid account of how she was subjected to sexual harassment and the intercourse, the same can be placed reliance upon and the conviction can be recorded.

In State of Maharashtra v. M.N. Madikar, AIR 1991 SC 207- The Supreme Court has opined, that even a woman with easy virtue is entitled to privacy and no one can invade her privacy as and when he likes. So also, it is not open to any and every person to violate her person as and when he wishes. Therefore, merely because she is a woman of easy virtue, her evidence cannot be thrown overboard. It has been empathically laid down that there is rule or prudence requiring corroboration of the victims in a case of rape.

The apex court in the case of State of H.P. v. Mange Ram, AIR 2000 SC 2798, has laid down that if the prosecutrix submits her body under fear or terror, the same would never amount to consent. In the said case their lordships also held that in the absence of any violence to the body of the victim in all circumstances would not give rise to inference of consent.

In State of Rajasthan v. N.K. AIR 2000 S.C. 1812, wherein the supreme court held that the absence of injuries on the person of the prosecutrix is not necessary to falsify the allegation or be regarded as an evidence of consent on the part of the prosecutrix.

Despite the categorical stand taken by the highest court of the land in placing the maximum reliance on the statement of the victim and the circumstances surrounding the episode in question, so many rape cases fail at the trial stage itself. Sometimes the trial courts give emphasis on absence of physical injuries, lack of corroboration by medical evidence, non-raising of alarm, no evidence of showing resistance and such other ancillary factors. From these angles the prosecution is disbelieved or the court arrives at the conclusion that there is consent.

Rape is not only a crime against the person of a woman; it is a crime against the entire society. Courts are therefore expected to deal with sexual crimes against women with utmost sensitivity. "A socially sensitized judge is a better statutory amour in cases of crimes against women than long clauses of penal provisions containing complex exceptions and provision. An unmerited acquittal encourages wolves in society."

Cehat AndOrs. vs Union Of India: 2003 (10) SCALE 11, (2003) 8 SCC 412 in light of the alarming decline in sex ratios in the country to the disadvantage of women, this petition was filed seeking directions from the Supreme Court for the implementation of the Pre-Natal Diagnostic Techniques Act which regulates the provision of pre-natal diagnostic technology. In this case, the Court took on the unique role of actually monitoring the implementation of the law and issuing several beneficial directives over the course of 3 years during which the case was proceeding in court. This petition put the issue of sex selection and sex selective abortion on the national agenda and as a consequence there have been heightened activities on this issue by government and non-governmental agencies alike.

Approach towards safety of women-Need of the hour:

1. To increase reporting of rape and assault cases: A wider social movement of educating women of their rights, to conquer the menace, is needed more particularly in rural areas where women are still largely uneducated and less aware of

their rights and fall an easy prey to their exploitation.

2. Women must be educate on their rights and encourage them to come forward to register the cases. There are many violent cases but due to stigma in the society very few are reported.
3. Making criminal proceedings more gender-sensitive: Standards for criminal proceedings, including rules of evidence and procedure, should be conducted in a gender-sensitive manner to ensure that women are not re-victimized. This includes the development and application of rules of evidence and procedure to ensure that they are not too onerous or based on harmful stereotypes that would inhibit women from testifying. It also requires simplification of legal procedures; ensuring victim confidentiality through in camera proceedings where appropriate; victim support; protection measures; and trained personnel at all levels of Criminal Justice delivery system.
4. Sensitivity training: should be provided to the entire criminal justice machinery on handling cases of sexual abuse and rapes. This should start with the Police and state-run Medical fraternity, where majority of the cases are first reported.
5. Law enforcement agencies:Most of the time police refuse to file a FIR and force the victim to 'settle' the matter. Cases reported to the police are not registered because police performance in prevention and detection of

crimes is judged on the basis of statistics. Victims are also harassed and pressurized to withdraw complaint. Irresponsible remarks by police officials and politicians often hurt traumatized victims. Law enforcement agencies should be well trained to react swiftly and with sensitivity in cases concerning offences against women and children.Gender insensitive police officers heighten the trauma of the victims by asking embarrassing questions. There is utmost need for gender sensitization of police personnel of all ranks.Police response to women victims of crime is callous and insensitive. Masculine and patriarchal culture of police is a reflection of the gender insensitive culture of the Indian society where women do not enjoy respect and consideration they deserve.Justice Verma Commission set up after the incident of gang rape, in its report, has strongly pitched for police reforms recommended by the National Police Commission and further reiterated by the Supreme Court in Prakash Singh's case.It says that urgent reforms are needed "in order for India to attain a standard of policing which is based upon a positive and cooperative relationship between civil society and the police service".

6. Exemplary punishment and Quick Justice delivery System: Social impact of the crime, where it relates to offences against women, cannot be lost sight of and per se requires exemplary treatment. Public abhorrence of the

crime needs reflection through imposition of appropriate sentence by the court. Campaigning of, 'Zero- tolerance 'of sex offenders. Establishment of more and more fast track court with time bound disposal of cases. It is expected that the courts should deal with cases of Crimes against woman in a more realistic manner and not allow the criminals to escape on account of procedural technicalities or insignificant lacunae in the evidence as otherwise the criminals would receive encouragement and the victims of the crime would be totally discouraged by the crime going unpunished.

7. Comprehensive campaigns must be initiated by NGOs to educate and inform the masses of the current problems that women face, highlighting statistics.
8. Media organizations should keep reporting on any new cases across the country and relentlessly keep the pressure up on the government machinery to investigate & prosecute the abusers.
9. Citizen organizations should work with existing public institutions like schools, colleges, industry bodies, religious institutions etc. in running the above campaigns through social media and offline workshops, seminar and help changing the mindsets from within.

We have just to remember in the words of Guru Nanak DevJi,"It is inside women that we are conceived, and it is from her that we are born.

It is to women that we are engaged and married.

It is a woman that is our life-long companion and it is she who keeps our human race going.

It is a woman again who is sought when one loses one's previous wife.

It is a woman through whom we establish our social ties.

Then why abuse her from whom even kings and great men are born?"

References

The British Crime Survey 2007-08 and 2006-07, Sugar Magazine and the NSPC.

Thomson Reuters Foundation poll, 2012.

Crimes In India, National Crime record Bureau, GOI, 1999 to 2012.

Note: Court cases discussed by the author of the paper are self written and are part of their experience as a senior Judge. Thus, references of the court cases have not been mentioned.

12

READING INTO CRIME AGAINST WOMEN IN INDIA: SOME ISSUES AND PERSPECTIVES

R. G. Dastidar

Protection from violence may be thought of as one of the "capabilities" that contribute to the quality of life (Sen, 1985).India is often portrayed as a progressive and developing country although rift with paradoxes, inequality and one prominent area of implications is crime against women. In recent times the issue of crime against women has been harshly brought into public perception both at home and abroad by spiraling crime rates and bizarre and incessant incidents, and increasing political voicing. "..amid public outrage over gang-rape and murder of two girls in Uttar Pradesh, the Narendra Modi government .... vowed "zero tolerance" policy towards violence against women and reform of criminal justice system, simpler, quicker and more effective delivery of justice" (PTI June 09.2014).

All this while, most of India is a culture which venerates the feminine. All Hindi words for power are feminine. Islam, theoretically is a religion that grants women most rights vis a vis most other religions of the world. Jainism and Buddhism shun all kinds of violence. But culture is hardly a variable that allows for a clear and complete understanding of crime against women in India. Statistics on crime against women show an increasing trend of violence, inequality and repressed rights. In some states, it is actually a night mare.

Much of the violence against Indian women is in the form of domestic violence, dowry deaths, acid attacks, honour killings, harassment, rape, abduction, and cruelty by husbands, in-laws, relatives, employers, (known persons), etc. Although, this may seem related to mostly the private space but it is equally appalling in public space as well, specially' when viewed against the perception of violence and responses to it by the power structures in society. The comments of some politicians in this regard on various occasions is if anything a window to our social conception of women, state and justice.

Women of all caste, community, age, religion, or social group etc. have been noted to be vulnerable to violence although it may show greater vulnerability to certain kind of violence in some communities, age and regions. Rising standards of education, income, political participation do not seem to provide any insulation from violence! Studies show a complex set of social, cultural, political and economic factors contributing to women's vulnerability to violence which is far more than that faced by men in the same context. Women in India like in most other societies seem disposable and are a lesser title in so far as the state is concerned! On a larger canvas the boundaries that define womenhood in India today are global. Women's trafficking and the missing girls report points to the nexus of the local to the global.

What does the Indian social reality of crime against women tell us about the society and times we live in and its social distribution of rights, justice, power , human values, culture, etc. What are the lessons here for India and the world? Few studies have covered these concerns. Holistic and continuous studies are mostly missing. While most of psychological studies focus on individual attributes of vulnerability, sociological studies have only started to focus on various issues, thanks to the feminist nudge. It is anyway presumed to be a symptom of power imbalance or administrative concern and therefore studying power relations remains the major concern with scholars of political science, administration etc. Studies on power treat violence as a residue category. It is seen as being used to snatch or maintain power, and thus it does not form the focus of study. It is widely recognized that even today, a lack of reliable and continuous data is an obstacle in having a clear picture of violence against women.

Drez in making a case for more studies on violence from the developmental perspective argues, ... "Violence also affects human wellbeing in indirect ways, as when armed conflicts undermine economic growth or the functioning of public services. If development is concerned with improving the quality of life, the issue of violence should be a major interest of the discipline. Yet, it tends to receive little attention outside specialized circles" (Drez, 2000). Another problem as most scholars would acknowledge comes from the data in this area which is either unreliable or simply unavailable. Government statistics come under fire in this area mainly on two counts-1. Under reporting and 2. Faulty statistics. There is an underreporting of the crime due to social and cultural factors as much as due to an insensitive police force and an intimidating judicial process (Gangoli, 2007). Methods of data collection, cultural constructs of women's modesty and the social repercussions of voicing victimization are high. Most sexual crimes go unreported due to stigma, fear and humiliation. In some areas certain crimes are seen to have social acceptance.

Other factors too have prevented any full analysis and study. The present article tries to look at some issues of crime against women in India by reviewing sociological and feminist literature.

According to National Crime Record Bureau (NCRB) in India, the number of reported rapes has increased with 700% since 1971 when it started to be recorded (NCRB, 2007; Gangoli, 2012:101). The rate of crime committed against women was 41.7 in 2012 according to NCRB report 2012. The proportion of IPC crimes committed against women towards total IPC crimes has increased during last 5 years from 8.9% in the year 2008 to 10.2% during the year 2012. Why is there this increase despite an environment of increased concern? The answer to this is a complex picture. Some scholars have explained this by arguing that the broadening of the definition of crime, better statistics, and also increased reporting have contributed to the picture. One example is the increased use of neutral terms as intimate partner abuse, family violence etc, which not only makes for better statistics but is also reflective of changed perception of domestic violence and includes the possibility that either sex may be a victim.

The U.N. declaration on the Elimination of Violence Against Women states that "violence against women is a manifestation of historically unequal power relations between men and women" and that "violence against women is one of the crucial social mechanisms by which women are forced into a subordinate position compared with men". India is a signatory partner to the convention. Under this, the issue is increasingly been addressed by the international forums and the Government of India. The United Nations General Assembly (UNGA), in its resolution on the Declaration on the Elimination of Violence Against Women, defines "violence against women" as "any act of gender-based violence that results in, or is likely to result in, physical, sexual or mental harm or suffering to women, including threats of such acts, coercion or arbitrary deprivation of liberty, whether occurring in public or in private life(CEDAW :1979).

However violence against women is a highly politicized topic of debate. Broadly speaking more men are victims of crime than women, but there is a basic difference in the type and pattern of violence faced by women. Besides, the statistics are increasing and no part of the world is free. With increased resources devoted towards scientific study of crime, there is a tendency to categorise it along various heads, including gender , which in some sense is also reflective of the new consciousness and sensibilities of our age. On the other hand since crime against women reflects on governments, the social structuring of families , social and cultural values and conceptions the definition of what constitutes violence and therefore subsequently crime and its definitions are contested. Violence however has been a pervasive social reality right from the hoary past. What can be broadly said is that it has existed in all societies and cultures and all times. In some it has been legally sanctioned, in others it has been quietly accepted or underplayed or fiercely contested.

Scientific treatment of crime against women has been strongly criticised for being biased, lopsided, incomplete and arbitrary as is the very definition of violence itself and what constitutes it. Recent studies with the advantage of global observations have however started to distinguish between the various forms of violence against women as being distinct and different from the violence generally observed on account of the genesis of it being specifically directed towards women on account of their gender. While Marx attributed it to the evolution of private property, the feminist attribute the patriarchal social evolution as the prime factor in its perpetuation, other theoretical formulations see it along various other interpretations, clearly it has indeed been an area of serious and long ongoing debates in the social sciences . All these theoretical explanations as well as codification of this social reality raises various questions with regard to what really constitutes it? What factors are responsible for it? How it can be eliminated ? How can a society be practically formulated on basis of human rights? These issues also raises consciousness about culture as a mediator of power and social justice and spaces as much as how dependence in a global world increases inequality , a factor known to contributing towards violence.

Some of the complexity of this issue can only be apprehended by the spectrum of individual case studies on violence against women which clearly defy interpretation along any single theory added to which are factors of a plural society. Crime against women in Government statistics come from a narrow legally defined part of a more pervasive and myriad social reality of violence against women. The Indian Penal Code enumerates it along broad seven heads of

(i) Rape (Sec. 376 IPC)

(ii) Kidnapping & abduction for specified purposes (Sec. 363 - 373 IPC)

(iii) Homicide for dowry, dowry deaths or their attempts (Sec. 302/304-B IPC)

(iv) Torture - both mental and physical (Sec. 498-A IPC)

(v) Assault on women with intent to outrage her modesty (Sec. 354 IPC)

(vi) Insult to the modesty of women (Sec. 509 IPC)

(vii) Importation of girl from foreign country (upto 21 years of age) (Sec. 366-B IPC)

There are additional enumeration along special and local laws which are gender specific laws for which crime statistics are recorded throughout the country. Some of these are:

(i) Immoral Traffic (Prevention) Act, 1956

(ii) Dowry Prohibition Act, 1961

(iii) Indecent Representation of Women (Prohibition) Act, 1986

(iv) Commission of Sati Prevention Act, 1987.

(v) Pre-natal Diagnostic Techniques (Regulation and Prevention of Misuse) Act 1996

Some other acts like harassment of women, factory act, etc. tend to create space for legal representation of women's rights.

Government definitions have administrative, research, political implications and hence they are often conservative. Most broadening of definitions in India have happened under activist pressures nationally or internationally. Activist working in this area have contested the conservative government formulation of crime against women time and again and lobbied for greater space, mostly legal and administrative changes modeled along positive discrimination and citizenship, with the aid of both local and international support. The Supreme Court Of India has intervened on behalf of public litigations and pointed the way to broader interpretations of laws benefiting women. The Government however, has often been flayed for tardiness and lack of political will in pushing women issues. The reasons for which have been analysed by scholars like Yuval-Davis (1997) who argue that (since) the influence of gender relations (can) be seen in national reproduction (biological, social, symbolic), national culture and national citizenship, which is often why political conservatism has resulted in the maintenance of second class citizenship for women. "Notions of the Ideal Society are often linked to notions of the Ideal Woman" (Papanek: 1994), and nationalism, identity and citizenship have reflected the social relationships of gender (as well as class and ethnicity). Thus the Indian women often have found themselves with constitutional equality but little practical equality in their day to day lives. Worse feminist protest and decent have been silenced and their rights sacrificed in the name of nationalism. Indian feminist face allegations of being run by western feminism and therefore anti-family and also anti- national.

"While domestic violence can be understood in terms of certain acts of usually direct physical or sexual physical violence, not least in law and in many prevalence surveys (see Martinez and Schröttle et al., 2006), to focus only on these is not enough. Who defines violence and how it is defined is crucial. Women experiencing violence in intimate relations recognize a vast array of violence's that are separate or merged, as: physical and threats thereof; sexual; emotional/verbal/psychological; economic/nutritional; reproductive/medical; social; spatial, temporal; and representational" (Hanmer: 1996). Studies show that acts of violence against women can be seen as the direct demonstration of a long process of threatening or control of women and in continuation of other indirect non codified violence. Women are taught to fear and therefore controlled discounted.

Feminist critics also assert that "the con-text in which violence is experienced is crucial. Women are much more likely than men to use violence in self-defence, more likely to be injured by acts of intimate violence directed against them, more likely to feel seriously threatened by it, less likely to be able to effectively defend themselves, and less likely to have the resources to leave violent relationships" (Britton, 2000).

Recent years have seen an increase in the public outcry and activism for women's issues through development initiatives mostly under our government's commitment to world organizations. Though approaches to the problem, solutions offered and their impact differ and are highly contested. Globalization for example is seen to have further marginalised women. This is because " ...definitions are used politically as tools in social struggles. Together with poverty, unemployment, terrorism, and other social problems, violence against women is a highly politicized topic of social scientific inquiry, and definitions of this harm and reflect this reality" (Ellis, 1987). It also leads to the developed vs. developing dialogue and global market forces promoted by international agencies. To sum it would be to say as Kilpatrick (2004) correctly points out, the debate around defining violence against women is "old, fierce, and unlikely to be resolved in the near future."

The definition of the problem is further carried forward in how this inequality is created and then perpetuated. Feminist literature in this area ranges from studies of culture ,religion, language, social structure and processes to political and economic systems. Some feminist for instance argue that law and judicial practises legitimise women's subordination and undermine women (Gangoli, 2007). Thus asserting that inequality is in fact intrinsic to how nationalism is defined and in the conception of the nation itself. ..."

while women's activism at the national and global levels has sought changes in the structure of those social relationships and in the meaning of citizenship" (Moghadam, 1999).

The concept of patriarchy in its many avatars is seen by many to explain inequality as a basic form of inequality defining society along with other stratification structures. Feminist literature establishes that social construct around patriarchy world over tend to elevate the male and subjugate the female. "Violence against women is a product of patriarchal social arrangements and ideologies that are sustained and reinforced by other systems of domination" (Hunnicutt, 2009).

Feminist movements in India have posed challenges to established patriarchal institutions such as the family, and to dominant social values and structures, most significantly in the arena of legal interventions and in the areas of violence against women. "Feminists have intervened in the area of law in at least three ways. One, to expose the working of patriarchal controls and structures within law, for instance, critiquing civil marriage and divorce laws that extend more rights to men than women. Two, to unpack the plural ways in which law operates, including offering some redress to women in situations of domestic violence and finally, to campaign to extend rights to women, such as campaigns against sexual assault and rape (Gangoli, 2007). It is also expressed that laws on violence against women are still not offering enough protection because certain violent acts are not considered crimes under some laws, for example marital rape is not considered a crime under the rape law "(Gangoli, 2007), Also (Ghosh and Choudhuri, 2011).

This can be further related to the fact that women do not form a vocal vote bank in their own right. If the loudest voice in any democracy is of patriarchal institutions and organizations then issues of violence against women are likely to be glossed over. Political trade off often end up in not being able to put women issues first. This is evident in how blatantly "khapp panchayats" can actually use media to voice anti women opinions and openly threaten all modern interpretations and change in rural areas that may lead to women's empowerment.

The prevalence of men´s violence against women is related to the ideological and institutional strength of unequal intersectional gender structures (Lundgren *et al.*, 2001; Walby, 2009), including such structural violence, as effects of state and related institutions; war and inter-communal violence; poverty and inequalities, including globally; and social structural relations of institutions that historically have been violent or have underwritten or been underwritten by violence. (Jeff, 2013).

Also some would argue that in a traditional society social conceptions promote this type of violence, shield the perpetrator or make little of the victim all of which has been instrumental in stalling an effective social response in favour of women. "Victims of rape are often persuaded that such things are either normal or justified, and their victimization may not be apparent, even to themselves" (Britton, 2000). Especially, when the aggression stems from within the family or community the stand often supported is that the outside world is far worse; family honour and support is essential to survival; living alternative are nonexistent; therefore accommodating aggression is the only alternative; etc. Structural factors such caste class community etc. have an impact on women's rights , freedom and safety (Gangoli, 2007). Studies have shown that sexual violence is more widespread in societies and groups where women's rights are lacking and are neglected (Koenig *et al.*, 2006; Kimua *et al.*, 2012; Sassen, 2000; etc.). The woes of domestic migrant labour is one such example.

An addition to the debate is the nature and role of women themselves that facilitate victimization. National data reveals that one in five women have experienced some form of violence from their husbands, or other members of their families since age 15, and there is a high degree of acceptance of domestic violence among women, with 57 per cent of married women aged between 15-49 accepting that a man is justified in beating his wife if she does not fulfil accepted gender roles (Gangoli, 2007) . "Right now, there is an important battle being waged over the nature of women's behaviour and its role in woman abuse" (Schwartz & De Keseredy, 1993). Feminist literature labels this as blaming the victim syndrome. Crime has been attributed to lifestyle changes like greater participation of women in public spaces which has impacted these issues in at least two ways. First is the increased exposure rate and second it is also seen as a backlash by displaced masculine dominance. Hackett (2011:265) observed from her statistical crime study in India that women who challenge the traditional gender roles can become a target for men's violence. Bennett and Manderson (2003:11) argue that, "at the heart of violence lies the abuse of power in the maintenance or creation of inequality". This is why some feminist ask for stricter and more laws and compliance.

While other studies point the problem relates more prominently to the inequalities stemming from global economic structures. The processes of globalization have in fact increased the social and economic stratification (Sen, 1996; Kishwar, 1996; etc.). Others feminists have suggested that some of these forms of violence against women are less specifically 'Indian' than reflecting a wider global trend of patriarchal oppression of women (Talwar Oldenburg, 2002). Studies around the world about increased reports of domestic violence as well as sexual violence in public spaces put it in relation to rapid social changes (Momsen: 2006; Foley: 2003; Maitse: 1998; Harris :2013); (Sideris : 2007).

One way of interpreting this problem would be to look at the status of women in India. This too is not without its problems. Scholars like : Devi, 1993; Kishor and Gupta, 2004, etc. agree that the diversity and complexity of parameters do not result in direct interpretations. This position is supported by studies that try to interpret violence against women along two or more indicators. For example in the conclusion of a study on crime gender and society it is asserted that "....First, murder rates in India bear no significant relation to urbanization or poverty. Second, education appears to exercise a moderating influence on criminal violence. Third, the strongest correlate of the murder rate is the female-male ratio: districts with higher female-male ratios have lower murder rates.....What seems clear is that there is a strong link of some kind between gender relations and criminal violence not just violence against women, but violence in the society as a whole." (Dreze and Khera, 2000).

In conclusion it may be said that there is a need for more intensive research in this area, but more importantly looking at the correlation of crime with poor governance and rights there is a strong case for working towards them. This issue therefore is a global and pervasive and has its roots in global governance, economic and social structures. Its understanding therefore needs to be negotiated at all levels. No wonder then it is often a litmus test of societies.

References

Britton, D. M. (2000), "Feminism in Criminology: Engendering the Outlaw", *Annals of the American Academy of Political and Social Science, 571*(1).

DeKeseredy, Walters (2011), *Violence against women: Facts, myths, controversies*, Toronto: Univ. of Toronto Press.

Dreze, Jean and Khera, Reetika (2000), "Crime, Gender, and Society in India: Insights from Homicide Data", *Population and Development Review*, Vol. 26, No. 2 (Jun. 2000).

D. Radha Devi (1993), "Status of Women in India : A Comparison by State", *Asia Pacific Population Journal*, Vol. 8 No. 4.

Ellis, D. (1987), 'Post –separation Women Abuse: The Contribution of Social Support, *Victimology*, 13.

Ellis, D. (1987), *The Wrong Stuff: An Introduction to the Sociological Study of Deviance*, Toronto: Collier Maclillan.

Foley, R.: (2003), *Violence against Women: The Challenges for Malaysian Women*, London: Routledge Curzon.

Gangoli, Geetanjali (2007), *Indian Feminisms: Law, Patriarchies and Violence in India*, Ashgate pub ltd. Hampshire.

Gangoli, G. (2012), "Controlling Women's Sexuality: Rape law in India. Ch.6. pp. 101-120", in: Westmarland, N, and Gangoli, G. ; (eds), *International Approaches to Rape*, Bristol, UK: The Policy Press.

Ghosh, B., and Choudhuri, T. (2011), "Legal Protection against Domestic Violence in India: Scope and Limitations", *Journal of Family Violence*, 26.

Hackett, M. (2011), "Domestic Violence against Women: Statistical Analysis of Crimes Across India", *Journal of Comparative Family Studies*. 42. (2).

Hanmer, J. (1996), "Women and Violence: Commonalities and Diversities", in B. Fawcett, B. Featherstone, J. Hearn and C. Toft (eds) ,*Violence and Gender Relations*, London: Sage.

Hearn, Jeff: (2013), "The Sociological Significance of Domestic Violence: Tensions, Paradoxes and Implications", *Current Sociology*, 61 (2).

Hunnicutt, G. (2009), "Varieties of Patriarchy and Violence Against Women: Resurrecting 'Patriarchy' as a Theoretical Tool", *Violence Against Women [Sage Journals]*, Vol. 15, iss. 5.

Kilpatrick, D. G. (2004), "What is violence against women? Defining and Measuring the Problem", *Journal of Interpersonal Violence*, 19.

Kimuna, S.R., Djamba, Y.K., Ciciurkaite, G., and Cherukuri, S. (2012), "Domestic Violence in India: Insights from the 2005-2006 National Family Health Survey", *Journal of Interpersonal Violence*, 28(4).

Kishwar, Madhu (1996), "Women and Politics Beyond Quotas", *Economic and Political Weekly*, Vol. XXXI No. 43, October 26, 1996.

Koenig, M.A., Stephensen, R., Ahmed, S., Jejeebhoy, S.J., and Campbell, J. (2006), "Individual and Contextual Determinants of Domestic Violence in North India", *American Journal of Public Health*, 96(1).

Lundgren, E., Heimer, G., Westerstrand, J., and Kalliokoski, A.-M. (2001), *Captured Queen: Men's Violence Against Women in 'Equal' Sweden – A Prevalence Study*, Stockholm: Fritzes Offentliga Publications.

Manderson, L., and Bennett, L. R. (eds). (2003), *Violence against Women in Asian Societies*. London, UK: RoutledgeCurzon.

Martinez, M. and Schröttle, M. *et al.* (2006), State of European Research on the Prevalence of Interpersonal Violence and its Impact on Health and Human Rights, EU FP6 Co-ordination Action on Human Rights Violations.

Moghadam, Valentine M. (1999), "Gender, National Identity and Citizenship: Reflections on the Middle East and North Africa", *Comparative Studies of South Asia, Africa and the Middle East*, Vol. XIX No. 1.

Momsen J., H. (2006), *Gender and Development*, 2 nd ed. New York, USA: Routledge Taylor & Francis Group.

NCRB (National Crime Records Bureau), Ministry of Home Affairs .2010.*Crime in India:* NCRB (National Crime Records Bureau), Ministry of Home Affairs (2010).

Neuman, Sandra. (2013), *The Issue of Sexual Violence against Women in Contemporary India*, Linnaeus University.

Papanek, Hanna (1994), "The Ideal Woman and the Ideal Society: Control and Autonomy in the Construction of Identity", in Valentine M. Moghadam ,eds., *Identity Politics and Women: Culture Reassertions and Feminisms . International Perspective*, University of Virginia: West view Press, p. 43.

PTI: Crime exposes the nature of governance systems. Zero Tolerance Policy Towards Violence against Women: Govt. 09th June 2014.

Saskia Sassen (2000), "Women's Burden: Counter-geographies of globalization and the feminization of survival", *Journal of International Affairs*; Spring; 53, 2.

Saskia Sassen (2000), "Unstoppable immigrants: Special report: Refugees in Britain",*The Guardian* 12.09.2000.

Schwartz, M. D., & DeKeseredy, W. S. (1993), "The Return of the "battered husband syndrome" through the typification of women as violent", *Crime, Law and Social Change*, 20.

Sen, Amartya. (1985), *Commodities and Capabilities*, Amsterdam: North-Holland.

Sen, A and DrPze, J. (2002), *India Development and Participation*, 2nd ed. New York, USA: Oxford University Press.

Sen, P. (1998), "Violence in Intimate Relations: A Research Project in India. Ch.8 pp.134-154" in: Afshar, H. (ed.) *Women and Empowerment: Illustrations from the Third World*, London: Macmillan Press LTD.

Sideris, T. (2007), "Post-Apartheid South Africa – Gender, Rights and the Politics of Recognition. New Avenues for Old Forms of Violence?", in: Buur, L., Jensen, S., and Stepputat, F., (eds) *The Security-Development Nexus. Expressions of Sovereignty and Securitization in Southern Africa*, Cape Town, South Africa: HSRC Press.

Sunita Kishor and Kamla Gupta. (2009), "Gender Equality and Women's Empowerment in India. National Family Health Survey (NFHS-3), India, 2005-06. Mumbai: International Institute for Population Sciences; Calverton, Maryland, USA: ICF Macro.

Teboho Maitse. (1998), "Political Change, Rape, and Pornography in Post-Apartheid South Africa", *Gender and Development* Vol. 6, No. 3, [Violence against Women] (Nov., 1998).

UNDP (United Nations Development Programme). (2011), *India Factsheet: Gender and Social Exclusion Indicators*, UNDP.

United Nations Committee on the Elimination of Discrimination Against Women. (1989), *The Work of CEDAW: Reports of the Committee on the Elimination of Discrimination against Women,* New York: United Nations.

Veena Talwar Oldenburg. (2002), *Dowry Murder. The Imperial Origins of a Cultural Crime,* Oxford University Press, New York.

Walby, S. (2009), *Globalization and Inequalities: Complexity and Contested Modernities,* London: Sage.

Yuval-Davis (1997), Nira. *Gender and Nation,* Thousand Oaks: Sage.

13

PRIVATE AND PUBLIC DICHOTOMY ABOUT DOMESTIC VIOLENCE: THE STATE OF THE ART LITERATURE ON ISSUES AND CONCERNS

R. K. Mohanty

There are a couple of current heuristic concerns about domestic violence in India, nay the world over. What is the content of current public discourse in relation to domestic violence? Is Domestic violence a Private Family Disputes or Open Public Crime against Women? Can domestic violence be understood only in terms of violence perpetrated by intimate male against the female partner? Do men / women experience violence in the same way? Does the government or law enforcement agency have a say in something that happens in the home? This paper through extensive survey of literature attempts to capture the issues accordingly under the following heads (1) the concepts, (2) World scenario on domestic violence, (3) Dualism in Domestic Violence: Private or Public, (4) A Feminist revision of the Public/Private, (5) Nature of violence perpetrated against men, (6) Degree of victimization of women and men. The Paper concludes with an overview of the state of the art.

Several terms are used to denote domestic violence (DV) such as domestic abuse, spousal abuse, battering, and family violence. It is broadly defined as a type of abusive behaviors by one against other partners in an intimate relationship such as marriage, dating, family, or cohabitation. It is inflicted against the will of the person, with the purpose being to humiliate, intimidate, coerce and control the victim, and very often the victim is left without recourse to any remedies: the police and law enforcement mechanisms are often gender-insensitive, hostile or indifferent (Copelon, 1994). Domestic violence includes forms of violence that perpetuate and exploit the dichotomy between women and men in order to assure the subordination and inferiority of women and everything associated with the feminine. Domestic violence, not only includes physical aggression or assault or threats thereof; but also sexual abuse; psychological abuse; controlling or domineering; intimidation; stalking; passive/covert abuse and economic deprivation (Shipway, 2004). Economic violence can be both a means to make the victim more vulnerable to other forms of violence, but can also be the reason why other forms of violence are inflicted. World economic figures show that (Ferree, 2004) women are generally more economically vulnerable than men. Most typical forms of socio-economic violence include taking away the earnings of the victim, not allowing them to have a separate income ('housewife' status, working in the family business without remuneration), or making her or him unfit for work through targeted physical abuse.

DV and IPV

The term "intimate partner violence" (IPV) is often used synonymously with domestic abuse/domestic violence. Domestic violence is a broader concept, often used to include child abuse, elder abuse, and other violent acts between family members (Wallace, 2004). Wife abuse, wife beating, and battering are descriptive terms that have lost popularity recently for at least two reasons: (1) many victims are not actually married to the abuser, but rather cohabiting or in other arrangements (Waits, 1985) and (2) males as well as females are victims of domestic violence (Johnson, 2005).

The U. S. Office on Violence against Women (VAW) defines domestic violence as a "pattern of abusive behavior in any relationship that is used by one partner to gain or maintain power and control over another intimate partner". The definition adds that domestic violence "can happen to anyone regardless of race, age, sexual orientation, religion, or gender", and can take many forms, including physical abuse, sexual abuse, emotional, economic, and psychological abuse.

The Children and Family Court Advisory and Support Service in the United Kingdom in its "Domestic Violence Policy" reads domestic violence to refer to a range of violent and abusive behaviors, defining it as patterns of behaviour characterized by the misuse of power and control by one person over another who are or have been in an intimate relationship. It can occur in mixed gender relationships and same gender relationships and has profound consequences for the lives of children, individuals and service providers in the families. Distinctions are made among the types of violence, motives of perpetrators, and the social and cultural context based upon patterns across numerous incidents and motives of the perpetrator.

In 1983, domestic violence was recognised as a specific criminal offence by the introduction of section 498-A into the Indian Penal Code. This section deals with cruelty by a husband or his family towards a married woman. The recognition of domestic violence as a crime has resulted in broadening the understanding of what domestic violence is, who may seek protection under the Domestic Violence Act, 2005, and what type of protection may be sought (Mohanty and Mohanty, 2012). Laws in India to deal with domestic violence do exist and they include Section 113(a) of the Indian Evidence Act, Section 498(a) and 304(b) of the Indian Penal Code and the Dowry Prohibition Act, 1961 as amended in the year 1986.

Johnson (1995,2000,2006[1] and 2006[2]) argues for three major types and one rare type of intimate partner violence. Types of violence (IPV) identified by Johnson are: 1) Common Couple Violence (CCV) is not connected to general control behavior, but arises in a single argument where one or both partners physically lash out at the other, 2) Intimate Terrorism (IT) may also involve emotional and psychological abuse. Intimate terrorism is one element in a general pattern of control by one partner over the other. Intimate terrorism is less common than common couple violence, more likely to escalate over time, not as likely to be mutual, and more likely to involve serious injury. IT batterers include two types: "Generally-violent-antisocial" and "dysphoric-borderline". The first type includes men with general psychopathic and violent tendencies. The second type is men who are emotionally dependent on the relationship. Support for this typology has been found in subsequent evaluations (Hamberger, et. al, 1996), 3) Violent Resistance (VR), sometimes thought of as "self-defense", is violence perpetrated by victims against their abusive partners, 4) Mutual Violent Control (MVC) is rare type of intimate partner violence occurs when both partners act in a violent manner, battling for control (Johnson and Ferraro, 2000; Saunders, 1988). Types of male batterers identified by Holtzworth-Munroe and Stuart (1994) include "family-only", which primarily fall into the CCV type, who are generally less violent and less likely to perpetrate psychological and sexual abuse.

According to the Duluth Model (2008), women and children are vulnerable to violence because of their unequal social, economic, and political status in society. The Duluth Model suggests that "violence is patriarchal". The model focuses solely on the men's use of violence in abusive relationships, rather than on the behavior of all parties concerned. This helps the men to focus on changing their personal behavior in order to be nonviolent in any relationship. The model relates to a "Power and Control Wheel" to illustrate this: it has power and control at the center, surrounded by spokes (techniques used), the titles of which include: coercion and threats, intimidation, emotional abuse, isolation, minimizing, denying and blaming, using children, economic abuse, male privilege. The model attempts to address abuse by challenging the misuse of power by the perpetrator. The power wheel model is not intended to assign personal responsibility, enhance respect for mutual purpose or assist victims and perpetrators in resolving their differences. It is an informational tool designed to help individuals understand the dynamics of power operating in abusive situations and identify various methods of abuse.

Use of Power and Control in Domestic Violence

S. No.	*Use of Power and Control*	*Type of Violence*
1	Using Male Privilege	Treating her like a servant • making all the big decisions • acting like the "master of the castle." • being the one to define men's and women's roles.
2	Using Economic Abuse	Preventing her from getting or keeping a job • making her ask for money • giving her an allowance • taking her money, not letting her know about or have access to family income.
3	Using Coercion and Threats.	Making and/or carrying out threats to do something to hurt her • threatening to leave her • threatening to report her to welfare • making her drop legal charges • making her do illegal things.
4	Using Intimidation	Making her afraid by using looks, actions, gestures • yelling, throwing furniture • smashing things • destroying her property • abusing pets • displaying weapons.
5	Using Emotional Abuse	Putting her down • making her feel bad about herself • calling her

		names • making her think she's crazy • playing mind games • humiliating her • making her feel guilty.
6	Using Isolation	Controlling what she does, who she sees and talks to • what she reads • where she goes • limiting her outside involvement • using jealousy to justify actions.
7	Minimizing, Denying and Blaming	Making light of the abuse and not taking her concerns about it seriously • saying the abuse didn't happen • shifting responsibility for abusive behavior • saying she caused it.
8	Using Children	Making her feel guilty about the children • using the children to relay messages • using visitation to harass her • threatening to take the children away.

Source: The Domestic Abuse Intervention Project in Duluth, University of Minnesota 2008 (Compiled).

World Scenario on Domestic Violence

Domestic violence is one of the few phenomena which cut across all the cultural, socio-economic, educational, ethnic and religious barriers. Violence against wives has a very long history: laws authorizing husbands to chastise their wives date back to 753 B. C. , when Romulus ruled in Rome (Kelly, 2002; Okun, 1986:2). Domestic violence occurs across the world, in various cultures, (Watts and Zimmerman, 2002) and affects people of all economic statuses (Waits, 1985). Modern attention to domestic violence began in the women's movement of the 1970s, particularly within feminism and women's rights, as concern about wives being beaten by their husbands gained attention. The first known use of the expression "domestic violence" in a modern context, meaning "spouse abuse, violence in the home" was in an address to the Parliament of the United Kingdom in 1973. Then, the world's first domestic violence services federation (Women's Aid) was set up in 1974, providing practical and emotional support as part of a range of services to women and children experiencing violence in England. With the rise of the men's movement of the 1990s, the problem of domestic violence against men has also gained significant attention. Harvard Psychology Professor Steven Pinker argues that feminism has reduced domestic violence, especially against men as their likelihood of being killed by a female intimate partner has decreased six-fold (Pinker, 2011). According to one study, the percentages of women who have reported being physically abused by an intimate partner vary from 69% to 10% depending on the country (Heise et. al. , 1999). Evidence that wife abuse was common can be found not only in legal codes but also in religious documents, personal testimonies from victims, court records, newspaper accounts, and published discussions by authors such as Cobbe (1878), "Wife Torture in England," and John Stuart Mill, The Subjection of Women, ed. Wendell Robert Carr (1989).

In the United States, according to the Bureau of Justice Statistics in 1995 women reported a six times greater rate of intimate partner violence than men (Bachman and Saltzman, 1995). The National Crime Victimization Survey (NCVS) indicates that in 1998 about 876,340 violent crimes were committed in the U.

S. against women by their current or former spouses, or boyfriends. According to the Centers for Disease Control, in the United States 4. 8 million women suffer intimate partner related physical assaults and rapes and 2. 9 million men are victims of physical assault from their partners. However studies have found that men are much less likely to report victimization in these situations. According to some studies, less than 1% of domestic violence cases are reported to the police (Roberts and Springer, 2007). In the United States 10–35% of the population will be physically aggressive towards a partner at some point in their lives (Archer, 2000; Fiebert, 2011). As abuse becomes more severe women become increasingly overrepresented as victims (Straus, 1999).

Violence by intimate family members is one of South Asia's darkest legacies. In a survey on violence against women in India, 94 percent of the cases involved an offender who was a member of the family (Ibid). Freedom not only from violence but also from the threat of violence is the first indicator of rise in women's capacity for survival and empowerment (Seth, 2010). The United Nations Declaration on the Elimination of Violence against Women states in its Preamble that violence against women is a product of the "unequal power relations" that characterize gender relations in all parts of the world. Violence against women is a universal reality but at the same time it is invisible. The UNDP's gender development index ranks India 108 among 174 countries in terms of gender equity.

In the North-Eastern states women related violence is highest among the *Khasi* society in Meghalaya which is a matriarchal society where the status of women is higher than that of men. Women inherit all family properties and brings her husband into her home. However, the other issue which deserves further investigation is whether hyper-masculinity or hyper-femininity inbreeds more violence against women. Next to Meghalaya comes Mizoram which is a patriarchal society. The MHIP (Mizo Hmeichhe Inzawmkhawm Pawl), the most active woman organization in the state, has been trying to eradicate the commercialization of bride-price, the dowry system, sexual exploitation of women of any kind and inequality between men and women. However, in spite of this movement launched by the MHIP, violence against woman is still higher leaving a great concern (Coomaraswamy, 2005).

Fighting the prevalence of domestic violence in Kashmir has brought Hindu and Muslim activists together in 2009. Additionally, aspects of Islamic law have been criticized for promoting domestic violence (Constable Pamela, 2007). One study found that half of Palestinian women have been the victims of domestic violence (Alexander, 2000). 80% of women surveyed in rural Egypt said that beatings were common and often justified, particularly if the woman refused to have sex with her husband. The Human Rights Watch found that up to 90% of women in Pakistan were subject to some form of maltreatment, within their own homes. Unofficial statistics estimate that 97% of Indian women experience violence at some point in their lives. Up to two-thirds of women in certain communities in Nigeria's Lagos State say they are victims to domestic violence. Statistics published in 2004; show that the rate of domestic violence victimisation for Indigenous women in Australia may be 40 times the rate for non-Indigenous women (Wikipedia). In Turkey, 42% of women over 15 have suffered physical or sexual violence (Tahir, 2011).

Dualism in Domestic Violence: Private or Public

Abuse and violence is a widespread problem which lies hidden within communities irrespective of class and race. It occurs behind closed doors and the most common victims are women, often because standards set by society restrict them from speaking out or seeking help. Women may fear the stigma to their families or humiliation and loss of reputation in society. The dualism between public and private spheres of action has been identified as a key feature of Western, liberal thought. Dualism is the desire to see our world in term of opposites, such as good and bad, success and failure, heaven and hell, daughter and son, left and right, light and dark, past and future and so on. One of the greatest challenges facing the domestic violence movement is the widespread perception that spousal abuse is a "private matter. " There is a felt need in order to move a private matter into the sphere of public concern and to translate that public concern into a widespread social consensus for action (Ghez and Marin, 2002). It seems that out of this thinking a lot of our assumptions, concepts and expectations materialise. Sometimes this leads to stress, disappointment and unhappiness. According to Carole Pateman (1989), the feminist critique of the dualism between public and private "is central to almost two centuries of feminist writing and political struggle; it is, ultimately what the feminist movement is about". Although the terms public and private are used quite differently in feminist debates, there are two assumptions that can be considered as common grounds. On one hand, the dichotomy itself is criticized as it implies a hierarchical, sexualized and gendered binary order. On the other hand, the assumption of a clear distinction between these two spheres is called into question. The representation of the public world as superior to the private, and the traditional location of women within the latter, renders them largely invisible in public life.

For a long time in history, the inferior position of women or certain ethnic or racial minorities was considered natural. Therefore, acts that are now considered human rights violations were not widely condemned because the victims of these violations were not acknowledged by those in power in society to have those rights. Civil and political rights (the so-called first-generation rights) (Titley, 2007), for example, are mainly concerned with violence in the public sphere and with limiting the state and its representatives in perpetrating violence as a means to abuse power. This has meant that specific forms of violence against women have gone unnoticed, or have only been gradually addressed. The very terms 'husband' and 'wife' embody gendered relationships, based on male dominance and female submission. The meaning of 'wife' is embodied in traditional culture as 'gendered property'. There has been long debate about the privacy of the family (Pagelow 1984). There are those who support the sanctity of the privacy of the family, and resist the intrusion of outside forces, viewing intrusion as anti-family. Correlated with this attitude is support for traditional gender relations within the family. The opposing argument is that the distinction between private and public is artificial and serves the interests of those with power. The family is often not a haven of happiness and safety, and may require outside forces to assist and protect less powerful family members.

The context in which men abuse their partners is complex because intimate relationships are sites of highly charged emotions involving a multitude of tangled, subtle meanings, many supported by cultural prescriptions. The emotional nature of intimate relationships and their location in the private/domestic sphere makes it difficult, if not impossible, to develop a simple single solution to the problem. What may be effective in assisting one victim/survivor may be rejected by another. What may be effective in stopping one abuser may backfire with another. Assault and violence in the private/domestic context is at least as criminal as violence in a public context and must be dealt with by the criminal justice system. Abuse and violence in intimate relationships is not the result of normal conflict between two equals.

According to Pagelow, (1984:13) "some of the insistence on maintaining family privacy is based on the historical establishment of patriarchal marriage and common law rights and privileges". Marriage under the common law of England (a heritage adopted in USA and Australia) was the merger of husband and wife into a single legal identity, that of the husband. Until relatively recently, wives had no right to sell, sue or contract without their husband's approval. This notion of a single legal identity has provided immunity from testifying against or suing a spouse and maintained the fiction that there is no such thing as spousal rape.

"Today, domestic assault is illegal in every state. However, confusion about whether this is a public or a private problem has not disappeared. On the one hand, the criminalization of domestic violence transforms into a problem warranting intervention and even sanctions. On the other hand, very low reporting levels, police and judicial indifference, and a pattern of blaming the victim all suggest that many people, including some victims, continue to see domestic violence as a private matter" (Kelly, 2003:2). Kelly argues that our misguided notion of privacy, derived from Locke, undergirds this confusion. Drawing upon feminist theory and interviews with professionals who work with battered women, she theorizes a more nuanced version of privacy that would permit or perhaps even require public responses to domestic violence. Notably, these "public responses" go beyond legal intervention to include community forces and organizations.

Kelly discusses Locke's distinction of public and private. A closer examination of Locke's theory reveals two different models of public and private. The first separates the family from politics; the second separates the individual and the state. The first model is premised on his exhaustive discussion of the difference between political and paternal power. Here he creates a picture of social relations in which the domestic realm is defined as paradigmatically private and the political realm of state power is defined as public. The second model arises from Locke's efforts to explain how individuals, who supposedly are born into a state of freedom and equality, are able to consent to a government without relinquishing the natural freedom that is theirs by God's intention. Locke solves this dilemma by reducing the government's involvement in citizens' lives to that of a referee in cases of direct conflict between individuals. Within this second model, the family plays a crucial role: Locke depicts it as a relatively peaceful association that in contrast to civil society does not require the continuous presence of a neutral arbitrator with the power over life and death to maintain order. Thus, the domestic realm provides Locke with the conceptual and the physical space for individuals to realize their potential as rational free beings even after they have consented to partial rule by government.

An important thread to this argument is that Locke presents two models of public and private that we conflate—one operating to separate the family from political life, and one operating to separate the individual from the state (Ibid:20). From the first model, we conceive of family life as a private matter, and from the second we conceive of privacy as being left alone. Kelly argues that a family of liberal individuals, who seek to develop themselves, in part through connection to others in this primary and private unit, poses a problem. All is well when we assume a harmony of interests among family members, but Locke's models of privacy are inadequate for helping us to conceive of responses to the pervasive reality of family violence.

In contexts, where rigid gender roles are more determining, the batterer has more freedom to deny responsibility. The set of gender roles that we are taught to belong to as women and men contain many contradictions or demands that cannot be fulfilled. At the same time, part of the hegemonic male gender role is to oversee women and children in fulfilling their roles, and if necessary, discipline them. These two conditions combine to create a common justification for those who are abusive in relationships because they can easily find something or another to (a) blame the woman for the violence committed against her, and (b) to claim the right to inflict it (Titley, 2007).

The ideology of patriarchy has viewed the family in 'ideal* terms as a place of private succor (particularly for men who experience the vicissitudes of the 'public' arena). Writers such as Lasch (1977) and Donzelot (1979) have eulogised the family as a 'haven in a heartless world' and railed against what they saw as intrusions by the state into this 'private' domain. In so doing they endorsed the 'rule of the father' as the legitimate 'head of the household' with the authority and responsibility to have power and control over women and children. The dominant religions of Christianity, Islam, Hinduism and Judaism have long supported patriarchy. The ideology of possessive individualism and self-reliance also supported the notion of the home being the realm of the 'private'. The development of suburban living with individual, self-contained, nuclear households has meant that 'privacy' is even more possible – and culturally seen as desirable. Thus, there are three key notions that permit wife abuse to occur with little or no 'interference' from outside. First is the 'idealised' notion of the home as a haven from the outside world, a place of security, happiness and contentment with stereotypical male and female gender roles. Second is the notion that what occurs in the home is 'private' and is not the province of outsiders, particularly agencies of the state and third is notion of the individual who is self-determining and unconnected to society (Gardiner,1996: 23).

The reasons behind women staying in a violent relationship (Titley, 2007) include financial dependence on the abuser, social constraints, and a lack of alternatives such as shelters for abuse victims. Domestic violence often involves isolation of the victim from the family and friends, deprivation of personal possessions, manipulation of children, threats of reprisals against her and her children or other family members. Furthermore, common social pressures regarding the nature of the family – 'some kind of father is better than no father for your children' - makes getting out of an abusive relationship not only difficult but also extremely dangerous.

The residual area of domestic jurisdiction has been greatly reduced by human rights law which itself adds another layer of public/private opposition through its traditional applicability only to the relations between the state and individuals, through the acts of public ofûcials. Human rights discourse thus largely excludes abuses committed by private actors. The idea is to delineate the reserved area from international intrusion. Feminist writers argue that the liberal opposition between public life, the domain of business, economics, politics and law, and private life, the domestic sphere of the family, has both supported and obscured the structural subordination of women. The separation of public and private spheres has traditionally been supported by the state. This parallels the traditional distinction between male and female roles in our society. The private or domestic sphere has been associated with women's 'expressive' roles while the public sphere has been popularly understood as men's 'instrumental' sphere of activity and influence (Parsons and Bales 1955). Domestic violence, or intimate partnership violence, is very different from violent incidents that occur among strangers. Consideration of domestic violence as a private, domestic issue has significantly hampered recognition of the phenomenon as a human rights violation. The invisibility of the phenomenon was exacerbated by the fact that traditionally, international human rights law was believed to be applicable to relations between individual and the state and human rights organisations focused only on politically motivated violations (such as torture or the inhumane treatment of prisoners). However, it has gradually become recognised that state responsibility under international law can arise not only from state action, but also from state inaction where the state fails to protect its citizens from violent crimes.

A Feminist Revision of the Public/Private

Kelly (2003) divides feminist theories into three camps, all of which criticize liberal theory's public/private dichotomy. In this ideological division, women are typically relegated to the private realm, thereby denying them opportunities for development as citizens, removing women's voice from public policy decisions, and aiding the characterization of domestic violence as a private affair (pp33-34). Dividing these feminist camps is their responses to the public and private dichotomy. Radical feminists such as MacKinnon (1984) propose the elimination of the public/private distinction, on the grounds that the dichotomy will always lead to women's subordination. Conservative feminists such as Elshtain (1981) criticize the radical feminists for undercutting the family. Elshtain (1981:38-41) holds the family to be necessary; happily, it is also a possible site for women, through their mothering, to transform the public realm through the development of values such as compassion and sensitivity. While liberal feminists also reject the radical feminist project of obliterating the public/private dichotomy, they tend to focus on reducing barriers to equal participation in the public realm by women. The trouble with all three camps, according to Kelly, is that they are essentialist, treating all women alike: "The differences among feminist theorists concerning the public/private split can be traced to a fundamental disagreement among them regarding the aspect of women's lives most in need of liberation. Is it women as mothers, women as individuals, or women as sex objects?" (Ibid: 49). Kelly's own position then emerges from the complexity of and tension between women's multiple identities and roles.

As mentioned above, it is possible to identify some common ground between those feminist positions which, despite being critical of the public/private dichotomy, still think of it as a useful framework. After all, the definition of what is private and what is public is decisive for the allocation of power and resources (Fraser, 1997). In this context, public/private is often considered as an analytical concept, rejecting the "mechanistic separation of the two spheres" (Bargetz, 2009), while not denying the real consequences following from the dichotomy. Bargetz, Brigitte (2009) analyses three criticisms on public/private distinction. Firstly, the public/private distinction has been criticized to reproduce a dichotomous thinking that it was meant to overcome in the first place (Chris and Squires, 2002:161). As critics point out, dichotomies like public/private, mind/body, reason/emotion, etc. are not neutral and innocent but imply powerful and exclusionary hierarchies. Starting from a critique of the opposition reason/emotion, Prokhovnik, seeks to elaborate an alternative to dichotomous thinking by exploring the potential of a relational theory. Dichotomous thinking, she posits, inevitably entails an opposition between two identities that are hierarchically ordered. Subsequently, she identifies four specific problematic aspects: Because dichotomous thinking is gendered and sexualized, it "leads specifically to the denigration of women" (Prokhovnik, 1999:37). An additional conceptual problem occurs when the dichotomy is accepted as dominant cultural metaphor and thus powerfully determines further ways of thinking and acting. A third problem arises with dichotomy when it is applied to the conception of truth, which presupposes "that only one party can be right" whereas "the other must be wrong" (Ibid: 33). Finally, Prokhovnik argues, thinking within a dichotomous frame leads to constituting two and just two parts of a whole, and therefore rejects a "prospect of heterogeneity" (Ibid: 31-38).

Whereas Prokhovnik's critic of androcentric dichotomous thinking relates to its epistemological and philosophical foundations, Chris and Squires (Ibid) question the empirical-analytical value of the dichotomy. They doubt that the public/private distinction may be an adequate instrument for keeping up "with the current means by which sexual inequalities are perpetuated" (Ibid). Conceiving the distinction rather as empirically irrelevant and politically ineffective, they share Diana Coole's (2000: 347) suggestion that the categories of public and private should be discarded and replaced by "new maps".

The usefulness of the public/private frame has been criticized by Black feminists as a liberal and white concept. Pointing out that public/private does not mean the same thing for different women, these critics reveal the concept's Eurocentric bias. Collins (1991), for example, argues that for African-American communities, public and private may not be useful categories, since they rely on the "archetypal white, middle-class nuclear family". Since racial oppression has impoverished many Black families, Black women and other women of color seldom fit this model. Poor families, she argues, do not have the same distinction, equating private with home and public with work, as Black women's paid labor is often domestic labor. Therefore, black women's labor has also often been neglected by feminist discourses.

The dominant feminist critique of the liberal public/private distinction focuses on the patriarchal oppression of women in the realm as well as through the existence of the separated realm of the private. However, some feminists question this conception because of its devaluation of the private. While acknowledging the private as a place of deprivation and violence – historically as well as at present – they enhance a more ambivalent vision of the private by emphasizing its empowering potentials. Thus, Bell Hooks (1990:42) points out that home can constitute a site of resistance and of "self-conscious constructed identity". "Historically," she concedes, "African American people believed that the construction of a home place, however, fragile and tenuous (the slave hut, the wooden shack), had a radical political dimension". That the gendered and sexualized distinction of "public man and private woman" cannot be maintained empirically has been strongly disputed by feminists pointing for example to the active participation of women in public in different historical contexts, to current movements of girl power, or to the feminization of the workforce. Emphasizing the "critical liberating potential" (Young,1997:134) and therefore a more positive vision of the home, both Hooks and Young, reject a public/private opposition that mainly focuses on the private as the sphere of deprivation, and instead bring forward a more ambivalent conception of the private.

Feminists argue that people are often reluctant to use the power of the state in cases of domestic violence. To them, many victims are reluctant to report abuse, and many law enforcement and court personnel are reluctant to use their discretion and resources to pursue these matters they conceive of as private. The criminalization of domestic violence and the sensitizing of criminal justice agents should by no means be abandoned (Ghez and Marin, 2002). Nancy Fraser (1990:56-80) .points out that "there are no naturally given, a priori boundaries" between matters that are generally conceived as private i. e. of "individual concern", and ones we typically label as public (i. e. of "common concern"). As an example, she refers to the historic shift in the general conception of domestic violence, from previously being a matter of primarily private concern, to now generally being accepted as a common one: "Eventually, after sustained discursive contestation we succeeded in making it a common concern". Domestic violence and communal violence are acquiring disturbing dimensions - one within the private sphere of the household and the other in the public domain of civil society (Shabana Azmi, 2003). She says "In fact all other freedoms lose their shine and become meaningless unless all individuals are ensured a life without fear' (Ibid).

Studies suggest that the most common causes for women stalking and battering include dissatisfaction with the dowry and exploiting women for more of it, arguing with the partner, refusing to have sex with him, neglecting children, going out of home without telling the partner, not cooking properly or on time, indulging in extra marital affairs, not looking after in-laws etc. In some cases infertility in females also leads to their assault by the family members. The greed for dowry, desire for a male child and alcoholism of the spouse are major factors of domestic violence against women in rural areas. There have been gruesome reports of young bride being burnt alive or subjected to continuous harassment for not bringing home the amount of demanded dowry. Women in India also admit to hitting or beating because of their suspicion about the husband's sexual involvement with other women. The Tandoor Murder Case of Naina Sahni in New Delhi in the year 1995 is one such dreadful incident of a woman being killed and then burnt in a Tandoor by his husband. This incidence was an outcome of suspicion of extra marital affairs of Naina Sahni which led to marital discord and domestic violence against her (Seth, 2010).

Violence against Men: Is it an Issue?

Awareness, perception, definition and documentation of domestic violence differ widely from country to country, and from era to era. Findings of studies regarding the prevalence of domestic violence vary significantly, depending on specific wording of survey questions, how the survey is conducted, the definition of abuse or domestic violence used, the willingness or unwillingness of victims to admit that they have been abused and other factors. Straus (2005) conducted a study which estimated that the rate of minor assaults by women in the United States was 78 per 1,000 couples, compared with a rate for men of 72 per 1,000 and the severe assault rate was 46 per 1,000 couples for assaults by women and 50 per 1,000 for assaults by men. Neither difference is statistically significant. He claimed that since these rates were based exclusively on information provided by women respondents, the near-equality in assault rates could not be attributed to a gender bias in reporting (ibid).

There is no question that domestic violence directed against women is a serious and bigger problem, but domestic violence against men is also increasing gradually in India. The supremacy of men in the society makes one believe that they are not vulnerable to domestic violence. Battering of men by their spouse and family members has become a latest issue and is another form of domestic violence under purview of judiciary. In India, compared to violence against women, violence against men is less frequent but it has already taken a deadly shape in many of the western countries by now (Martin, 1999:418). Males have reported incidences of assault against them like pushing, shoving, slapping, grabbing, hitting which are intended to harm them and also take their lives on many occasions. Recently, hundreds of husbands gathered in Chandigarh and Shimla to voice their opinion for men's rights and protection against domestic violence subjected to them by their wives and other family members. It reflects the need for a special law for curbing domestic violence against men in present times (Ibid).

Studies reveal some of the possible causes such as not abiding by the instructions of the wives', inadequate earning of men, infidelity towards wives, not helping the partner in household activities, not taking a proper care of children, abusing the spouse's family, infertility of men, spying the activities of partner, doubting the partner all the time and not trusting her, revolt by the wife when asked to look after in-laws etc. On many occasions the spat between men and women becomes public thereby influencing the society around especially in the villages. In urban areas such forms of violence may go unreported because of greater privacy. Also the families find their reputation at stake in urban areas.

One analysis found that "women are as physically aggressive or more aggressive than men in their relationships with their spouses or male partners" (Wikipedia). However, studies have shown that women are more likely to be injured. Archer's meta-analysis (Archer, 2000) found that women in the United States suffer 65% of domestic violence injuries. A Canadian study showed that 7% of women and 6% of men were abused by their current or former partners, but female victims of spousal violence were more than twice as likely to be injured as male victims, three times more likely to fear for their life, twice as likely to be stalked, and twice as likely to experience more than ten incidents of violence (Time Magazine, 1995). However, Straus notes that Canadian studies on domestic violence have simply excluded questions that ask men about being victimized by their wives (Straus, 2005).

Determining how many instances of domestic violence actually involve male victims is difficult. Male domestic violence victims may be reluctant to get help for a number of reasons. Another study has demonstrated a high degree of acceptance by women of aggression against men (Straus, 2006). Problems in conducting studies that seek to describe violence in terms of gender is the amount of silence, fear and shame that results from abuse within families and relationships. Another is that abusive patterns can tend to seem normal to those who have lived in them for a length of time. Similarly, subtle forms of abuse can be quite transparent even as they set the stage for further abuse seeming normal. Finally, inconsistent definition of what constitutes domestic violence makes definite conclusions difficult to reach when compiling the available studies. Theories that women are as violent as men have been dubbed "gender symmetry" theories (Archer, 2000; O'Leary, 2000; Frieze, 2000; White *et al.*, 2000 and Johnson, 2005).

Straus and Gelles (1990) found that in couples reporting spousal violence, 27% of the time the man struck the first blow; in 24% of cases, the woman initiated the violence. The rest of the time, the violence was mutual, with both partners brawling. The results were the same even when the most severe episodes of violence were analyzed. In order to counteract claims that the reporting data was skewed, female-only surveys were conducted, asking females to self-report, and the data was the same. The simple tally of physical acts is typically found to be similar in those studies that examine both directions, but some studies show that male violence may be more serious. Male violence may do more damage than female violence. Women are more likely to be injured and/or hospitalized. Wives are more likely to be killed by their husbands than the reverse (59% to 41% per Department of Justice study), and women in general are more likely to be killed by their spouses than by all other types of assailants combined (Angela and Kirk, 1989).

A 1997 report says significantly more men than women do not disclose the identity of their attacker (Rand and Strom, 1997). One researcher, however, says that there is no evidence that male victims are more likely to under-report than female victims. In fact, men tend to over-estimate their partner's violence and under-estimate their own, while women do the reverse

(Kimmel, 2001). A 2009 study showed that there was greater acceptance for abuse perpetrated by females than by males (Robertson and Tamar, 2009). Several studies have confirmed that women's physical violence towards intimate male partners is often in self-defense (Swan and Snow, 2002; Muelleman and Burgess, 1998).

Degree of Victimization of Women and Men

Domestic violence is a significant problem. Measures of the incidence of violence in intimate relationships can differ markedly in their findings depending on the measures used. Survey approaches tend to show parity in the use of violence by both men and women against partners than do approaches using data from reports of domestic violence that tends to show women experiencing violence from male partners as the majority of cases (over 80 percent). Research based on reported domestic violence or on police records show men to be responsible for the majority of domestic violence and the high frequency of women as victims. The problem of under-reporting is believed to be substantial.

There are a number of reasons (Gardiner,1996: 28) for the lack of reporting or recording: a) victim/ survivors feel shame and humiliation at revealing that the person who society expects to love them, actually despises them enough to hurt them, b) The privacy in which the abuse occurs means there are no supporting witnesses, except perhaps children c) Cultural attitudes that condone 'wife* abuse d) Denial that what is occurring is abuse or is a serious problem e) Economic dependence on the abuser f) Lack of access to information and services g) The perception that nothing can be done to stop the abuse. h) Belief that the victim/ survivor may have deserved it or the husband had the right to be violent i) Emotional attachment to the abuser, particularly if he is the children's father.

Although reliable, gender-sensitive statistics are still rare, there is evidence to suggest that women and men experience violence in different ways (Titley, 2007). The World Health Organisation's World Report on Violence and Health notes that whereas men '...are much more likely to be attacked by a stranger or an acquaintance than by someone within their close circle of relationships...one of the most common forms of violence against women is that performed by a husband or male partner' (Ibid). In other words, women experience more violence in the private sphere, whereas for men it is more likely to occur in the public sphere.

Erin Pizzey (1982), the founder of an early women's shelter in Chiswick, London, expressed an unpopular view in her book, Prone to Violence, that some women in the refuge system had a predisposition to seek abusive relationships. She also expressed the view that domestic violence can occur against any vulnerable intimates, regardless of their sex. In the same book, Erin Pizzey stated that, of the first 100 women to enter the refuge, 62 were as violent, or more violent, than the men they were, allegedly, running away from.

The statistics cited by Women's Aid and Ahimsa are that violence by women against men is a tiny proportion of all domestic violence is rejected by advocates for male victims of domestic violence. They claim that this finding is based in the situation that many studies report only male-on-female violence because that is all they ask about, those studies that do examine prevalence in both directions overwhelmingly find little difference by gender. Martin S. Fiebert of the Department of Psychology at California State University, Long Beach, has provided an analysis (2011) of 195 scholarly investigations: 152 empirical studies and 43 analyses, which he believes demonstrate women are as physically aggressive, or more aggressive, than men. The aggregate sample size exceeds 175,700.

The U. S. National Family Violence Survey has consistently indicated, in repeated surveys over more than 30 years, that women are more than twice as likely as men to initiate domestic assault, and more than twice as likely to use weapons. Other studies have demonstrated a high degree of acceptance by women of aggression against men. The available data (BBC Survey on 16. 06. 2006 indicates that million men experience "minor" abuse (such as "pushing, grabbing, shoving, slapping, and hitting") per year. In the United States, approximately 800,000 men per year (3. 2 percent) are raped or physically assaulted by their partner. At least 371,000 men are stalked annually. 3 percent of nonfatal violence against men stems from domestic violence. In 2002, men comprised 24 percent of domestic violence homicide victims. Over 20 years, the instances of homicide from domestic violence against men decreased by approximately 67 percent. Approximately 22 percent of men have experienced physical, sexual, or psychological intimate partner violence during their life (Center for Disease Control and Prevention, Intimate Partner Violence: Fact Sheet,

Atlanta Georgia, 2006). There are many reasons why there is not more information about domestic abuse and violence against men. A major reason is the reluctance of men to report incidents to the police, unless there are substantial injuries. Data indicate that although mutual violent behavior is quite common in intimate relationships, men are rarely seriously harmed.

The Australian Bureau of Statistics Personal Safety Survey (2006) show that overall, more males than females are victims of physical assault (10. 8 per cent vs 5. 8 percent). However, women are most at risk of assault in the home and from men they know, while men are most at risk of assault in public spaces and from men they don't know. Among the large numbers of men physically assaulted each year, close to 70 percent were assaulted by strangers. Less than five per cent were assaulted by a female partner or ex-partner. In contrast, among the female victims of physical assault, 31 percent were assaulted by a male partner or ex-partner. Thirty percent of people who had experienced violence by a current partner since the age of 15 were male, while 70 percent were female. In the European Union (EU), one in five women suffers some form of domestic violence. Ninety-five percent of this violence occurs in the home. According to Respecting Accuracy in Domestic Abuse Reporting (RADAR) report in USA, women are just as likely as men to engage in partner aggression. Men experience over one-third of domestic violence-related injuries (Archer,2000). Men are far less likely to report domestic violence incidents than women (Stets and Straus, 1990). The myths about domestic violence are numerous (Gelles 1997). Many of these myths are based on domestic violence studies that use biased survey methods (Arriaga and Oskamp 1999).

According to a report produced by Southern Connecticut State University: In 95% of family violence cases the victims are women beaten by male partners. In 1% of the cases the reverse is true. There are an estimated 28 million battered women in the U. S. , more than half of all married women in the country. In the U. S. , one woman is beaten by her husband or partner every 9 seconds. Battering is the single major cause of injury to women between the ages of 15 and 44 in the U. S. ; more than car accidents, muggings, and rapes combined. 70% of the assault victims seen in the emergency room of Boston City Hospital are women who have been attacked in their own homes (www. southernct. edu/womenscenter/domesticviolence). Research published in the Journal of Family Psychology says that contrary to media and public opinion women commit more acts of violence than men in eleven categories: Throw something, push, grab, shove, slap, kick, bite, hit or threaten a partner with a knife or gun (Capaldi, D. M., *et. al.*, 2004). A study reported in Washington Times (12. 06. 2006), which is based on interviews with 1,615 married or cohabiting couples and extrapolated nationally using census data, found that 21 percent of couples reported domestic violence.

An Overview

When violence occurs within the context of these competing goals, a wide range of troublesome questions result. For instance, should a victim's primary concern be to protect her by leaving, or should she stay to try to work things out so that the family is not torn apart? How far should the external agencies go to protect victims or potential victims from violence? What is the role of neighbors, the church, and/or the community more generally in addressing instances of domestic violence? If a victim does not want to leave or prosecute her abuser (even in extreme cases), should she be allowed to stay in a situation even if it means subjecting herself and her children to continued abuse?

Most speculation has focused on the individual recipients of abuse. The emphasis is not surprising, for the victim most clearly embodies and expresses the associated tensions. The battered woman who protects her abuser by denying the abuse (sometimes in the presence of the police) embodies the contradictions that occur when an individual seeks simultaneously to protect herself and her family. The apparent dilemma/trauma in such behavior rivets the heuristic attention on why she responds in the manner that she does. Many people simply are not able to get past such questions as "Why does she stay?" and "What did she do to cause a person who loves her to commit such violent acts?" Unfortunately, the widespread lack of awareness about the nature and depth of the (frequently irresolvable) tensions that are inherent in domestic violence has made it easier to blame the victim than to acknowledge our lack of clarity on situational dynamics about what is happening.

Blaming the victim can take a number of forms, including holding her directly responsible for causing the violence or distancing ourselves from the situation with thoughts like "I would never allow it to happen to me." Another common reaction is to explain domestic violence as the product of external factors such as unemployment or alcohol and/or drug abuse. Although external factors may contribute to particular instances of domestic violence, such explanations are fundamentally incomplete. These accounts fail to appreciate the tensions as embedded within the origins of the liberal construction of the family as a private institution. The development of a working knowledge of the derivation and operation of these tensions is crucial to contemporary efforts to address domestic violence. When we replace idealizations of the family that presume familial peace that recur in Locke's theory with an understanding that the domestic sphere is a site of significant conflict and/or repetitive acts of violence, we recognize the need for an understanding of the relationship between public and private that is capable of accommodating the paradoxes and contradictions that arise in instances of familial conflict. Failure to fully engage these tensions results too easily in a pattern whereby the interests of some individuals are systematically subordinated in order to achieve a level of clarity that simply may not be possible.

Jean Elshtain argues that traditional liberal models such as Locke's fail to provide women with a vocabulary to articulate their position in the family. According to Elshtain (1981), women were left with only two choices; to identify themselves with the rationalistic self-interest of the public sphere or the sentimentality of the private sphere. This observation helps to explain the double bind that is created for so many victims of domestic violence. If a woman's role in the family is identified with the rational sphere, then failure to leave an abusive husband is likely to be portrayed as irrational. Furthermore, according to this standard, it becomes much easier to blame women for getting into the situation in the first place—because they "should have known better." If, on the other hand, a woman's role in the family is viewed through the sentimental lens, we are likely to assume that as the moral beacon of the domestic sphere she should put family above all else. According to this interpretation, if she leaves she is a failed wife and if she stays she can be blamed for endangering her children. The feminist critique of the public/private dichotomy has been an important contribution to feminist research. Exposing the gendered and sexualized dimensions and the inherent hierarchies, feminists have revealed the public/private distinction as an influential liberal power mechanism of modernity. In particular, in view of some androcentric and Eurocentric biases, it is suggested that taking into account the concept of everyday life makes it possible to overcome some of the public/private framework's analytical shortcomings.

Coming to Indian scenario, while the Domestic Violence Act, 2005 is an important first step in terms of the concepts it introduces into the Indian legal system, the viability of its implementation may be contested on certain grounds. Many laws are gender neutral, however, their application is gender biased. The effects of this public/private divide in the international law are more evident in domestic violence, which literally happens in the private. Moreover the economic and social context of its (laws) application has not been considered seriously by both the governmental and at the same time non-governmental organizations, all over the world. Opposition to the introduction of this Act has also been expressed on the grounds of its interference with the private sphere—that of the home and family. Interference into domestic privacy; has traditionally been seen as a greater evil than actual violence inflicted upon a wife. However further step came in understanding domestic violence as a violation of human rights itself and attempts were made to dissolve the same. However, any purported intrusion enabled by the Act is necessary for the increased recognition of domestic violence as a valid social concern. And it is a reading of the provisions of the Domestic Violence Act in this light that will enable it to play a significant role.

References

Alexander, Doug. (2000), "Addressing Violence Against Palestinian Women", *International Development Research Centre* , Ottawa, Ontario.

Angela B and K R. Williams. (1989), "Exploring the Effect of Resource Availability and the Likelihood of Female-perpetrated Homicides", *Law and Society Review*, 23 (1): 75–94.

Archer, J. (2000), "Sex Differences in Aggression between Heterosexual Partners: A Meta-analytic Review", *Psychol Bull* 126 (5): 651–80.

Arnot, ML. and U, Cornelie. (2003), *Gender and Crime in Modern Europe,* London: Routledge. p. 123.

Arriaga, XB and S Oskamp. (1999), *Violence in Intimate Relationships*, Sage Publishers.

Bachman, RT and L E. Saltzman. (1995), *Violence against Women: Estimates from the Redesigned Survey*, Bureau of Justice Statistics, US.

Bargetz, Brigitte. (2009), "The Politics of the Everyday: A Feminist Revision of the Public/Private Frame" In ed. , I. Papkova, *Reconciling the Irreconcilable*, Institute of Human Sciences, Osterreich, Austria.

Bell Hooks. (1990), "Homeplace: A Site of Resistance", in: ibid, *Yearning: Race, Gender and Cultural Politics*, Boston (South End Press), p. 42

Capaldi, D. M., Kim, H. K., & Shortt, J. W. (2004), "Women's Involvement in Aggression in Young Adult Romantic Relationships", In K. L Putallaz & K. L. Bierman (Eds.), *Aggression, Antisocial Behavior, and Violence Among Girls* (pp. 223-241), New York: Guilford.

Carole Pateman. (1989), "Feminist Critiques of the Public/ Private Dichotomy", in: ibid. , *The Disorder of Women. Democracy, Feminism and Political Theory*, Cambridge (Polity Press), p. 118

Chris Armstrong and Judith Squires. (2002), "Beyond the Public/Private Dichotomy: Relational Space and Sexual Inequalities", *Political Theory*, No. 1, p. 261.

Cobbe Francis Power. (1878), "Wife Torture in England," *Contemporary Review*, Vol. 32.

Collins, Patricia Hill. (1991), "Work, Family, and Black Women's Oppression", in *Black Feminist thought: Knowledge, Consciousness, and the Politics of Empowerment*, London (Routledge), p. 46.

Constable, Pamela. (2007), "For Some Muslim Wives, Abuse Knows No Borders",*Washington Post* (May 8, 2007).

Coole, Diana. (2000), "Cartographic Convulsions: Public and Private Reconsidered", *Political Theory*, Vol. 28, No. 3, p. 347.

Coomaraswamy, Radhika. (2005), 'Human Security and Gender Violence', *EPW*, Oct 29, pp. 4729-36.

Copelon, R. (1994), 'Understanding Domestic Violence as Torture' in Cook, R. (Ed.) *Human Rights of Women: National and International Perspectives*, University of Pennsylvania Press. (p. 116- 152).

Donzelot, J. (1979), *The Policing of Families*, New York, PAN.

Elshtain, Jean. (1981), *Public Man: Private Woman*, Princeton: Princeton University Press.

Erin Pizzey. (1982), *Prone to Violence*, Jeff Shapiro: Books.

Ferree, M. M., (2004), 'Assessing the Science: Key Issues for Research on Violence against Women'. Paper presented at the *Conference :Everyday Violence and Human Rights* in Osnabrück, Germany.

Fiebert, Martin. (2011), *References Examining Assaults by Women on their Spouses or Male Partners: An Annotated Bibliography*, California State University.

Fraser, Nancy. (1997), *Justice Interruptus: Critical Reflections on the "postsocialist" Condition*, London/New York (Routledge).

Frieze IH. (2000), "Violence in Close Relationships—Development of a Research Area: Comment on Archer (2000)", *Psychol Bull*, 126 (5): 681–4.

Gardiner, G. (1996), *From Private To Public: Creating A Domestic Violence Community Intervention Project*, School of Social Work, Curtin University, Australia.

Gelles Richard J. (1997), *Intimate Violence in Families*, Sage Publications.

Ghez M and L Marin. (2002), "Domestic Violence" ,*Encyclopedia of Public Health*, Ed. Lester Breslow. Vol. 2. Gale Cengage.

Hamberger, L. K., *et al.* (1996), "A Large Sample Empirical Typology of Male Spouse Abusers and its Relationship to Dimensions of Abuse", *Violence & Victims*, 11 (4): 277–92.

Heise, Lori; *et al.* (1999), "Ending Violence Against Women", *Population Reports*, Series L. No. 11.

Holtzworth-Munroe, A., and G. L. Stuart. (1994), "Typologies of Male Batterers: Three Subtypes and the Differences Among Them", *Psychological Bulletin*, 116 (3): 476–97.

John Locke. (1988), *Two Treatises of Government*, ed. Peter Laslett, Cambridge University Press.

Johnson MP. (1995), "Patriarchal Terrorism and Common Couple Violence: Two Forms of Violence Against Women", *Journal of Marriage and the Family* (National Council on Family Relations) 57 (2): 283–94.

Johnson MP. (2000), "Conflict and Control: Images of Symmetry and Asymmetry in Domestic Violence". In Booth, A. , A. C. Crouter, and M. Clements, *Couples in Conflict*, Hillsdale:NJ: Erlbaum.

Johnson MP. (2005), "Domestic Violence: It's Not About Gender—Or Is It?", *Journal of Marriage and Family* ,67 (5): 1126–30.

Johnson MP. (2006[1]), "Conflict and Control: Gender Symmetry and Asymmetry in Domestic Violence",*Violence against Women*, 12 (11): 1003–18.

Johnson MP. (2006[2]), Violence and Abuse in Personal Relationships: Conflict, Terror, and Resistance in Intimate Partnerships In A. L. Vangelisti & D. Perlman (Eds.), *Cambridge Handbook of Personal Relationships* (pp. 557–576), Cambridge University Press.

Johnson MP and K J. Ferraro. (2000), "Research on Domestic Violence in the 1990s: Making Distinctions", *Journal of Marriage and the Family*, 62 (4): 948–63.

Kelly K A. (2002), Private Family, Private Individual: John Locke's distinction between Paternal and Political Power, *Social Theory and Practice*, Vol 28 No 03.

Kelly, K A. (2003), *Domestic Violence and the Politics of Privacy*, Ithaca: Cornell University Press, 2003.

Kimmel, M. S. (2001), "Male victims of Domestic Violence: A Substantive and Methodological Review". *Report to the Equality Committee of the Dept of Education and Science,* Ireland. pp. 10–11.

Lasch, C. (1977), *Haven in a Heartless World: The Family Beseiged,* New York, Basic Books.

MacKinnon, Catharine. (1984), *Feminism Unmodified: Discourses on Life and Law,* Cambridge: Harvard University Press.

Martin L. S. *et al.* (1999), "Domestic Violence in Northern India", *American Journal of Epidemiology,*150(4): 417-426.

Mill, John Stuart. (1989), The Subjection of Women, ed. Wendell Robert Carr. Cambridge, Mass:MIT Press.

Mohanty RK and S Mohanty. (2012), *Criminology Penology and Victimology,* Mumbai, Himalay Publication.

Muelleman, R. L.; Burgess, P. (1998), "Male Victims of Domestic Violence and their History of Perpetrating Violence", *Academic Emergency Medicine,* 5: 9.

O'Leary, K. Daniel. (2000), "Are Women Really More Aggressive than Men in Intimate Relationships? Comment on Archer", *Psychological Bulletin,* 126 (5): 681–684.

Pagelow, M. D. (1984), Family Violence, New York, Praeger.

Parsons, T. and R. Bales. (1955), *Family. Socialisation and Interaction Process,* New York, Free Press.

Pinker, Steven. (2011), "Women's Economic Power Decreases Domestic Violence Against Both Genders", *Forbes,* December 5, 2011.

Prokhovnik, Raia. (1999), *Rational Woman. A Feminist Critique of the Dichotomy,* London/New York (Routledge), p. 37.

Rand M, Strom K. (1997), *Violence-Related Injuries Treated in Hospital Emergency Departments,* Washington (DC): Bureau of Justice Statistics, U. S. Department of Justice: 1997.

Roberts, Albert R.; Springer, David W., eds. (2007), *Social Work in Juvenile and Criminal Justice Settings* (3rd ed.), Springfield, Illinois: Charles C Thomas. p. 270.

Robertson, K and M, Tamar. (2009), "Attitudes and Attributions Associated With Female and Male Partner Violence", *Journal of Applied Social Psychology*, 39 (7): 1481.

Saunders DG. (1988), "Wife Abuse, Husband Abuse, or Mutual Combat? A Feminist Perspective on the Empirical Findings", In Bograd ML, Yllö K, *Feminist Perspectives on Wife Abuse*, Thousand Oaks: Sage Publications. pp. 90–113.

Sen, S and A, Sanhita. (2006), "The Domestic Violence Act, 2005: A New Direction", *Advocacy Internet*, 8(5): p. 3-8.

Seth Sunmit. (2010), "Domestic Violence as a Human Rights Issue", *Legal Services India*, November 03.

Shabana Azmi. (2003), "Domestic Violence is not so Private", *Deccan Herald (India)*, 13th August.

Shipway, Lynn. (2004), *Domestic Violence: A Handbook for Health Professionals*, New York: Routledge.

Stets, JE and MA Straus. (1990), Gender Differences in Reporting Marital Violence and its Medical and Psychological Consequences, In Straus and Gelles (eds), *Physical Violence in American Families*, NJ: Transaction Publishers.

Straus, M A. (1999), The Controversy over Domestic Violence by Women: A Methodological, Theoretical, and Sociology of Science Analysis, In X. B. Arriaga & S. Oskamp (Eds.), *Violence in Intimate Relationships* (pp. 17–44), Thousand Oaks, CA: Sage.

Straus, M A. (2006), "Paper Presented at Conference on Trends in Intimate Violence Intervention", New York University.

Straus, M A. , and Gelles, R. J. (1990), *Physical Violence in American Families*, Somerset, NJ: Transaction.

Strauss M A. (2005), "Women's Violence toward Men is a Serious Social Problem" , *Current Controversies on Family*

Violence, Ed by R J. Gelles and D R Loseke. Newbury Park: Sage. .

Swan, S. C. ; Snow, D. L. (2002), "A Typology of Women's Use of Violence in Intimate Relationships". *Violence Against Women,* 8: 286–319.

Tahir, Fahrettin. (2011), "Behind the veil", *The Economist,* 12th May.

Time. (1995), "Women: Killed by Greed and Oppression, ", *TIME Magazine,* Sept 11, Volume 146, No. 11.

Titley Gavan (Ed). (2007), *Gender Matters,* Council of Europe, Publication Division, Hungery, Budapest.

Waits, Kathleen. (1985), "The Criminal Justice System's Response to Battering: Understanding the Problem, Forging the Solutions", *Washington Law Review,* 60: 267–330.

Wallace, Harvey. (2004), *Family Violence: Legal, Medical, and Social Perspectives,* Allyn & Bacon. p. 2

Watts C and Zimmerman C. (2002), "Violence against Women: Global Scope and Magnitude", *Lancet* 359 : 1232–7.

White JW, *et. al.* (2000), "Intimate partner aggression—what have we learned? Comment on Archer (2000)", *Psychol Bull,* 126 (5): 690–6.

Wikipedia, (2012), *Domestic Violence,* Wikipedia. com (Retrived January 2012)

Young, Iris Marion. (1997), "House and Home. Feminist Variations on a Theme", in: ibid, *Intersecting Voices, Dilemmas of Gender, Political Philosophy, and Policy,* Princeton (University Press), p. 160.

14

A STRING OF STIFLED WOMANHOOD (SUICIDES BY ECONOMICALLY INDEPENDENT GIRLS — AN ISSUE OF CONCERN)

SUDHA ARORA

If women don't share, doesn't mean, they don't suffer

About hundred and fifty years back from today, the women were incapable of identifying their own sufferings and social status. They never had any expectations from life. Suffering within the four walls of their homes, without complaining, was their fate and dealing with household problems and moving ahead was their duty. As there was no alternative for them outside their homes hence whatever they got was accepted by them. Tolerance and sacrifice were their ornaments. They considered it fortune if respected and destiny if humiliated. If a middle-class woman happened to be talented and creative, she would knit a border, cushion cover, and embroider bed sheets, pillow cover or a sari or make wall hangings from the left out stuff in the house kept as garbage, in the spare time of the afternoon — after taking care of her kitchen and children. They spent their time, decorating the area within the four walls of their homes.

Lack of awareness of their rights, looking down on their domestic labour, child marriage, denial of a normal lifestyle on becoming a widow — are some of the social system which made it essential to educate the women during that period. Women became literate. Awareness followed. However, their presence in the outer space remained limited mostly to teaching in a school. The onset of education for women led to second generation of women who were made aware about self independence which further led to their involvement in Banks, Govt. offices, Corporate houses and many other fields of social, economic and political activities. Most of the Indian middle class women, who had been dependent for their monetary needs on their husbands earnings, also began to contribute to the household expenditure. However this did not make any difference in their laborious routine and household chores. They managed to deal with this double responsibility with efficiency. Although the equations within the marital relationships in the Indian society have changed for betterment but it is only in a small segment of the women where there have been positive changes among their male counterparts. For an average middle class woman, the situation is even more complex than it was earlier.

The scenario for a middle class woman, still seem to be depressing. Everyday a new incident of molestation comes with the morning newspaper but with the increasing insensitivity of modern times, the hammering that we feel the first day of shocking news get simmered slowly. As the news shift from first page headline news to the fourth page corner, they stop being our concern leaving just a small scar on our mind.

In the Year 2011, On International Women's Day – from 8th March to 28th September 2011, there was a string of four suicides and homicides of girls, between 22-32 years of age, in suburbs of Mumbai which ropes in some important issues all over again. These were the recorded headline news, but there are so many cases of molestation and battered woman which are not brought into the picture by the family members themselves due to social taboos/stigmas. Let's have a look on these four incidents of suicides —

27th September 2011 – Usha Singh(name changed), A 24 year old resident of Andheri (East), A Graduate from IIT Kanpur and a MBA hanged herself to death leaving behind a cell video recording, saying she was frustrated and she did not want to bother her parents and husband with her problems !

26th July 2011 – Geeta Verma(name changed), a MBA Graduate — resident of Mulund (East) killed herself by hanging leaving behind her one and a half year old daughter.

16th April 2011 – Rama Singh(name changed), a 34 year old woman killed herself by jumping off a seven storey building in Dahisar (East) after flinging her six year old son Siddhesh, from the terrace. Rama was a house wife and her husband Nilesh, a stock broker.

8th March 2011 — On the morning of International Women's Day, came the shocking news of the murder of Prema Gupta (name changed) of Delhi and suicide of Kiran Verma (name changed) of Mumbai, a chartered accountant and guest lecturer at Saraf college, preparing for her MBA. Kiran had jumped from the 19th floor of her residence Sahyadri Housing Complex, Malad (East) after throwing her 6 year old son Gaurav and 3 year old daughter Mihika to death — an act of suicide and homicide — in legal terms.

All these incidents of suicides have some shocking similarities. Coming from the middle class, these girls were professionally qualified and had a job before their marriage. They chose to marry boy of their own choice. They could have earned their own living and create their own space but unfortunately, education and financial independence could not stop them from ending their own precious life. Why ? The question is disturbing for all the feminist organisations and social science students.

Few months back, UN Women – a newly created body dedicated to gender equality and empowerment of women – gave its report titled 'Progress of the World's Women: In Pursuit of Justice ' said 'India significantly lacks behind the rest of the world in representation of the fairer sex in judicial system and justice is still out of reach for majority of the community.' There was news of the ratio about Domestic violence that 45% of men approve of wife beating necessary as a step to control the women !

To get into such a desperate situation like suicide, one doesn't act in a sudden fit of depression. It has to be a deep rooted struggle of making adjustments, compromises, looking for a breathing space, unable to share with anybody and finally taking a step of total destruction of lives.

As for Usha Singh, She has left a video clipping prior to her decision to end her life, holding her frustration responsible for suicide and apologised to her parents and her husband – Ratan Singh (name changed). Her husband said – while he was leaving for his job, she was pleading to talk to her for 10 minutes but he was getting late for work. Reaching office, he got a SMS from his wife saying "Sorry !" He did not take it seriously and never thought, his wife is going to end her life ! It was a love marriage in February this year – just seven months back ! Usha was working but she left her job after marriage and was at home. Four months back they had shifted to this new house Golden Apartments, Kondivita lane in Andheri East. Just after her husband Ratan left for work, she hanged herself in the morning of 28th Sept, between 9.45—10 A.M.

If we go through each cases of suicide, there is definitely a 'cry for help' from the victim to their friends, parents or partner — which is normally unattended and not taken seriously, thinking that it's a passing trait. Every suicide leaves behind a trail of clues and incidents of lingering depression which does consist a 'cry for help' to close relatives or friends or husband, who are not able to figure out its intensity. Even after the incident, hardly do they come out with the 'truth' that they were getting warning signals but were ignoring it, thinking it's a common phenomena when a newly married girl has to make adjustments to the newly acquired environment and they start narrating the behavior of the victim as a very 'happy' and 'pleasant' personality and that nobody could ever judge from her contented image that she will take such a drastic step !

In the case of Kiran Verma, a CA and visiting lecturer in Poddar College, the family members and friends have stated that Kiran was a 'normal' person. She did not look sad and never showed any signs of depression. There were no fights heard or seen in the Verma household although it was a joint family.

The in-laws stick to their statement of 'Everything was fine. There was no tension in the family. They are unable to figure out the motive behind Kiran's decision. This was an unexpected step' and 'Nobody knows why she had taken such step ! '

Kiran Verma's suicide on the eve of her wedding anniversary speaks volumes about her agony. It is a clear indication of the rift in the relationship which always remains unidentified at the surface. Women who put up with silent abuse or constant negligence from their partners, try to compensate for it by chatting with friends or colleagues at the workplace, making themselves busy in their career, looking after their children, getting their homework done – there are umpteen household chores to keep them engaged.

No woman, specially a mother of two kids, would like to share her misery with friends, least of all with parents .... thinking that she will be able to solve it on her own. Most women think they are able to handle their problems themselves. Although deep down in their hearts such women are quite upset and can feel the gravity of the pressure gradually building up inside them, they prefer to keep it a secret. They are aware of the fact that the trauma is too much to handle but they know the need to handle it on their own. That is one big reason for not sharing it with parents or with friends.

Moreover, they don't want their parents to get worried for their well-being since all girls assume that their parent's responsibility is over once they educate their daughters and send them to ' their' home after getting them married to the boy of their choice.

Even today, a middle class young girl gives her hundred percent to the family she is married to. After marriage, the family, husband and children become her first priority. Generally her own career and ambitions take a back seat. In a joint family, often the husband leaving his newly married wife all alone becomes partial to his own family. In such a situation the girl becomes the victim of double setback injury. Neither does she get the love of her in-law's family nor does she want to burden her parental family by sharing her own tragedy. When they are not able to generate within themselves the energy and strength, the roots of their sorrow penetrate so deep that under their 'All is well' appearance they quietly keep dying within themselves. Such girls under extreme depression think that killing themselves is the only option left for them.

So, why does a woman refuses to share the trauma she is going through ? In our age old tradition, girls are handed down this unwritten code of conduct that after marriage it's their life and they have to take charge of the situation, however grim it may be.

With increasing higher education and girls holding attractive degrees of MBA, Engineering and other professions, it becomes all the more essential that the girl is capable of taking care of her problems with in-laws, husband and kids.

We have made our daughters financially independent but have we trained them well to be emotionally independent? They still look upon their counterpart to give them moral support ... It's good to rely on your partner to a certain point but from the saturation point onwards they should stop begging for emotional support or moral boost !

No woman ever goes to a counseling centre, unless she undergoes domestic violence or physical abuse which leaves black and blue bruises on her body. Emotional abuse remains unidentified even by the woman herself for a long period of time.

Some Cases and Instances

In the year 2010 on Monday 28th June, there was a news in all the papers about Kirti Wadhera (name changed) – who jumped off the 27th floor of Runwal Pride Tower at Mulund just after 13 months of her love marriage to Sumit Wadhera (name changed). Kirti was forced to give up her job with a leading share broking firm as a pre condition for the marriage. She hailed from a middle class family while Sumit was from an affluent home.

Just after a few months of marriage, she was not given proper food to eat and was also beaten. She stayed with her parents for two and a half months and then returned to her in-laws assuming that the situations will improve. Her assumptions went wrong. Loosing her financial independence with no job in hand and treated as a maid in the house with a totally hostile atmosphere, Kirti was unable to take it any more. Jumping off the 27th floor seemed to her to be the only way out the miseries, she had brought upon herself by marrying the boy of her own choice !

I am reminded of the case of Akanksha (name changed) – who was a talented stage actor and a child psychologist by profession. She had a inter-caste love marriage with the boy who was an ardent fan of her theatre. After her marriage, she had to move with her husband who had a transferable job. Finally when they got settled in Mumbai, she wanted to join theatre.

Not only was her idea strongly opposed, she was threatened with termination of marriage if she returns to the stage. She started helping out her husband in his research work but felt exhausted to the core. Initially she did everything to support her husband in his professional commitments but there came a saturation point and she came to me for counseling. As Akanksha had married against her parent's wishes, they had cut off all relations and the door of the parental house was closed upon her. She voiced her total desperation to the extent that she wanted to kill her daughter before committing suicide as she felt her husband was not capable of bringing up a kid, and she did not want her lovely daughter to be tortured in the hands of a step mother. Now she has one more daughter to look after and she has made herself happy in a role of a full time mother and home maker. Of course she has to deal with the tantrums of her husband, but she has managed to pull on. Her husband is still not very cooperative and often dictates his terms to run the house.

Like most of the women, Akanksha also has the ingrained capability of handling all odds. She is doing her best to keep life going. Both the daughters keep her busy. Her own aspirations or identity are no more her priority. After all it's the future of her two daughters which is of greater concern. So, Is this a precondition to save one's marriage — leaving all aspirations for oneself and dedicating one's life to looking after children in their growing period? Akanksha, as I see her, will definitely find her way to fulfill her own dreams and pursue her career – either as a stage person or a child counselor once her daughters are on their own and Akanksha finds time for herself.

Then there are umpteen cases where women don't share their depression even with their closest friends. I can never forget the case of my neighbour Shweta Khanna (name changed), my morning walk partner for 9 long years, with whom I used to discuss some of the battered women cases occasionally and who knew about my association with a counseling centre. Still she never ever complained about her husband till one late night we heard a loud scream and finally came to know what she had been undergoing for the last 33 years. Agreed, She belong to the older generation where woman used to link their pride with their husbands. The generation which used to scream only when they were not able to take violence on their ageing body which was growing weaker with time.

So if women don't share, doesn't mean, they don't suffer. It's only that their shock absorbers fail completely after a certain point of time and the steps like suicides are out of total exhaustion and desperation on hitting the dead end. It is not merely in a fit of abnormal depression that they take such a drastic step as suicide.

From Usha Singh of Andheri to Kirti Wadhera of Mulund to Kiran Verma of Malad in Mumbai, All from metro city – It's a long string of stifled womanhood !

Unfortunately, we have not been able to make our education degrees, enough relevant, to blend with the social crisis and emotional upheaval which a girl from a middle class background, goes through after an arranged or love marriage. Her world of dreams is shattered in no time and the time to redefine dreams is not taken by her with a sense of responsibility towards her own survival. The symptoms of depression arising from subtle kind of negligence of the partner are not taken seriously to be a reason to visit a psychiatrist or a psycho-analyst, who could have been of great help to evade the self destructive moment. Efforts should be taken before they reach the ' dead end ' by themselves or by the parents, relatives, friends and counterparts !

A comment from the Bombay High Court Judge on the status of married daughters, is shocking – ' When a daughter gets married and leaves the house of the father to reside with her husband, She ceases to be a member of the family of father. After marriage when she goes to the house of the parents, legally she is only a guest in the house ! ' Such statements only strengthens the mindset of our Patriarchal society and sex selective abortions in India.

Dealing With It

The tragedy can be arrested and hurdles can be crossed if only we realize that we have to break the culture of silence on various levels.

- All educated and well qualified women in desperate situation need to be given a message that there are always alternatives and there is always hope. This is the social responsibility of each and every woman.
- The immediate agency to give this message is parenting of children. All the parents need to give loud and clear message to their daughters that their relationship don't cease once the girl is married off and goes to a new atmosphere with new relatives around who may not be very co-operative too. So the message should be given, 'If you face humiliation or adverse situation after marriage, we are always there for you. Do not ever suffer in silence.'
- The other agency is our education and media. Education does not make young girls independent, instead it just creates capacity to earn money. The life skills are not instilled in individuals. Financial independence is not enough, Emotional independence is required too.
- Government should make it compulsory for all schools and Colleges to appoint a permanent trained counsellor who can make students more responsible towards their life, make them aware of the mindset of Indian society and give respect to their life partners after marriage.
- Media constantly glorifies the image of the 'silent suffering woman' which it has to stop doing. The image of the 'silent suffering

woman' has to be discredited at all levels like in our religious dictates and rituals.

- All girls should know that life is not a bed of roses once they get married. Life is full of struggle and one should try one's level best to adjust and make marriage work, but not at the cost of one's life. An educated girl has to learn to live on her own terms, keeping her self-respect intact and not succumb to social taboos regarding single and divorced women.
- Women themselves have to understand that life is very precious. If marriage fails, it is not end of the world ! There are many new paths to tread on, many new avenues to explore.
- All of us have to break the culture of silence !

These incidents forced me to pen down a poem for the parents of daughters —

One Single Door, At Least !

It could be a carved antique door
Or a door made of cut pieces of wood
Maybe with a ethnic handle on it
Or a metal hasp

The door should open to a home where
Parents of a daughter —
who eloped with her lover against their wishes
would say...
" We know that whatever you have done
Is wrong, yet we pray

You to be happy with the one
you have chosen

Don't ever forget
If at any time
The decision of yours goes wrong
And your feet want to turn where you belong
This door is always open for you ! "

When all doors seem closed
To daughters
Let there be at least one single door
Always open for them!

Reference

Turquet Laura. (2011), 'Progress of the World's Women: In Pursuit of Justice ', UN Women, Newyork, USA.

15

EVOLVING ROLE OF WOMEN CELLS

SUMAN NALWA

The pressure of women movement in response to the increasing incidents of bride-burning, enactment of special category of offences relating to domestic violence and dowry harassment and dowry death culminated in establishment of CWCs in various states in India . Even the central government through the Ministry of Home Affairs asked the states to adopt appropriate measures for dealing with increasing crime against women including setting up 'crime against women cell' in districts where they do not exist. The mandate given to these cells was to enquire, investigate and supervise the cases arising out of violence perpetuated on women. Even the Supreme Court of India in case of Joint Women's Programme vs. State of Rajasthan, directed the States of Rajasthan and Haryana to create a Special Dowry Cell at the State level to investigate into the dowry deaths through specialised investigative units.

The main objective of setting up such Cells was to give focus to the crimes committed against women and give them a platform to come forward and complain against the perpetrators in confidence. Also it was felt that like other specialized cells, the investigation of such cases will be of highest standards and the women victims will be dealt with much more sensitivity in a congenial manner then in police station where the CAW had the tendency to be treated as a low priority area compared to other law and order duties.

However, over a period of time, the CAW Cells have acquired an additional role of conciliation and mediation which has been sanctioned and approved by the High Courts (mostly High Court). Even the administrative instructions have sanctified this role of CAW Cells. High courts/ Supreme Court observations on the working of women cells In Joint Women's Programme vs. State of, the Supreme Court directed the States of Rajasthan and Haryana to create a Special Dowry Cell at the State level to investigate into the dowry deaths through specialized investigative units. One or two women social workers dealing with Social Welfare and Women's problems may be associated with such dowry cells In S. Hanumantlia Rao v. S. Ramani, the Supreme Court held that approaching the Women Protection Cell for reconciliation of the estranged spouses did not amount to mental cruelty since the cell only made efforts to bring about conciliation between the parties but failed. In Raj Kumar Khanna v. The State and others, the division bench of the High Court had observed: "police headquarter framed the procedure to be followed by the CAW Cell with the intention of preventing abuse of the process of law. But in this case police committed abuse of the process established by the Commissioner.

No attempt was made to resolve the difference between Manoj Kumar and respondent no. 5 nor efforts were made to bring about amicable settlement for which purpose crime against women Cell was created. This cell is meant to safeguard the marriage and not to ruin it by registering case immediately on the asking of the complainant. Once an FIR is registered it becomes difficult to solve matrimonial tangles and things reaches such a pass that it cannot be restored back." In Crl. W. No. 127/1992, the Police filed an affidavit to the effect that the 'Crime Against Women' Cell was created by the Commissioner of Police to receive such complaints and then make efforts to ascertain facts and try for reconciliation. It is thought advisable in cases where the differences have not reached the stage of tragedy, the attempt should be made to forge unity between the two spouses so that they are brought about to make the marriage a success.

On failure of these reconciliation attempts, the law should be permitted to take its course. ......the proceedings taken up by the CAW Cell are mainly directed to bring about a reconciliation between the strained spouses. On the failure of reconciliation, resort to the provisions of law is taken too. If the respondent chooses not to take part in the proceedings before the Crime Against Women Cell, it is his sweet will. No action is taken for non appearance. There is no compulsion for the respondent to take part in the proceedings. The proceedings are in the nature of enquiry to find out the truth as to the allegations made in the complaint before registering a case. For example, it also becomes necessary to ascertain the factum of marriage even, and also the allegations of cruelty and "stridhan."

In Crl. W. No. 663/1995, the Police affidavit stated that "the proceedings by the Crime Women Cell are in the nature of enquiry to find out the truth as to the allegations made in the complaint before registering a case. For example it becomes necessary to ascertain the factum of marriage, even and also the allegations of cruelty and Stridhan. .....enquiry by the CAW Cell is in the nature of a primary enquiry with the sole object to make the marriage success and in case the matter is not reconciled between the parties the complaint is proceeded in accordance with law. In case the allegations made in the complaint are not found to be true the complaint is dropped/ closed."

In Savitri Devi vs. Ramesh Chand, the Delhi High Court while commenting upon section 498a, 406 IPC stated at para 23 that .....once a complaint is lodged under sections 498a/406 IPC whether they are vague, unspecific or exaggerated allegations or there is no evidence of any physical harm or injury inflicted upon woman that is likely to cause grave injury or danger to life, limb or health, it comes as an easy tool in the hands of police and agencies like Crime Against Women Cell to hound them with the threat of arrest making them run here and there and force them to hide .... 25 (para) the judgment went on to add that "it was primarily a social problem and social evil but has been allowed to be dealt with iron and heavy hands of the police.

In Rajender Singh vs State of NCT of Delhi, the Delhi High Court while quashing an FIR under 498a, stated that in case of matrimonial disputes it becomes the duty of the court to encourage genuine settlement of matrimonial disputes. Reliance was placed on the judgement in the case of G. V. Rao v. L. H. V. Prasad and Ors wherein the Supreme court stated "there has been an outburst of matrimonial disputes in recent times. Marriage is a sacred ceremony, the main purpose of which is to enable the young couple to settle down in life and live peacefully. But little matrimonial skirmishes suddenly erupt which often assume serious proportions resulting in commission of heinous crimes in which elders of the family are also involved with the result that those who could have counselled and brought about rapprochement are rendered helpless on their being arrayed as accused in the criminal case. There are many other reason which need not be mentioned here for not encouraging matrimonial litigation so that the parties may ponder over their defaults and terminate their disputes amicably by mutual agreement instead of fighting it out in a court of law where it takes years and years to conclude and in that process the parties lose their "young" days in chasing their "cases" in different courts."

In Beldev Singh vs State of , the petition was recalling the record of the CAW cell while framing the charge sheet. The High Court observed that CAW Cell is the amalgam of investigating agency which is also entrusted with the function of attempting to reconcile the parties. The proceedings before the CAW Cell are initiated pursuant to the complaint filed by the complainant in which there may be allegations of harassment on account of demand of dowry, etc., on the basis of which complaint generally is under section 498-a/406 IPC.

There is therefore no harm in summoning the record of the CAW Cells and while hearing the arguments on the charge, the learned trial court should be prudent enough to see as to which documents contained in the record before the CAW Cells are to be considered and parties allowed to rely thereupon. In Jasbir Kaur vs State, the petition was regarding the abolition of CAW Cells. The High Court opined that "the creation of CAW Cells for investigation of crime pertaining to women, does not cause any discrimination on the basis of sex for the CAW Cells have been constituted with a social purpose so that the crimes relating to women are dealt with sensitivity.

CAW Cell is like any other specialized wing of Delhi Police like Special Cell, Crime Branch, etc., where firstly an attempt is made to bring about unity between the two spouses so as to make the marriage a success. On the failure of these reconciliation attempts, the law is allowed to take its course. Thus no fault can be found with the creation of CAW Cells." In Harish Arora vs. State of , the petitioner filed the petition for dropping the proceedings before the CAW Cell. The High Court saw no reason to pass an order with respect to CAW cell proceedings stating that the proceedings before the CAW cell are not judicial or quasi judicial or proceedings in the investigation of the crime. They are only reconciliatory proceedings. CAW Cell is an agency created to make efforts for reconciliation between the families before initiation of criminal proceedings on the complaint of the wife. The petitioner is at liberty not to appear before the CAW cell. No coercive action can be taken by the CAW Cell, compelling an unwilling person to put in appearance before it. CAW can conduct proceedings only where both the parties are ready and willing to join the proceedings voluntarily.

In Crl. M. No. 9052/2007 and W. P. (Crl)1045/2007, the High Court on CAW Cell stated that "CAW Cell has no power to investigate the crime. It is not a police station where FIRs are registered. Investigation in any crime can be done only after registration of FIR. CAW Cell only makes reconciliatory efforts between the parties that also upto the stage of pre-registration of FIR. The investigation can also be done by CAW Cell, if it is referred to it after registration of FIR. Since FIR is not registered, no direction can be given to CAW Cell for investigation. " In W. P. (Crl) No. 1031/2007 and Crl. M. A. No. 8989/07, the High Court on the authority of CAW Cell stated that " CAW Cell has no authority to secure the presence of any person either by coercion or by threat. CAW Cell is only a conciliatory body where efforts are made for conciliation with the free will of the parties. If any person is not willing to go to CAW Cell, he cannot be compelled. It is also directed that CAW Cell, in future, instead of issuing summons to the parties shall send request letters asking them to appear for the purpose of conciliation and not for the purpose of investigation. The petitioner is at liberty not to appear before the CAW Cell."

In Harpal Singh Arora vs State, the Delhi High Court commenting on the nature of enquiry of the CAW Cell observed that CAW Cell, which has now become a notified police station, is a kind of pre-litigation alternate dispute resolution mechanism that might help in resolving a dispute before the Criminal Justice process is set in motion by registering an FIR. This may not be a statutorily recognised device. Never the less, given the nature of matrimonial disputes, straightway registering an FIR, which triggers the Criminal Justice process, can place the parties in an inflexible position and thereafter less inclined to reconcile their differences. ....the reference of the complaint to CAW Cell has the effect of postponing the activation of criminal justice process by facilitating dialogue between the parties with the help of the police.... The enquiry by the CAW Cell is at pre-FIR stage and is therefore only a preliminary enquiry. Further commenting on the final enquiry reports of the CAW Cell the court observed that though the conclusion of the CAW Cell is not binding on the magistrate during hearing under 156(3), he cannot brush aside the conclusion of the CAW Cell and must give observation on why he inclined to order investigation notwithstanding the report. In a recent landmark judgement in the case of Chander Bhan vs, State, the Delhi High Court gave broad guidelines and directions in such matters (498a, 406 of the IPC) in order to salvage and save the institution of marriage and matrimonial homes of the couple. Guidelines:

1. Social workers/NGO: there is no doubt that most of the complaints are filed in the heat of the moment over trifling fights and ego clashes. It is also a matter of common knowledge that in their tussle and ongoing hostility the hapless children are the worst victims. Before a wife moves to file a complaint with the women cell, a lot of persuasion and conciliation is required. (a) The Delhi legal Service Authority, National Commission for Women, NGO's and social

worker's working for upliftment of women should set up a desk in crime against women cell to provide them with conciliation services, so that before the State machinery is set in motion, the matter is amicably settled at that very stage. But, if ultimately even after efforts put by the social workers reconciliation seems not possible then the matter should be undertaken by the police officials of Crime Against Women Cell and there also, serious efforts should be made to settle the matter amicably. Police Authorities: (a) Pursuant to directions given by the Apex Court, the Commissioner of Police, Delhi vide Standing Order No. 330/2007 had already issued guidelines for arrest in dowry cases registered under sections 498A/406 IPC and the said guidelines should be followed by the Delhi Police strictly and scrupulously.

(i) No case under Section 498-A/406 IPC should be registered without the prior approval of DCP/ Addl DCP.

(ii) Arrest of main accused should be made only after thorough investigation has been conducted and with the prior approval of ACP/DCP

(iii) Arrest of the collateral accused such as father-in –law, mother-in-law, brother-in-law or sister-in-law etc should only be made after prior approval of DCP on file.

(iv) police should also depute a well trained and a well behaved staff in all the Crime Against Women Cells especially the lady officers, all well equipped with the abilities of perseverance, persuasion, patience and forbearance.

(v) FIR in such cases should not be registered in a routine manner.

(vi) The endeavour of the Police should be to scrutinize complaints very carefully and then register FIR

(vii) The FIR should be registered only against those persons against whom there are strong allegations of causing any kind of physical or mental cruelty as well as breach of trust.

(viii) All possible efforts should be made, before recommending registration of any FIR, for reconciliation and in case it is found that there is no possibility of settlement, then necessary steps in the first instance be taken to ensure return of stridhan and dowry articles etc. by the accused party to the complainant.

Thus in the present scenario the CAW Cells are working as conciliation platforms with a view to give a woman a chance to explore the possibility of negotiating a violence free future with the perpetrators of violence without necessarily opting a criminal action. In some states the capacity building in this regard has been done by augmenting the CAW Cells with qualified social workers. Model has been a success in this regard where the police partnership with an academic institute like TISS to harness the social workers to work in coordination with police has been successful to a large extent. At other places like, it has remained an ad-hoc arrangement wherein the NGOs have been roped in without any specific MOU or policy statement.

CAW Cells under the Police

Pursuant to its policy of ensuring better and humane treatment of women victims and to have a high quality investigation unit to investigate crimes against women, Crime Women Cells were created. One central cell was set up in the police headquarter in 1983, headed by a DCP, as the first police response to deal exclusively with the crimes against women. The experience of this cell while dealing with the women victim projected the need for specialized attention for crimes committed against women which it was felt the traditional police could not handle with sensitivity. In 1986 separate cells were set up in all the police districts. Counselling of spouses and their family members became an integral part of functioning of these cells where in it was realized that a woman does not essentially want to take criminal action against the spouse but wants to negotiate non violence within the marriage. There has been criticism by many women groups as a non police role ill fitted to be done by unqualified generalist. However till the year 2008, it had no power to register the criminal cases. It was felt that there was inadequate and improper investigation of cases with late referrals and other delays. The infrastructure and facilities were inadequate at the police station level to deal with women victim which sometimes was augmented by inadequate and abusive examination.

Keeping this in mind a separate police station was notified in the Centralized CWC in 2008 march to register and investigate cases relating to matrimonial disputes including cruelty, harassment and any other cases of crime against women. At present there are 11 CWC in the 11 districts of Delhi Police headed by an ACP and a Central Crime Women Cell at Nanakpura headed by and officer of the rank of Joint Commissioner of Police and one police station Crime Against Women.

Slowly and steadily the CWC has been providing other non police services to the women victim be it the professional legal, psychological counseling or the services of the protection officer under the Domestic Violence Prevention Act. Crisis Intervention Centers have been institutionalized in the system to provide holistic relief to the rape victims through specialized assistance for trauma, counseling and rehabilitation.

In its ever expanding role the Cell started a round the clock 'Women Helpline 1091' in 2002, in coordination with the 'Police Control Room', with a view to improve the response to women in distress who seek police intervention. The unique feature of the helpline was the response of the Women Police Team to these calls who are equipped to provide counseling and options on support services to the women victim. The CWC also has many outreach programs like self defense training in various schools and colleges with an objective to make women more confident when exposed to a threatening situation. The CWCs have evolved from being a starting point of litigation to mediation over a period of time. The move has been towards a solution oriented policing. With this changing role there has been a lot of criticism of police performing non police functions, however the high courts have increasingly recognized this role of police in its various judgments. Further, the police have increasingly started associating social workers in this role and limiting their mandate to the policing (investigative) duties. The Police have started giving options in alternate dispute resolution to the warring couples through the services of the trained mediators. High Court has also set up a mediation centre in the central CAW Cell to exclusively deal with marital complaints at prelitigation stage and offer an alternate solution outside the criminal justice system.

There is a trend of softening stand of High Courts in dealing with marital disputes or complaints under 498a IPC. The division bench of High Court ,in Raj Kumar Khanna vs State while finding no fault with creation of CAW Cells stated that "police Headquarter framed the procedure to be followed by the CAW Cell with the intention of preventing abuse of process of law. But in this case, police committed abuse of the process established by the commissioner. No attempt was made to resolve the difference between Manoj and respondent no. 5 nor were efforts made to bring about amicable settlement for which purpose CAW Cell was created. This cell is meant to safeguard the marriage and not to ruin it by registering case immediately on the asking of the complainant. Once an FIR is registered it becomes difficult to solve matrimonial tangles and things reach such a pass that it cannot be restored back." However, the mandate of the original CAW cells as laid out on the standing order 281 of the Police does not envisage reconciliation/ amicable settlement as role/ duty.

Administrative guidelines for the CAW Cells, police

1. Standing Order (SO) -281 of Delhi Police issued vide No. 2980-3230/Crime (W) Cell, dated 18/5/1989:vide this SO the mandate of the special Cell was for investigating cases and enquiring into complaintsof Crime against Women. The duties assigned were

    A. Investigate all cases of murder for dowry and death of women where dowry is the motive behind the crime.

    B. Investigate all cases of rape of women

    C. Monitor investigation of or investigate itself any other case of crimes against women such as cases under 304, 305, 306, 498A IPC and Dowry Prohibition Act.

    D. may enquire into complaints received by it and, where necessary, direct the local police to register and investigate cases which may rise out of such enquiries

2. Circular on arrest by Delhi Police: while issuing the guidelines on making arrest in cases under investigation in light of Supreme Court of India in Joginder Kumar case specifically mentioned that "no hasty action should be tolerated in cases of marital disputes where old and infirm parents or relatives not living at the alleged place of harassment are accused of cruelty." The experience of Police has been unique and most commented upon by the High Court . Questioning the authority of the CAW Cells in settling domestic disputes the court has grudgingly accepted the Cells and the pre-litigation

platform it offers to the warring couples. Increasingly it is gaining the confidence of the courts which is evident with the High Court operating from within the centralized CAW Cell their Mediation Centre. The association of NGOs and greater transparency and SOPs has further increased its credibility so much so that it can be suitably replicated in other States as well. Police organisation has the mandate to protect the rights of the people.

However, when it comes to responding to the needs of the women the supportive response desired is not available. Being masculine by nature the police personnel are also carrying the same patriarchal gender norms as the rest of the society with a result that they do not offer unconditional protection to women from all kinds of male violence. They may or may not intervene in a domestic violence case. In all societies because of the low status of the women, the violence against women is treated as low priority areas.

The police personnel deployed in the women cells are treated as dignified social workers within the police subculture. Further, the capacity to be responsive to the needs of the women victim is a specialized skill which is not inherent in the police personality. Further, within the districts the staff earmarked for dealing with CAWs is also roped in for important law and order duties which are considered more important than the CAW duties. NGOs are increasingly being associated with the working of the CAW Cells. However any joint institutionalized response requires the involvement of credible NGOs to forge a partnership with the police.

Looking at the various high court/ supreme court rulings with regard to CAW cells it is evident that the high courts have been critical of their role and have from time to time tried to define their role from an investigative to counselling body. The stress has been to set it up as a pre litigation stage conciliation medium with a view of saving the families from break ups. Role of CAW has over the period of time remained reactive at large. The euphoria of the women advocacy groups has to a large extent turned into despondency at the CAW Cells inability to play a more proactive role in dealing with the issues relating to women. The stand of CAW cells in assuming the role of family counsellors without any specialization in this regards has to a large extent been vindicated by high courts accepting this role of CAW Cells in their various judgements. They have recognized this pre-litigation role of CAW Cells in settling trifling issues between warring couples by giving them a platform to renegotiate their relationship. The police leadership has also risen to this felt need and increasingly the social workers and specialist from legal, psychological and medical field have been incorporated in the system to deal with this duty at a professional level. However, there is a need to institutionalize these practices to bring about role clarity of all the stakeholders. The future mandate of CAW cell has to be all encompassing, creating a conducive and safe environment for women in all spheres of their life so that they can enjoy their rights of being human to the fullest. However, crime against women has its roots in the social system and other social institutes have to take up their responsibilities in combating the CAWs in a multidisciplinary approach to device strategies for prevention and rehabilitation. From the police perspective in its futuristic vision it should ensure a gender friendly environment and a professional response at all the police stations and having a clear cut policy on violence against women so that the need of a separate Cell for the women does not remain.

Note: Court cases discussed by the author of the paper are self written and are part of their experience as a senior Police Officer. Thus, references of the court cases have not been mentioned.

16

ACID ATTACK : AN ANTI WOMAN BURNING SOCIAL MENTALITY-AN ANALYSIS

SYED MUBIN ZEHRA

Introduction and Background

Can a mother say that it is impossible for me to have a sight of my daughters face .This seems to be the most atrocious injury on an individual women when even her mother would deny to see her face. Or even atrocious would be when she herself refuses to have a glimpse of herself in the mirror. Now when would such negating situation arise is the question in concern here. These references seem to serve the reality of an acid attack victim woman .Yes, if we just think over it with slightest of sensitivity what would be the life of an acid attack victim it sure does sends a griping shrill down your heart.

Acid attack is a minute reflection of the many more crimes that have been a part of our civilized society that has been haunting the social progress and movement of women. Here I discuss the seriousness of crimes like acid attacks on women and also investigate through its manifestations and silent sufferings across its victims and pose several unanswered questions too in curbing this crime against women.

Women and the crimes that curb their social mobility are serious concern areas of people working for the emancipation and rehabilitation of victims of crime against women. There has been an active surge of historical, anthropological and social scholarly work resolutions and solutions on women and crime against them. Here I touch upon the most inhuman and also a neglected crime against women. That is the acid attacks on women. Acid attack clearly is an anti women burning social mentality and deserves an analysis and solutions too in curbing this serious crime that seem to have been ruining many beautiful lives.

As we were growing up in the 80s acid attacks were heard of rarely or even say 10 years back acid attacks were rare and heard of once in a while .However in recent times, it has become a serious concern with regards to crime against women. This crime against women has a special geographical domain and is rampant in our south Asian subcontinent and committed in countries like Pakistan, India and Bangladesh. However we do find it cropping up in some African countries as well. There have been some cases in United Kingdom and Italy too.

Acid attacks are found happening in rural as well as urban scenario both and its victims are in majority the women only. It has touched and hurt women from a small village to even the most urban working women in a metro city too. Such acid attacks are reflections of the serious criminal minds that surrounds us woman unknowingly.

There has been a serious call for action on the part of police, society and lawmakers in checking this crime against women. Some inroads have been made which we discuss in detail here in curbing this crime but the question arises are they enough in completely checking this crime. Such and many more questions are to be answered as we follow in this paper.

Acid Attack: A Social Crime Against Women

What is an Acid Attack?

It is a social crime against women. It is the deliberate use of acid to attack another human being. The victims are overwhelmingly women and children. Attackers often target the head and face in order to maim, disfigure and blind. Acid violence rarely kills but causes severe physical, psychological and social scarring, and victims are often left with no legal recourse, limited access to medical or psychological assistance, and without the means to support themselves.

This is a gender crime and often a crime of honor and inequality that prevails regarding the female section of our society. The common reasons for this crime could be as follows.

1. Male honor
2. Rejection in love
3. Family and marriage related issue
4. Land disputes
5. Dowry
6. Jealousy
7. Social punishment
8. Revenge

These are few to list of many reasons that could just lead to an acid attack on an innocent woman anytime anywhere and in any situation. The acid used is mostly sulphuric and nitric acid that is easily available in the market. Bangladesh has highest reported incidents of acid attack .Sometimes it is also referred to as crimes of passion.

Acid Attack Victim's Apathy and Pain

Acid attack or throwing of acid lead to blindness, permanent scarring of face or body and along with such physical injury it leads to far reaching social, psychological and economic difficulty for the victim.

The most notable effects of an acid attack are the lifelong bodily disfigurement. According to the Acid Survivors Foundation in Pakistan, there is a high survival rate amongst victims of acid attacks. Consequently the victim is faced with physical challenges, which require long term surgical treatment, as well as psychological challenges, which require in-depth intervention from psychologists and counselors at each stage of physical recovery. These far-reaching effects on their lives impact their psychological, social and economic viability in communities.

According to London based charity- 'ACID SURVIVORS TRUST INTERNATIONAL', some 15,000 acid attacks are reported worldwide every year. While the physical, psychological and emotional cost of suffering acid trauma is incalculable, the actual cost of surgery and medication to mend the resulting disfigurement totals around 3.5 million rupees, or close to $57,000 USD.

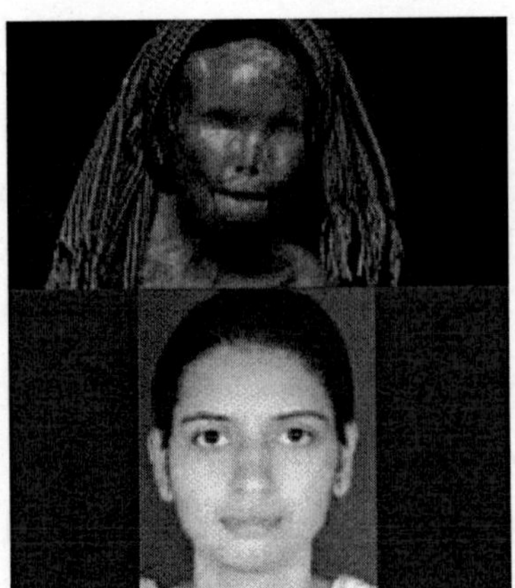

A picture of an acid attack victim before and after the attack. This image is self expressive about the pain and apathy of the victim.

Laxmi, 24; Nisha, 22; Sonam, 16; Ruby, Tabassum and so many young names that keep knocking and tell the tale of their horrific experience of this attack . One such individual is 25-year-old Laxmi, who was attacked in 2005 when she was just 16, has taken it up herself to lead her own campaign in the movement to fight acid attacks, and has been a fierce advocate. In the years since her attack, Laxmi has been the face of the movement, having appeared for television interviews, and sought out over 27,000 signatures to control acid sales. Where most victims hide their face because of trauma, Laxmi was courageous in taking a public stand against acid violence. Such courage has led her to be successful in petitioning the Supreme Court to order the Indian Government to regulate the sale of acid and to support

women in successfully prosecuting their attackers. But the question that keep knocking is that acid attacks victim apathy never seems to end .What is the reason behind such attacks? why are they targeted only towards woman in particular is one major question that need answers . This picture of Laxmi the acid attack survivor and crusader is a symbol of strength for many.

Acid Attack : A Great Weapon Used Against Women Development and Empowerment

Throughout recorded history, violence against women has been ignored, excused or accepted as a seemingly intractable part of the human condition. In the 1990s, however, momentum began to build around the idea that women's rights were human rights, thanks in large part to the tireless efforts of women's organizations around the world.

The 1993 UN Declaration on the Elimination of Violence against Women was a landmark acknowledgement that violence against women is a human rights violation no matter where it occurs. Social norms in much of the world lead people to turn a blind eye toward violence against women and girls. In some cases, women are even thought to "ask for" violence themselves even simply by dressing in a particular manner .Whatever the situation, it is the design of society to stop women from coming in the forefront or a tool to stop women development.

Acid attacks are also one such tool that stands as a tool to curb women development and freedom. The scars that are left on the faces of these victims are scars of our society that does not give security and freedom for the woman to live and move freely and such attacks are used to scare her from moving freely in the society .These scars of acid victims are a shame for our society, shame on India and shame on humanity. There are people and community working for the rehabilitation and support of acid attack victims. Organizations like ASF was formed in 1999 with the growing concern of the rising trend of acid violence in Bangladesh. Acid violence is a form of gender based violence that reflects and perpetuates the inequality of women in society. Gender based violence is a common scenario in Bangladesh. This form of violence cuts across cultural and religious barriers and impede on women's right to fully participate in society. It has the effect of denying women important rights such as economic well being, social well being, political participation, personal fulfillment and self worth.

Acid attack and life after that is the most traumatizing and hard to live for its victim. In the words of one of the victims "when the criminals who did this to me are free wearing fancy sunglasses and driving in a car why should I hide myself in a room! Yes this spirit and strength inside a victim can give her the strength to collect the broken pieces of her soul and self to start a new life again. However due to ignorance of society and the government and civil society the majority of victims stay aloof and lonely and stay like an outcast.

The most important criteria or necessity for the rehabilitation of the acid attack victims are that they need a concern family friend society and above all the support of government too. Fast justice is best in fighting back to check the irreparable damage of the tragedy.

Compensation and medical support too is an important need.

Majority of the acid attacks are directed against women only. Hence the concerns should be based on the female gender issue level. As per the honorable Supreme Court of India order on acid attacks criminal writ petition129 of 2006 Laxmi versus union of India dated 6th December 2013, there is a provision of compensation of three lakhs of rupees to be provided and check on sale of acid.

We need to have strict and effective laws against acid attack. In Bangladesh, reported attacks have fallen since the government tightened up the rules on the sale of acid and introduced the death penalty for attackers. Even where laws are tightened, convictions can be hard in male-dominated societies. In an incident in Pakistan, a woman died after an acid attack and left a mobile phone video message denouncing her attackers. But the suspects - her husband, mother-in law and father-in law - were acquitted. So it is the society also to be blamed.

The prevalence of attacks in South Asia can be explained by the easy availability of acid. Acid is widely used in the cotton, rubber and jewellery industries. Hence attacks are also seen in rubber-producing areas like Cambodia. Acid attacks appear to be disproportionately common in South Asia.

It is not about religion or culture; it takes place in parts of the world where women are not empowered. It's an extreme form of violence against women. It is a crime with a marked gender skew. Experts say that women and girls are victims in 75-80% of cases. Of the female victims, about 30% are under 18.

The case of Shivi Khanna (name changed), a 23-year-old woman from New Delhi with dreams of becoming an Indian navy nurse, alights from a train in the bustling Bandra station in India's financial hub of Mumbai on May 2. She wâs to join the Colaba Naval Hospital as a staff nurse and fulfill her lifetime dream to eke out a secure life for herself. But as soon as the young woman got off the train, a man appeared from nowhere, tapped her back and as she turned round, threw acid into her face. The attacker then melted away into the crowd. Her eyes were damaged, her liver and kidneys were affected and she suffered excruciating pain for a month before breathing her last on June 2, 2013 in Mumbai.

This case brings to light the ignorant attitude of our society also where no one runs to save Shivi Khanna from this attack in a crowded railway station hence our society also need to be active and supportive in checking such crimes against women.

Acid attack, Women and Some Unanswered Questions

1. **Elusive Justice**: it still seems justice is a long way for these victims of acid attacks. It has indeed been a long road to justice for these acid attack victims.
2. **Tougher Punishments**: The Justice Verma Committee submitted its "path-breaking" recommendations on January 23, 2013 to the Home Ministry, calling for tougher punishments, including life imprisonment for sex crimes against women, but stopped short of the death penalty. According to activists, the easy availability of acid in the retail market also needs to be addressed.

3. **Reforms in Society:** It is important that the society also look up to the acid attack victims in a positive manner and give them full support to live a normal life. It is important that these women find love and compassion and support rather than pity from society. The story of Laxmi an acid attack victim finding love in Alok an activist is one such example.

4. **Rehabilitation:** The one most important aspect of such acid attack victim is their rehabilitation and proper medical and economic support .The amount of three lakhs of rupee directed for compensation seem a drop in the ocean of these victims necessity hence this issue should be taken care of and directives for medical facility and care should be given by government .The question of rehabilitation and government concern in this matter should be a serious issue of debate in policy making.

It is high time that all channels working for the rehabilitation and support of acid attack victims should check sensitize and bring awareness in the society against this crime .As acid attack is an attack on the beauty and integrity of a woman and the society and the system need to answer several such questions.

References

National Crime Records Bureau. 'Report on Crime Against Women in India, 2013', *National Crime Records Bureau,* Government of India.

http://www.acidviolence.org/index.php- Acid Survivors Trust International London Pictures of acid attack victim taken from– www.stopacidattacks.org

Zehra Syed Mubin. (2013), 'Column on Acid Attack', *Jansatta,* 21st July, 2013.

17

DECLINING CHILD SEX RATIO IN INDIA

UPASANA BEHAR

Declining sex ratio has emerged as a serious problem in India. The decline is continuing unabated. According to the Census 2001, the sharpest decline in the sex ratio was in the age group of 0 to 6 years. This is a matter of deep concern both for our society as well as the government.

A study of the Census reports from 1961 to 2011 reveals that the child sex ratio in 0-6 age group has been consistently falling since 1961. Over the last 50 years, the child sex ratio has fallen by 63 points. In 2001, the number of girls per one thousand boys in the 0-6 age group was 927. In 2011, it fell to 914 (a decline of 1.40 per cent). Notably, this is the lowest sex ratio ever in the country.

Child Sex Ratio in India[1]

Year	*1951*	*1961*	*1971*	*1981*	*1991*	*2001*	*2011*
CSR	983	976	964	962	945	927	914

According to a report of the Central Statistical Organization[2] of the Government of India, between 1991 and 2011, the number of girls in 0-6 age group has fallen by 3 million. According to the Census 2011, as far as child sex ratio is concerned, it is lower in northern and western states and higher in southern and eastern ones. In our country, every state has its distinct socio-economic-cultural identity. It is because of the social, cultural and economic differences that the child sex ratio also differs from state to state.

The states with the lowest child sex ratios are Haryana (830), Punjab (846) and Jammu & Kashmir (859) while those with the highest sex ratios are Mizoram (971), Meghalaya (970) and Andaman Nicobar (966). The lowest child sex ratio in the country is of Jhajjhar in Haryana (774). Kashmir recorded the highest decline -8.71% in the period 2001-2011. In Dadra, Nagar Haveli and Lakshadweep the decline was -5.62% and -5.32% respectively[3]. They are at the second and third positions in terms of quantum of decline in the 2001-11 period. Thus we can see that low child sex ratio has nothing to do with the richness or poverty of the State. The sex ratio in Punjab and Haryana is less than 900 whereas both these states are considered to be prosperous.

Child Sex Ratio in Madhya Pradesh

As far as the child sex ratio in Madhya Pradesh is concerned, according to the figures of Census 2011, released by the Directorate of Census, there has been a drop of 14 points in the child sex ratio between 2001 and 2011. The number of girls in 0-6 age group per 1000 boys stood at 918 (According to the preliminary report of Census 2011, this figure was 912, which was even less than the national average). Ten years back, the figure was 932. This is the lowest sex ratio since 1961. The situation in Rewa district has worsened at the fastest pace in the last ten years. The child sex ratio in Rewa was 926 in 2001, which fell to 883 in 2011[4].

Over the last three decades, child sex ratio has declined in all divisions of the state. In Gwalior and Chambal divisions, it is less than 900. This area of the state is known for female foeticide and infanticide. The area is backward on all developmental indicators. It is still in the grips of feudal mindset and hidebound traditions. Women and girls are not respected and are treated as second grade citizens. Being the father of a girl is considered a matter of shame while being the father of a boy is considered a matter of pride.

Reasons for Decline in Child Sex Ratio

It is important to study and understand the reasons for the consistent fall in the child sex ratio in the country. There are no natural causes behind the declining child sex ratio. It is a man-made phenomenon. This problem exists in all regions, castes, classes and communities of the country. The attitude of Indian society towards girls, its patriarchal mindset, cultural norms, prejudices, socio-economic pressures, insecurity and misuse of modern technology, among other things, are responsible for the falling child sex ratio.

Social Factors

Indian society is patriarchal and male-dominated with a keen desire to have a son. Shackled by narrow thinking, superstitions, orthodox traditions and practices and moribund social set-up, the people differentiate between sons and daughters. The birth of a girl in a family brings grief and disappointment. Even today, society gives more importance to boys than girls – whether it is a rich family or a poor one, whether educated or uneducated. It is because of this love for the boys that every year, lakhs of girls are killed before their birth. And this practice is growing instead of abating.

Generally, there is no problem if the first child of a family is a boy and the second turns out to be a girl. But if the first child is a girl, then there is an intense desire to have a son. The chart below makes it clear that if the first child is a girl, then the second is less likely to be a girl than if the first child is a boy.

Sex Ratio for Second Births[5]

S.N	*If 1st birth was female*	*Total*	*If 1st birth was male*	*Total*
1	All India	759	All India	1103
2	Punjab	614	Punjab	1003
3	Haryana	667	Haryana	968
4	Rajasthan	674	Rajasthan	1192

In our society, boys are considered the future head of the family and its bread winner. It is believed that only the boys continue the family tradition. They look after the parents when they grow old. The parents can live in the son's house in the evening of their life but not in the house of their daughter. The Indian society believes that girls belong to someone else. The family into which she marries will be her real family and her duties will be towards her in-laws and not towards her parents, who gave birth to her.

In India, especially among the Hindus, there is a belief that the soul attains salvation only if the last rites are performed by the son. Thus, boys are needed not only for earthly life but also for the afterlife.

Dowry is also one of the reasons why girls are abhorred. In most families, parents start worrying about the dowry right from the day the girl is born. Most parents have to take loans to give dowry and they continue to reel under the burden of the debt all their lives. According to the National Crime Records Bureau (2012), in the year 2002, 6822 cases of dowry deaths were registered in the country. By 2011, the figure had grown to 8618. In 2012, it fell marginally to 8233. In Madhya Pradesh, 743 cases of dowry death were registered in 2012[6] .These figures show that dowry continues to be a major problem in our country. Steps take to combat the problem are proving to be insufficient. Anti-dowry laws notwithstanding, the incidents of killing women for dowry are growing. The problem of dowry is rooted in our society. And the society will have to come forward to eliminate it.

The preference for a male child has an economic angle too. It is believed that a boy will earn after he grows up and thus will economically strengthen the family and extend monetary support to his parents and family. On the other hand, the girls will go to their in-law's place. In our society, the number of working women is still comparatively low.

Yet another reason is that in Indian society, daughter is perceived as the 'honour' of the family. Many families feel that of late, the country has become insecure for girls and in the present scenario, providing security to girls has become a challenge. Incidents like the Nirbhaya rape case of Delhi have only strengthened this view although they have also led to women becoming more vocal in protesting against their sexual harassment and / or molestation. According to 2012 report of the National Crime Records Bureau (NCRB), the number of rape incidents in the country went up from 22,172 in 2011 to 24,206 in 2011 to 24,923 in 2013. These figures show that rape cases are on the rise in the country. They also indicate that daughters are not safe in our society. This is also one factor responsible for the declining child sex ratio.

Sex Selective Abortion

One of the main reasons for the declining child sex ratio is sex selective abortion. Techniques like Ultra Sound, Amniocentesis etc were invented to detect abnormalities in the foetus during pregnancy. But slowly, they came to be used for determining the sex of the foetus and for aborting it, if it turns out to be a female.

Due to the patriarchal mindset of the society, the new technologies are being misused and this has become a serious problem in our country. According to Dr. Anita Raj, Professor in the Global Public Health, Department of Medicine at the University of California at Sandiego[7]while the overall rate of abortion in India was lower than in other countries, the rate of sex selective abortion was going up.

Before the advent of these modern techniques, the new-born girls were killed by strangling, by giving them poison or by burying them in the ground. Salt, Opium, Jaggery and Papaya seeds were used to kill the baby girls. This was very common in society. Even the couples who do not have access to the modern techniques or who do not abort female foetus due to fear of the law have an ardent desire that somehow they should have a son and not daughter.

Sex Selective Abortion in India: Historical Background

A peep into history reveals that in 1789, the Resident of Banaras State had tried to put a stop to the practice of female foeticide in the Rajikumar tribe. Acts banning female foeticide were promulgated in 1795 and 1804 but they were not effective[8].

British officials took note of the wide prevalence of female foeticide in India in the late 18th century. In 1870, the British government promulgated the 'Infanticide Act'[9]. In 1871, the first Census was conducted in the country and it proved the existence of the practice. Female foeticide was more prevalent in North India. The law, however, proved ineffective as most of the deliveries were done by midwives in homes. The British government then created 'Government dowry fund' and provided for fine and imprisonment for female infanticide[10].

With the advances in medical science came new techniques to determine the health of pregnant mothers and foetuses. These included Pre-natal Sex Determination Methods which were meant to assess whether the fetus was developing normally in the womb and to diagnose and treat any problems inhibiting its growth. But this technique started being used for Sex Selective abortions.

Various slogans were coined to promote population control including "Bacche Do Hee Acche" and 'Hum, Do Hamare Do". The 79th Constitutional amendment provided that those with more than two children will be disqualified from contesting elections. These measures also indirectly led to the lowering of the child sex ratio by promoting Sex Selective abortion. The provision was, however, done away with later.

Initially, Sex selective abortion was an urban phenomenon but slowly it spread its tentacles in the villages too. According to the figures released by the Directorate of Census, in 2001, the sex ratio in 0-6 age group was 923 in villages and 905 in cities. In 2001, the figures were 934 and 906 respectively.

Sex selective abortion in Madhya Pradesh- According to a report of the Public Health and Family welfare department of the state government, there has been a rise in the number of abortions in the State. Over the last 8 years, more than 2.5 lakh children could not come into this world for different reasons. Last year, there were 55,000 cases of abortion all over the state. Bhopal topped the list with 15,634 abortions. In the year 2005-06, the number of abortions in the state was 21,220 which grew to 55,333 by 2012-13.

It is often asked as to how a mother consents to the killing of her own unborn child. The answer is that patriarchal values permeate the entire society and affects the thinking of men and women both.

At the same time, women do not have right over their own bodies. Women who fail to give birth to boys have to face inhuman behavior ranging from taunts to beatings to burning alive to being thrown out from home by the families blinded by their love for the male child. We need to understand that the women are also born and brought up in the society where patriarchal values dominate, where sons are welcome and daughters are despised. Because of this, women start feeling guilty if they give birth to girls and they too start preferring boys to girls.

Female Child Mortality

One reason for the declining population of girls in the country is their higher mortality rate. And this has nothing to do with biological reasons. Biologically, girls are stronger and more likely to survive than boys. The reasons for this are social. The female mortality rate is going up because, after their birth, the girls are discriminated against in almost everything. They are not looked after well and are deprived of the nutrition and other facilities needed to lead a healthy life. That is why, as compared to boys, the girls suffer more from malnutrition and Anemia. According to SRS report 2012[11], the infant mortality rate in the country is 42, which were 44 in 2011. The lowest infant mortality rate is in Kerala (12) while it is highest in Madhya Pradesh (56). Even if slowly, the infant mortality rate in the country is coming down. But even now of every 24 children born, one dies before its first birthday. The figure is 1 of 22 in villages and 1 of 36 in cities.

Female Child Mortality in MP- According to SRS bulletin 2013[12], the infant mortality rate in the state is 56, which is the highest in the country. The figure is 54 for boys and 59 for girls i.e. the infant mortality is higher for girls than for boys.

In 1990, the child mortality rate in the State was 147.60, which was to be brought down to 49.60 under Millennium development goal. However, on the basis of the progress achieved till now, the Government of India estimates it will come down to only 76.37 by 2015. Similarly, the Infant mortality rate was 111 which were to be brought down to 37. However, estimates suggest that by 2015, the rate is likely to be 58.7[13].

Crimes Against Women

One reason why society does not prefer girls is the growth in crimes against them. This factor plays a key role in pulling down the child mortality rate. The crimes against women and girls are rising every year in the country. According to NCRB report, in 2012, the number of crimes against children was 38,172. The cases of kidnapping and abduction of girls and women were 29,796 in 2010 and 35,565 in 2011. In 2012, 38,262 cases were registered of which 16,373 pertained to minor girls. Security of children has become a major concern. No place is safe for girls and women. Cases of domestic violence, sexual violence, abduction, rape, teasing, trafficking, murder of women and honour killing are increasing in the country and this is one reason for the fall in child sex ratio.

Crimes against women in MP- The highest number of cases of female foeticide are registered in MP. According to the information furnished by the Union Health and family welfare in the Lok Sabha, MP is at the top in terms of female foeticide. In the last four years,

127 cases of female foeticide were registered in MP. The number of such cases was 39 in 2009, 18 in 2010, 28 in 2011 and 32 in 2012.

According to written information tabled by the then Home Minister in the Vidhan Sabha on March 6, 2013, 'In Madhya Pradesh, 29,828 minor girls went missing in the period from January 2008 to March 2013, of which 4,990 girls are still untraced'.

According to NCRB (2012), MP is first in the country in terms of foeticide (30%) and infanticide (20%). According to the report, MP is also first in terms of molestation of children and second in terms of crimes against children (13.5%).

According to the figures compiled by the police department, 43,920 children went missing from the state between 2006 and 2011. These included 23,969 girls and 19,969 boys. Of them, around 3,500 boys and 5,880 girls are still untraced.

Thus it is clear that security of girls has emerged as a major challenge for our society. Neither government nor society has been able to give a secure environment to girls. This is affecting child sex ratio.

Efforts made by Government to Improve Child Sex Ratio

The government has adopted a two-pronged approach to achieve this objective. On one hand, various schemes and programmes have been launched and on the other, laws are being made to deal with the problem.

(A) Through Schemes: In 2009, the government announced that January 24 will be observed as 'National girl child day'. Besides popularizing slogans like 'Love girl child', "Save daughters", "Stop killing girls" etc. At least 15 cash transfer schemes for girls like Dhanlaxmi, Ladli, Beti Hai Anmol, Kanyadaan etc have been launched[14].

SAARC had declared 1991-2000 as Decade of the Girl Child. As part of the SAARC endeavour, in 1992, India drew up a national plan of action focussing on survival, protection and development of the girl child. The scheme aimed at making equal opportunities available to girl child and at securing their freedom from hunger, illiteracy, exploitation and neglect. In 1992, the Central government constituted the National Women's Commission.

The Central government launched 'Balika Samridhi Yojana' in 1997. The key aim of the scheme was to bring about a change in the attitude of the family and society towards mother and girl child.

Efforts at Government level in Madhya Pradesh- For effective and systematic implementation of schemes and programmes for development and welfare of women and boys-girls, Women and Child Development Department was constituted in the State in 1988. The MP State Women's Commission was constituted on March 23, 1998.

The state's first women's policy was implemented in 1997, the second in 2003 and the third in 2008. In the 2008 policy, special provisions were made for the development of teenaged girls. These include ensuring availability of quality education, health and nutrition facilities for teenaged girls, combating their sexual and physical exploitation and developing life skills in them.

The state government has also launched schemes like Beti Bachao Abhiyan, Ladli Laxmi, Mukhyamantri Kanyadaan, Free Bicycle, Sabla, Gaon Kee Beti, Pratiba Kiran and Kanya Saksharta Protsahan. The state government has also brought forth a scheme for giving pension to couples having only daughters with a view to promoting birth of girl child.

(B) Through Laws: Section 312 and 313 of the IPC provide for fine and imprisonment up to three years or both in case of the foetus being destroyed with or without the consent of the mother, unless it is done for saving the life of the woman[15]. Section 315 provides for punishment for a person who knowingly does anything that leads to the death of the foetus before its birth[16].

In the 1980s, women's organizations all over the country launched a vigorous agitation as a result of which the then government promulgated the Pre-Natal Diagnostic Techniques (Prohibition of Sex Selection) Act 1994 (PCPNDT Act) which came into force on January 1, 1996. The law was amended in 2008 to make it more stringent. It made determining the sex of unborn child a criminal offence. The law provided for imprisonment and fine for the offenders. This law proscribed the doctors from revealing the sex of the foetus.

How serious the government is about implementing the new law is evident by the fact that the Central Supervisory board, meant to oversee the implementation of the PCPNDT Act, did not meet for three years. The board was reconstituted in March-April 2011 by the Union Health and family welfare Ministry[17].

The Supreme Court has called for proper implementation of the new law from time to time. The

Supreme Court in 'Centre for enquiry into health versus Government of India, 2001' opined that the Central and state governments were not implementing the provisions of the PNDT Act. It also called for launching publicity campaign against pre-natal sex determination and female foeticide through Press, Electronic Media and other means, review and reconsideration of the provisions and sending quarterly reports to the Board. In 2002, the SC again instructed the States to seize and seal all unlicensed Ultra sound machines being used for sex determination[18].

The Supreme Court has taken a strong view of police not taking proper action against those responsible for female foeticide. The Apex court said that it will monitor the issue itself. The court said that the sex ratio had drastically declined in the 2011 Census and hence the actions taken under PNDT Act will be reviewed every three months. Orders for monitoring the actions will be issued soon[19].

In November 2011, the Union women and child development ministry established 'Sectoral innovation council for child sex ratio'[20] .It remains to be seen what role the council plays in the future to push the sex ratio in the positive direction. Some provisions have been made in other laws like Dowry Prohibition Act, 1961 (Amended in 1986), Immoral traffic Prevention Act 1986 and Child protection Act 2012 regarding this.

Despite so many laws and schemes, the child sex ratio has gone from bad to worse and the situation has turned alarming. Many schemes are in operation in MP but it is first in the country in female foeticide and infanticide (20%). Why is the child sex ratio declining despite the governments doing so much to arrest its fall?

Are the governments not making efforts in the right direction? Are the governments not striking at the root causes of the problem? The governments need to seriously think and reflect on these issues.

If the persistent fall in child sex ratio is to be reversed, laws will have to be implemented strictly. But what is even more necessary is to bring about a change in the thinking of the society. The society should change in its mindset. The society will have to come forward to end the discrimination between the boys and the girls. We have to stop considering girls as inferior to boys. Both should be given equal opportunities in the fields of education, health and employment. Anti-dowry laws will have to be implemented strictly and sons and daughters should be given equal rights in property.

Recommendations

The Central and state governments have taken a series of steps to increase sex ratio through both schemes as well as laws. But instead of improving, the situation has only worsened. Hence, there is need for the governments to review their old laws and schemes.

Only laws and schemes cannot solve the problem of declining child sex ratio. The root causes of the problem are social viz patriarchal mindset of society, desire for sons, socio-economic conditions, sex-selective abortions, neglect of girl child, dowry etc. The society and the government need to strike at these social evils. In this context, some recommendations are as under:

- A comprehensive policy addressing all factors responsible for falling child sex ratio should be drafted.

- Governments should implement the laws strictly.
- Figures regarding every pregnant woman and every case of abortion should be provided by the hospitals to the governments. An online software should be prepared in which the family members can themselves feed figures and they should then be uploaded to the website of the health department. The health officer of the area should follow up each case for at least a year.
- The registration of the clinics of doctors caught performing sex determination tests or doing sex selective abortions should be permanently cancelled and they should be severely punished.
- Anti-dowry laws should be implemented strictly and social campaign should be launched against the evil of dowry. Those who marry without dowry should be felicitated and they should get preference in government schemes, bank loans etc.
- Government should encourage families with two daughters and it should bear the expenses on their education etc.
- PCPNDT Act should be widely publicized and the government should take help of NGOs in this work.
- Ads, slogans etc that promote patriarchal values or the language of which smacks of patriarchy should be immediately banned and a committee

should be formed to vet the ads before they are allowed to be aired / published.

- Before formulating any new scheme or programmes the government should keep our country's diversity in mind. Our country is divided into many religions, castes, communities and regions and people speaking many different languages live here.
- Most of the government schemes are meant for poor families. The government seems to link the problem of sex selective abortion with poverty. But that is not correct. Had it been so, the problem would not have existed in Punjab, which is one of the most prosperous states of the country. But the problem is most serious there. So the government should make schemes also keeping in mind rich and educated families.
- Gender equality should form part of the syllabi of schools, colleges and of government and private training programmes. Seminars and lectures should be held from time to time on this topic.

Notes

1. Ramaiah Janaki G., Chandrasekarayya T. and Murthy Vinayaga P.2011. "Declining Child Sex Ratio in India: Trends, Issues and Concerns", *Asia Pacific Journal of Social Sciences*, Vol 3, Jan – June 2011.
2. India's Lost Girls by Eric Bates from *www.article-3.com.*
3. *http://updateox.com/india/child-sex-ratio-in-india-state-wise-data.*

4. Census India, Provisional Population Totals, Gender Composition.

5. Ramaiah Janaki G., Chandrasekarayya T. and Murthy Vinayaga P.2011. "Declining Child Sex Ratio in India: Trends, Issues and Concerns", *Asia Pacific Journal of Social Sciences,* Vol 3, Jan – June 2011.

6. National Crime Records Bureau (NCRB) 2012.

7. Article on "Selective Abortion Female Foetuses India Creating Gender Imbalance Crisis" by Palash Ghosh September 19 2012, from *www.ibtimes.com*

8. Gupta Shrinivas.2004."Kanya Bhrun Ki Hatya: Karak Aur Kanun", *Stri Mukkti Ka Sapna-Vasudha,*Vol. 59-60.

9. Patel Rita, "The Practice of Sex Selective Abortion in India: May You Be the Mother of a Hundred Sons", Department of Maternal and Child Health, School of Public Health-source-/uploads/cgi.unc.edumedia_items/the-practice-of-sex-selective-abortion-in-india-may-you-be-the-mother-of-a-hundred-sons.original.pdf

10. *ibid.*

11. Sample Registration System Statistical Report 2012.

12. Sample Registration System Statistical Bulletin 2013.

13. *Bharat Sarkar ki Sahastrabadi Vikas Lakshya ki Stithi Report , 2011,* Bhojan ke Adhikar Abhiyan Dwara Bhopal Mein Bacchon ke Bhojan ke Adhikar Parr Doosra Rashtriya Adhiveshan 2012 ke Avsar Parr Jaari Report " Hum Kyon Sharmasar hain".

14. Naqvia farah and Kumar Shiva k., "Indian & the Sex Selection Conundrum" from *www.the hindu.com.*

15. Gupta Shrinivas. 2004."Kanya Bhrun Ki Hatya: Karak Aur Kanun", *Stri Mukkti Ka Sapna-Vasudha,*Vol. 59-60.

16. Gupta Shrinivas. 2004."Kanya Bhrun Ki Hatya: Karak Aur Kanun", *Stri Mukkti Ka Sapna-Vasudha,*Vol. 59-60.

17. Naqvia farah and Kumar Shiva k., "Indian & the Sex Selection Conundrum" from *www.the hindu.com.*
18. Gupta Shrinivas.2004."Kanya Bhrun Ki Hatya: Karak Aur Kanun", *Stri Mukkti Ka Sapna-Vasudha*,Vol. 59-60.
19. *http://adaalat.in*
20. Naqvia farah and Kumar Shiva k., "Indian & the Sex Selection Conundrum" from *www.the hindu.com.*

References

Arya Sadhna, Menon Nivedita and Loknita Jini(ed). (2001), *Narivadi Rajniti: Sangharsh Avum Mudde,* Hindi Madhyam Karyanvay Nideshalay, Delhi University.

Gupta Shrinivas. (2004), "Kanya Bhrun Ki Hatya: Karak Aur Kanun", *Stri Mukkti Ka Sapna-Vasudha*,Vol. 59-60.

Karant Vrinda (2008), *Bhartiya Nari: Sangharsh avum Mukti,* Granth Shilpi, New Delhi.

Kumar Sanjay and Sathyanarayana K.M. (2012), "District Level Estimates of Fertility and Implied Sex Ratio at Birth in India", *Economic & Political Weekly,* August 18, 2012.

Maitreyi Puspa (2005), *Khuli Khirkiyaan, Samayik Prakashan, New Delhi.*

National Crime Records Bureau (2012), "Crime in India 2012 Statistics" , *National Crime Records Bureau*,Ministry of Home Affairs, GOI.

Patel Rita, "The Practice of Sex Selective Abortion in India: May You Be the Mother of a Hundred Sons", Department of Maternal and Child Health, School of Public Health-source-/uploads/cgi.unc.edumedia_items/the-practice-of-sex-selective-abortion-in-india-may-you-be-the-mother-of-a-hundred-sons.original.pdf

Ramaiah Janaki G., Chandrasekarayya T. and Murthy Vinayaga P. (2011), "Declining Child Sex Ratio in India: Trends, Issues and Concerns", *Asia Pacific Journal of Social Sciences,* Vol 3, Jan – June 2011.

Society for Resource Integration and Development Action .Study Report on "Comparative Study Analyzing the Issue of female Foeticide in two Districts of Madhya Pradesh having Highest and Lowest Girl Child Sex Ratio with Reference to PCPNDT Act 1994 & with 2002 Amendment", *Society for Resource Integration and Development Action,* Madhya Pradesh.

State Planning Commission Madhya Pradesh. "Status of Children in Madhya Pradesh", *State Planning Commission Madhya Pradesh.*

Tandan Lata Sneh and Sharma Renu (2006), "Female Foeticide and Infanticide in India: An Analysis of Crime against Girl Children", *International Journal of Criminal Justice Sciences,* Vol 1 Issue 1 January 2006.

www.infochangindia.org-Wadia Havovi, " The Sex Selection killing Fields"

www.the hindu.com-Naqvia farah and Kumar Shiva k., "Indian & the Sex Selection Conundrum",

www.article-3.com- Bates Eric, "India's Lost Girls", *http://adaalat.in*

www.ibtimes.com-Article on "Selective Abortion Female Foetuses India Creating Gender Imbalance Crisis" by Palash Ghosh September 19 2012.

www.independent.co.uk-Sen Amartya, "The lost girls: Girls are still aborted in states with more educated women",

www.censusindia.gov.in. -"Gender Composition".

18

"SECUREPIC: SECURING PICTURES ON SOCIAL NETWORKING SITES"

VASIMA KHAN

Introduction

In the recent years, we have witnessed a dramatic rise in popularity of online social networking services, with several Social Network Sites (SNSs) such as Face book, Twitter, You Tube etc are now among the most visited websites globally. However, since such forums are relatively easy to access and the users are often not aware of the size and the nature of the audience accessing their profiles, they often reveal more information which is not appropriate to a public forum. As a result, such commercial and social site may often generate a number of privacy and security related threats for the members especially for women. The Internet is idealized as an equal-opportunity online community, but research shows that vulnerable groups such as women feel that security and privacy in use of internet is the most important area of concern which includes freedom of expression, privacy of communication and secure online spaces. It is important to mention that there have been a number of cases when women's online pictures have been misused and these cases have also led to humiliation and sometimes to a great extent such as suicide. One solution to this problem is that either women should ignore such threats or stop posting their pictures on such kind of sites. But this is not the ultimate solution as it affects a woman's freedom to live online. As a result we can say that there is tremendous need of a solution that preserve the privacy of one's profile on the social networking site, especially for women. In this paper, a software solution has been proposed that will prevent downloading or copying of pictures from one's profile.

Social Networking Sites (SNSs) are virtual communities where users can create individual public profiles, interact with real-life friends, and meet other people based on shared interests. They are seen as a 'global consumer phenomenon' with an exponential rise in usage within the last few years. There are a number of social networking sites which are being used these days. A few of these trendiest social networking sites people are using both on the web and on mobile right now are as follows-

Facebook

Not surprisingly, Facebook is the top social network on the web. It's a thriving beast of a social networking site on the web with its massive user base, but theories suggest that it's struggling to maintain the interest of younger users and may be losing them to newer apps and social networks. Despite these troubles, Facebook still remains number one... at least for now.

Twitter

Like Facebook, Twitter has also changed for the better over the years of its existence and continues to expand in popularity. Centered around micro blogging and a 140-character text limit, Twitter has become a popular social network of choice for mobile web users who own smart phones and tablet computers.

YouTube

Good old YouTube. Nothing quite compares to YouTube when it comes to video sharing. Although owned by Google, YouTube is still recognized as a separate social network all its own, and one that revolves entirely around video production, blogging, movie-making and music sharing.

Google+

As it made its debut in the early summer of 2011, Google+ was the fastest growing social network, the web has ever seen. It seems as if Google has finally created something that people are actually excited to use – unlike previously failed attempts at jumping on the social media bandwagon with projects like Google Wave and Google Buzz.

LinkedIn

Known as the social network where professionals can connect, LinkedIn is right behind Facebook and Twitter. Individuals can promote themselves and their businesses, make connections with other professionals, interact in group discussions, post job ads or apply for jobs.

Social media has changed the way people interact. In many ways, social media has led to positive changes in the way people communicate and share information; however, it has a dark side, as well. Social networking can sometimes result in negative outcomes, some with long-term consequences. Since such forums are relatively easy to access and the users are often not aware of the size and the nature of the audience accessing their profiles, they often reveal more information which is not appropriate to a public forum. As a result, such commercial and social site may often generate a number of privacy and security related threats for the members especially for women. The Internet is idealized as an equal-opportunity online community, but research shows that vulnerable groups such as women feel that security and privacy in use of internet is the most important area of concern which includes freedom of expression, privacy of communication and secure online spaces. It is important to mention that there have been a number of cases when women's online pictures have been misused and these cases have also led to humiliation and sometimes to a great extent such as suicide. One solution to this problem is that either women should ignore such threats or stop posting their pictures on such kind of sites. But this is not the ultimate solution as it affects a woman's freedom to live online. As a result we can say that there is tremendous need of a solution that preserve the privacy of one's profile on the social networking site, especially for women. In this paper, we propose a software solution that will prevent downloading or copying of pictures from one's profile.

Threats of SNS

Social networking privacy issues have dominated the headlines in the first half of 2011. With most social networks, the default settings share everything and users have to reset their options to make their accounts more private. This opens up a host of security issues because so many people—both friends and not—have access to your information. And to see just how many security issues social networks pose, we recently conducted a social media poll that asks whether respondents have seen spam, phishing or malware incidents. Of the nearly 2,000 people polled, 71% reported that they, or one of their colleagues, had been spammed on a social networking site, 46% had been phished and 45% were sent malware. The remaining respondents were divided—some were not victims, others were unsure.

Cybercriminals can steal information about you from your social networking profile and posts and then tailor their attacks based on your interests and likes. This is known as "social engineering" and it makes security threats much more difficult to recognize. Here's a closer look at some of the recent attacks and privacy issues plaguing three major social networking sites—Facebook, Twitter and LinkedIn, and a sneak peek at Google Plus.

Girls are uploading their pictures on social networking websites like Facebook, Twitter, etc, to be accessed by everyone. What is happening is that many people are taking those pictures and misusing them by creating fake profiles to defame the girls. On some, inappropriate messages about the girl are written. On others, the picture is altered with a nude body of someone else added to the face of the girl. Many webmasters of adult websites use girls' pictures from social networking websites to promote their business, with things like, "these girls are available." In reality, those girls don't even know that their picture is on a website of such a nature. Pimps are also hovering on social networking websites, trying to find pictures of good looking girls for their business. Many prostitutes also use those pictures for personal gain. Many girl's cell phone numbers are put on websites after being taken without their consent. Some websites have pictures along with the cell numbers. In reality, those pictures do not belong to the person whose cell phone number has been posted. The pictures have been taken from social networking websites.

Below are some real life stories of girls who went through a lot of misery because of photo tampering and fake profiles.

The father of a South Delhi school girl suffered from the fake profile of his daughter posted on some SNS that not only described the teenager as a 'sex teacher', but also contained obscene photographs and her contact details. The teenager's family had received the first call where the caller wanted to speak to the girl. Similar calls poured in later, the police said, adding all the callers referred to some SNS. Father of the girl lodged a complaint with the Cyber Cell of the Delhi Police's Economic Offences after his family started receiving calls following the appearance of the fake profile.

An air-hostess had moved a court alleging that someone has opened an account in her name on some SNS wherein she is being described as a "sex struck woman". The family had a harrowing time when two strangers knocked at their door a fortnight ago and told them the girl had invited them for sex, they added. Police said a case has been registered and investigations were on. The air-hostess claimed that act has lowered her reputation in the eyes of her family members and neighbors. She also said that she has written to the National Commission of the Women against her criminal defamation, but no actions have been taken so far.

It was one of those normal evenings when *****, a software engineer in Chennai, logged on to some SNS to unwind from work and catch up with friends. But one and a half minutes later, the evening turned shocking and miserable for her. What she saw was a cheeky scrap and forward to a profile that had her semi-nude photo in another girl's profile, tagged as her sister who flagged joint hints of intimate advances and indecent invites. Her photo had been brazenly and easily tampered with. After many weeks of tension and repeated requests to some SNS, the ID was removed. She vowed never to be vulnerable again.

Miss. Shetty found this same thing the hard way. Like millions of other girls of her age, she also innocently uploaded her picture on a popular networking site. Some boys started harassing her by posting photo-shopped nude pictures of her. Traumatized, she went into depression and became suicidal.

Related Work

In recent years, due to the increasing number of privacy and security threats on online social networks users, social network operators, security companies, and academic researchers have proposed various solutions to increase the security and privacy of social network users. Social network operators attempt to better protect their users by adding authentication processes to ensure that the registered user represents a real live person[1]. Many social network operators, like Facebook, also offer their users a configurable user privacy setting that enables users to secure their personal data from other users in the network[2].Additional protection may include defense against hackers, spammers, social bots, identity cloning, phishing, and many other threats. For example, Facebook users have an option to report other users in the network who harass others in the network[3]. Many commercial and open source products, such as Checkpoint's Social Guard[4], Websense's Defensio[5], United-Parents[6], RecalimPrivacy[7], and PrivAware application[8], offer online social network users tools for better protecting themselves. For example, the Websense's Defensio software aims to protect its users from spammers, adults content, and malicious scripts on Facebook. In recent years, several published academic studies have proposed solutions for different social network threats. De-Barr and Wechsler used the graph centrality measure to identify spammers. Wang[8] presented techniques to classify spammers on Twitter based on content and graph features. Stringhini et al [6]presented a solution for detecting spammers in social networks by using "honey-proûles". Egele et al.[4] presented PoX, an extension for Facebook which make all requests for private data explicit to the user. Sobh and Mostafa[9] presented the Reûective Policy Assessment tool which helps the user examine their proûle from the viewpoint of another user in the network. Recently, Hilmi[10] proposed a method for detecting fake proûles in online social network based on anomalies[11] in the fake users social structure.

Proposed System

Our proposed solution is to provide a software which provides security to the pictures posted on one's profile on social networking site. This is done by giving an option to each one's profile to secure the pictures on that profile. If the option is enabled by the user, then our software will allow others to see the pictures on that profile but they cannot access those pictures or copy them, or manipulate them. This is done by using an MMO based approach which uses an anomaly detection mechanisms which create a profile of typical behavior for every external user who access the profile and raise an alert when a user attempts an activity that does not fit his/her behavior. This approach tends to be highly complete in that it can detect a previously unknown attack pattern, but it requires significant effort to develop algorithms that can create accurate user profiles. The novel thing about the proposed technique is the idea of MMO (Means, Motive and Opportunity) which speedup the detection rate and enhanced the capability of catching unknown attacks by applying anomaly on them.

Conclusion

Social networking sites can be valuable sales and marketing tools, as well as fun diversions. Inherent in these applications are security risks that can put the individual or a company in a compromising position or at serious risk. Aside from not using these sites at all, end-user education, alongside documented policies and procedures, is the most fundamental protection that exists. In this paper, we presented the "SECUREPIC" software which aims to better protect users privacy in SNS. The software protects users privacy by using an MMO based approach which protects pictures posted on social networking sites which in turn provides security for women.

Notes & References

1. Cristian I. Pinzón, Juan F. De Paz, Martí Navarroc, Javier Bajo, Vicente Julián and Juan. M. Corchado.2011. "Real-time CBR-agent with a Mixture of Experts in the Reuse Stage to Classify and Detect DoS Attacks", *Science Direct Elsevier, Applied Soft Computing* 11 (2011) pp. 4384–4398.
2. Facebook-Newsroom, *http://www.facebook.com.*
3. Y. Boshmaf, I. Muslukhov, K. Beznosov, and M. Ripeanu. 2011. "The Socialbot Network: When bots Socialize for Fame and Money," in *Proceedings of the 27th Annual Computer Security Applications Conference ACM*, pp. 93–102.
4. M. Egele, A. Moser, C. Kruegel, and E. Kirda. 2011. "Pox: Protect-ing users from Malicious Facebook Applications," in *Perva-sive Computing and Communications Workshops*

(PERCOM Workshops), 2011 IEEE International Conference on IEEE, pp. 288–294.

5. Y. Liu, K. Gummadi, B. Krishnamurthy, and A. Mislove. 2011. "Analyzing Facebook Privacy Settings: User Expectations vs. Reality," in *Proceedings of the 2011 ACM SIGCOMM confer-ence on Internet Measurement Conference*, ACM, pp. 61–70.
6. G. Stringhini, C. Kruegel, and G. Vigna 2010. "Detecting Spammerson Social Networks," in *Proceedings of the 26th AnnualComputer Security Applications Conference*, ACM, pp. 1–9.
7. P. Garcý´a-Teodoro, J. Dý´az-Verdejo, G. Macia´-Ferna´ndez and E. Va´zquez. 2009. "Anomaly-based Network Intrusion Detection: Techniques, Systems and Challenges", *Computer and Security, Science Direct*.
8. Cheng-Yuan Ho, Yuan-Cheng Lai, I-Wei Chen, Fu-Yu Wang, and Wei-Hsuan Tai. 2012. "Statistical Analysis of False Positives and False Negatives from Real Traffic with Intrusion Detection/Prevention Systems", *IEEE Communications Magazine*, pp. 146-154.
9. Tarek S. Sobh and Wael M. Mostafa. 2011. "A Cooperative Immunological Approach for Detecting Network Anomaly", *Elsevier Science Direct, Applied Soft Computing* 11 pp. 1275–1283.
10. Hilmi Günes¸Kayacık, A. Nur Zincir-Heywood and Malcolm I. Heywood.2011. "Can a Good Offense be a Good Defense? Vulnerability testing of Anomaly Detectors through an Artificial Arms Race", *Elsevier, Science Direct, Applied Soft Computing* , 11, pp. 4366–4383.
11. S. Venkatesan , M.S. Saleem Basha, C. Chellappan, Anurika Vaish and P. Dhavachelva.2012. "Analysis of Accounting Models to Detect Duplicate Requests in Web Service", *Elsevier Science Direct, Journal of King Saud University – Computer and Information Sciences* (2012).

19

SEXUAL HARASSMENT IN THE WORKPLACE

VINITA BHATNAGAR

Introduction

A Professor of IIT has been suspended for sexually assaulting a research scholar on a trip to Poland in September[1]. This is a fresh addition to the spate of high profile cases involving the sexual harassment of women in the work place.

In November 2013 the Tarun Tejpal sexual assault scandal set the social media aflame. A celebrity recognized by Asia week as one of Asia's fifty most powerful communicators and by The Guardian as among the twenty which constitutes India's top elite or by Business week as one of the fifty most powerful people in India, Tejpal's identity before the scandal erupted was of a moral crusader against corruption.

That image came crashing down as excerpts of an email sent by a young journalist complaining of sexual molestation began to circulate. The incident took place in a lift on two separate occasions. The girl was the daughter of a colleague and also a friend of Tejpal's daughter.She complained to the Managing Director in an email and demanded that a committee be instituted as per the Vishaka Guidelines. This set off a series of events that spiraled out of Tejpal's control.

First, he wrote an unconditional apology where he admitted that he had forced himself upon the young woman despite her lack of consent and accepted that he had violated a long-standing relationship of trust and respect. He called this act a "shameful lapse of judgement" caused by a moment of insanity. He acknowledged the inherent disbalance of power between the editor-in-chief of Tehelka and an employee of the same organization.

Tejpal attributed his act to a lapse of judgment. Not a lack of ethical or moral sense but an act of judgement, which made him attempt a "sexual liaison"[2] .The play of words seeks to obfuscate the fact that it was not a case of an attempted sexual liaison but of sexual harassment.

The victim has since resigned from the job. She rejected the apology and especially the assumption that there had been a "liaison". She demanded the setting up of an inquiry committee. It is typically the women who face sexual harassment who resign and withdraw from the workplace, thus penalizing the victim rather than the culprit.

Nivedita Menon comments:

> *"The gutsy young Tehelka journalist who has blown the cover on the sexual assault she faced from TarunTejpal, and the principled and unambiguous support she has received from fellow staffers in the face of the Editor's attempts to 'manage' the crisis. (We haven't heard the last of that incident yet."[3].The*

fact that an organization that posited itself as a crusader against the ills of society should not have a redressal system for complaints regarding sexual harassment is itself revealing. The law against sexual harassment may have come into being but where is the mechanism to ensure that companies actually comply with the law and set up Complaints Committees and act promptly on the complaints they have received?

Even where complaints committees exist they are often toothless entities and cannot really punish the culprit. The intrepid journalist had been covering cases of sexual harassment and was aware of the norms and the policies that exist to protect women from sexual harassment in the workplace. The fact that even an avowedly progressive organization such as Tehelka had not instituted a mechanism for dealing with issues of this nature is itself a shocking revelation.

What Is Sexual Harassment?

In April 2013 the Sexual Harassment of Women at Workplace (Prevention, Prohibition and Redressal) Bill[4] came into existence. Till now the Indian Penal Code covered acts that might outrage or insult the "modesty" of women but did not recognize conditions that might create a hostile work environment.

Sexual harassment in the workplace became an increasingly important issue around the world in the 1970's as more and more women entered into the work-force. In USA, a report was submitted to the Chancellor and President of MIT by Mary Rowe in 1973 which officially used the term "sexual harassment" for the first time though the word had gained currency in women's groups during that time. Almost at the same time women activists in Cornell were protesting against sexual intimidation and coercion in the workplace. It was the Anita Hill versus Clarence Thomas case in the early nineties that really put the issue centre stage and saw America recognize the pervasiveness of the phenomenon and how deeply entrenched misogynistic and exploitatively "macho" the world of work was.

The European Parliament offers a comprehensive definition of sexual harassment:

> *Where an unwanted conduct related to the sex of a person occurs with the purpose or effect of violating the dignity of a person, and of creating an intimidating, hostile, degrading, humiliating or offensive environment.*
>
> *Where any form of unwanted verbal, non-verbal or physical conduct of a sexual nature occurs with the purpose or effect of violating the dignity of a person, in particular when creating an intimidating, hostile, degrading, humiliating or offensive environment*[5].

The individual experience of sexual harassment may be subjective but a key concept is that the sexual advances are unwanted. It involves an abuse of power and reflects the lower status of women within the workplace and within society. It is seen to symptomatic of organisations where there is great power differentials between employers and employees and which have a culture of disrespect for women.Sexual harassment is a social issue and afflicts women working in offices, industries, hospitals, the armed forced etc. It has negative repercussions in terms of the effect on the individual psyche of the harassed woman as well as the organizational culture. Those who have been harassed may experience illness, humiliation, anger, loss of self confidence and psychological damage. Sexual harassment may also lead to workplace problems such as decreased performance, lower job satisfaction and higher absenteeism. In many cases it leads to resignation.

For the organization, a public revelation of sexual harassment can provide a death knell for the public image of the organization. There have been a spate of resignations from Tehelka and a serious question mark over its future as a brand.

Young Working Single Women At Risk

On 22nd August a photojournalist was gang-raped in the early hours of the evening in central Mumbai. The woman was on a professional assignment and was accompanied by a male colleague who was beaten up and tied by the assailants. She made a detailed report to the police and the five suspects were arrested and confessed that they had raped a rag picker and a sex worker earlier who had not lodge a complaint. This had emboldened the rapists to attack again. Later a call centre worker came forward to say that she had also been raped by these men.

One of the rapists confessed to his mother that since the girl was out alone with a male, she must have been loose and therefore easy prey. The vulnerability of women in public spaces arises from the rampant misogyny of a culture that sees working women as "available" precisely because they are present in public space. Mumbai has traditionally been considered to be a "safe" city for women and has had a long tradition of working women. But the culture of the city is changing and this change has been made most starkly manifest in the brutal gang rape of the young woman.

Sameera Khan explored this notional sense of Mumbai as being a safe city for women and how this perception is changing in her article titled "Women, Safety and the City of Mumbai"[6] and concluded that the bulk of assaults go unregistered. She points out that the men had raped rag pickers and sex workers before this:

> *"It is no surprise that those women did not report the rapes-in the work they do they are usually harassed by the authorities, and to trust law enforcers to protect them must have seemed rather hopeless."*[7]

Manual workers are more vulnerable to sexual harassment than educated blue collar workers. The sensational case in which Shiney Ahuja raped his maid focused attention for a brief while on the vulnerability of the female migrants from states such as Bihar, Orissa, Jharkhand, Assam and Mizoram who migrate to larger cities for employment. They are isolated from their friends, families and relatives and unaware of their basic rights, primarily because of their illiteracy. On the other end of the spectrum, women serving in the armed forces are not exempted from sexual harassment. The case of Lata Singh (name changed) who complained against three senior officers and was subsequently dismissed from the army is a shocking example of how oppressed and harassed women officers feel in the male bastion of the armed forces. There have been instances of suicides by women officers who had complained of harassment and been punished by the Army brass for their courage[8].

The " casting couch, casting-couch syndrome or casting-couch mentality" is a term that refers to the trading of sexual favors by an aspirant, apprentice employee or subordinate to a superior in return for entry into an occupation, or for other career advancement within an organization."[9]

The casting couch is rampant in the glamour world of films, television and modeling. Ekta Kapoor's The Dirty Picture[10] was an honest look into the murkier side of stardom while Bhandarkar's Fashion [11] depicted the seamier side of the fashion industry. Bhandarkar himself had been accused of sexual exploitation by Preeti Jain who claimed that he had promised her a role in films and exploited her for five years. In 2005, India's Most Wanted caught Shakti Kapoor and AmanVerma in a sting operation and accused them of abusing power to force women to have sexual relations with them.[12]

Bureaucrats are not immune from sexual harassment. The case of Rupan Deol Bajaj v. K.P.S. Gill is well known. The then-Chief of Police in Punjab slapped a senior administrative services officer on the bottom at a dinner party. The general public opinion was that the officer was blowing the case out of proportion, and top officials in the state tried to suppress the case[13]. Despite this attitude, the Supreme Court found the officer guilty of offences under section 354 (assault or criminal force to a woman with intent to outrage her modesty) and section 509 (an act intended to insult the modesty of a woman).

Another well-known case was Radha Bai v. Union Territory of Pondicherry, in which the appellant was a government officer who was sexually harassed and molested by the Home Minister of Tamil Nadu when she exposed his illegal involvements with the inmates of a shelter home for women. When she complained, she was removed from service. Following additional complaints, the Supreme Court intervened in the investigation of the case almost seventeen years after the incident. Ultimately, the Supreme Court held that although the complainant was terminated from service, she would be entitled to full retirement benefits and directed the State and the harasser to compensate her for lost reputation and honor.[14]

Psychological Profile of a Sexual Harasser

Far from the lecherous producer stereotype, men who sexually harass women may sometimes display great charm and charisma. Typically they have deeply held traditional values about male and female roles, a sense of entitlement-of being above the law along with other narcissistic tendencies. . Since they are motivated by the power drive they may be viewed as displaying great leadership qualities by the world in general.

Phaneesh Murthy has often been identified as a game changer in the IT industry. As Global Sales Head at Infosys he was called the "other Murthy" and was widely credited with driving up the revenue of the firm from 2 million to 700 million. He was said to be taking home a salary greater than Narayan Murthy himself. He navigated iGate through the convoluted process of the take-over of Patni Systems.

In 2002 Murthy had to resign from Infosys because of sexual harassment charges brought against him by Rosy Menon (name changed). The case was settled out of court for over three million dollars and Murthy resigned from Infosys. He subsequently started his own company and then joined iGate as CEO.In May 2013, he was forced to resign from iGate because of charges of sexual harassment brought against him by AracellRoiz. What is surprising is that iGate chose to employ Murthy despite the taint of sexual harassment on him. It gave him a free hand in hiring and promotions, despite his history of using position and power to create coercive sexual relations. When Murthy was finally dismissed the statement issued by the company is sad and regretful:

> *"We recognize the significant contributions Mr. Murthy has provided over the past 10 years in helping to establish iGate as a leader in the IT industry. He has worked hard to improve the value of iGate, and we greatly appreciate his efforts. However, as a result of this violation of iGate policy, we asked Mr. Murthy to step down."*[15]

Sexual Harassment In University Spaces

On September 30th Roma Singh (name changed), formerly Lab assistant at Bhim Rao Ambedkar College, Delhi University was rushed to hospital with ninety percent burns. On October 7th she succumbed to her injuries. Prior to her dismissal Roma Singh had repeatedly filed sexual harassment complaints against the college principal, G K Arora, in 2009. She had been dismissed from service and the apex committee of the university ruled in favour of Arora. Roma Singh set herself ablaze in protest against the sexual harassment. She had endured as well as the weak grievance redressal mechanism which saw her tormentors being given a clean chit.

In the aftermath of the suicide the Delhi University Karamchari Union (DUKU) decided to hold a meeting of the non- teaching staff across seventy five colleges. The president of the Delhi University Teacher's Union commented "Instead of sacking the principal, the GB and administration penalized the victim, who then took the extreme step. We will join the protest and attend DUKU's meeting."[15]

Roma Singh had written letters to everyone including the chairman of the college, the National Commission for Women and the Delhi Police alleging that Arora, Principal of the College, demanded sexual favours from her. Her dying declaration states: " Principal GK Arora and lab- assistant Ravindra Singh used to force me to establish physical relations with them. When I refused to agree to their demands and complained against them, they got annoyed and leveled baseless charges against me to terminate my service contract. The principal and lab-assistant also threatened to kill my son."[16]

The dying declaration is considered sacrosanct in that the impending death is seen to ensure that the dying victim does not lie. If it is seen as reliable it can be admitted as evidence. It was on this ground that students, teachers and karamcharis protested against the police who did not even file an FIR against Arora. Eventually Arora was suspended from the college which had exonerated him on two separate occasions, and booked under Section 306 of the IPC for abetment to suicide.

In theory Delhi University has very strong ordinances against sexual harassment/ The complaints redressal mechanism consists of an Apex Complaint Committee, a College Complaint Committee and a University Unit Complaint Committee. There is a Central Pool Complaint Committee to deal with issues that cannot be taken up with the other complaint committees. The mandate given to the committees is to resolve any complaint within a period of a month. The ordinance suggests a range of disciplinary actions to punish the culprit including warnings, written apologies, bond of good behaviour, adverse remarks in the confidential report, debarring from supervisory duty, denial of membership to statutory bodies, denial of re-employment, stopping of increments/promotion, reverting, demotion, suspension, dismissal. For student/s culprits, the punishment could be in the form of warnings, written apologies, bond of good behaviour, debarring entry into hostels/campuses, suspension for a specific period of time, withholding results, debarring from exams, debarring from contesting elections, debarring from holding posts such as member of a committee, of courses, membership of a college union, expulsion, denial of admission, declaring the harasser to be 'persona non grata' for a stipulated period of time, and other such relevant actions.

Despite such stringent rules and regulations sexual harassment cases continue to dog the university.

Jawaharlal Nehru University

Jawaharlal Nehru University has often been considered a liberal oasis in a patriarchal society. Its GSCASH (Gender Sensitization Committee Against Sexual Harassment) was set up in 1999, a template that has been borrowed by universities and institutions nationally. The GSCASH wasn't set up through consensus or ideology alone. It took hunger strikes, marches and public debates to drive home the need for a committee to deal with gender issues. The GSCASH has three major functions — gender sensitisation and orientation, crisis management and mediation and formal enquiry and redress.

However JNU cannot claim to be a gender just campus. In 2012, a research student accused a senior professor of sexually harassing her. The professor and his supporters waged a campaign against GSCASH and hinted that the complainant was mentally unstable. This attack on the victim has the effect of dissuading women from lodging their complaints from the fear of public shame. Typically women who have lodged complaints against men in powerful positions have felt constrained to abandon their work or study. In effect, this means the victim is punished for the crime! Even though Nayar has been forced to retire, he will receive retirement benefits.

In August 2013, a JNU student axed his classmate and committed suicide. The crime was linked to his inability to face rejection. The whole of JNU has claimed collective responsibility and the Vice Chancellor has taken moral responsibility for the crime.

What enabled Akash to commit the crime with such impunity? Why didn't Geeta (name changed) complain earlier? The girl now must live with the traumatic memory of that bloody afternoon. She has suffered from grievous head injuries and will need extensive speech therapy, psychotherapy and physiotherapy sessions.[17]

What is shockingly apparent is that the oasis is an illusion. The campus reflects the same subterranean, terrifying impulses that afflict the nation. Violence in intimate relations is part of our culture and men typically have trouble dealing with rejection.

Vishaka Guidelines

The Vishaka Guidelines grew out of the shock and outrage felt by society when Bhanwari Devi was gang-raped in the presence of her husband. Bhanwari Devi was a "saathin", a grassroots worker and activist employed by the Women Development Project of the Government of Rajasthan. In 1992 the government launched a programme against child marriages and Bhanwari Devi tried to prevent the marriage of a one year old girl. In return the villagers harassed, threatened and socially boycotted her. Then she was gang raped.

The subsequent series of events revealed how deep rooted patriarchal notions can miscarry justice as the police and the local judiciary proved intractable in the face of Bhanwari Devi's attempts to get justice. The trial court in Rajasthan acquitted the five accused.

Five NGO's filed a Public Interest Litigation in the Supreme Court under the name "Vishaka" seeking detailed information on how sexual harassment of women in the workplace could be prevented through a judicial process.In response, the Supreme Court issued the Vishaka Guidelines which represents a landmark in the context of sexual harassment in the workplace.

The Vishaka Guidelines places the responsibility of preventing sexual harassment squarely on the shoulders of the Employers:

> *"It shall be the duty of the employer or other responsible persons in work places or other institutions to prevent or deter the commission of acts of sexual harassment and to provide the procedures for the resolution, settlement or prosecution of acts, of sexual harassment by taking all steps required."*[18]

The Sexual Harassment of Women at Workplace (Prevention, Prohibition and Redressal) Act, 2013

This act recognizes that sexual harassment is a violation of a woman's right to "Life and Liberty" and to "Gender Equality". It creates an insecure and hostile work environment which discourages women's participation in work and therefore affects their economic and social empowerment. It extends in reach to include students at schools and colleges, patients in hospitals, clients, workers and customers.

Every employer is to constitute an Internal Complaints Committee. The Presiding Officer will be a woman employed at a senior position in the office. Two members will be employees of the organization preferably with legal knowledge and awareness of women's issues. One member will be from an NGO preferably with knowledge and experience of issues related to sexual harassment of women at the workplace. The committee members will hold office for three years and the external members will be paid fees.

The Internal Committee has the same powers as a civil court:

1. Summoning and enforcing attendance of a person and examining them under oath.
2. Requiring the discovery and production of documents.

3. The inquiry needs to be completed within three months.
4. The Inquiry makes recommendations and the employer needs to act on these recommendations within sixty days.
5. There are provisions to deal with false complaints arising out of malicious intent.

If an employer fails to constitute an internal Complaints Committee or does not comply with the provisions of the act a penalty ranging up to Rs 50,000/-may be imposed. A repetition may lead to the penalty being doubled, a revocation of the statutory business license or a de-registration of the entity.

The employer needs to take responsibility for raising awareness among employees as to what constitutes sexual harassment and how to complain and seek redressal if harassment occurs. The law against sexual harassment in the workplace is a powerful statement by the government that sexual harassment of women will not be tolerated. However our experience of the implementation of the Vishaka Guidelines suggests that employers may hesitate to set up and publicise Complaints Committees. The option of conciliation before an inquiry will lead to pressure on the complainant to withdraw her complaint. After all the complaints committee will be constituted by the employees of the organization and they will tend to favour the boss if he has been the culprit. Lack of legal knowledge and a refusal to see sexual harassment as a criminal act are also certain drawbacks as are the exclusion of rules and regulations forbidding sexual harassment in the service rules of organizations.

Some Lacuna in the Sexual Harassment Act of 2013

On December 12, 2012 a young lawyer revealed that a retired judge of the highest court in the land had sexually harassed her. A Committee of three Supreme Court judges put forth its conclusion that the statement of the intern both written and oral, "prima facie discloses an act of unwelcome behavior". Justice Ganguly refused to step down as Chairman of the West Bengal Human Rights Commission on the ground that he had not been found guilty by an appropriate court.

On 2nd January, 2013 the Central government cleared the proposal for Ganguly's removal as chairman of WBHRC. Justice Ganguly has denied the allegation and in his defence will seek to prove that the allegation was false or malicious.

> *The Bill against Sexual Harassment provides that in case a committee arrives at a conclusion that the allegation was false or malicious, it may recommend that action be taken against the woman who made the complaint. The clause also provides that mere inability to substantiate a complaint or provide adequate proof need not attract action against the complainant.*

This could deter women from filing complaints. The National Advisory Council (NAC) has recommended that the entire clause be removed as it might deter victims from seeking protection of the proposed legislation.

The Justice Ganguly case also highlights the fact that those working as unpaid interns are not covered under the Sexual Harassment Bill. The gross power imbalance between a retired judge occupying a high constitutional position and an unpaid intern offers a startling revelation of how difficult it may be for a woman to name and shame the sexual offender in the workplace.

Notes & References

1. Times Nation, TOI Bhopal, Wednesday, December 25/12/2013.
2. Tejpal's letter-*http://www.indianexpress.com/news/tehelka-case-read-tarun-tejpals-letter-to-the-victim/1198662/*
3. Menon, Nivedita-*http://kafila.org/2013/11/21/sexualized-workplaces-predatory-men-and-the-rage-of-women/*
4. *http://wcd.nic.in/wcdact/womenactsex.pdf*
5. *http://ec.europa.eu/justice/gender- equality/files/your_rights/final_harassement_en.pdf*
6. Khan, Sameera. "Women, Safety, and the City of Mumbai" *Economic and Political Weekly*, Vol. XLVIII No. 36 September, 7, 2013. Pp 12-13.
7. *Ibid.* p 12.
8. *http://www.thehindu.com/todays-paper/tp-national/tp-karnataka/article2448547.ece*
9. *http://indiatoday.intoday.in/story/casting-couch-bollywood-rina-golan-subhash-ghai/1/155320.html*
10. Film- The Dirty Picture (2011). Director- Milan Luthria, Produced by ALT Entertainment and Balaji Motion Pictures.
11. Film-Fashion (2008) Director-MadhurBhandarkar, Produced by Bhandarkar Entertainment and UTV Motion pictures.
12. *http://articles.timesofindia.indiatimes.com/2005-03-17/news-interviews/27834189_1_police-complaint-india-tv-shakti-kapoor*
13. *http://www2.tau.ac.il/InternetFiles/news/UserFiles/J_Barak.pdf p180*
14. *Ibid.* p. 181.

15. Qtd. *http://nainakapur.blogspot.in/2013/05/workplace-sexual-harassment-and-igate.html*
16. *http://www.dailymail.co.uk/indiahome/indianews/article-2453011/Justice-Pavitra—Kejriwals-AAP-demands-investigation-college-principal-accused-sexually-harassing-DU-lab-technician-set-fire.html*
17. "Axe attack, suicide at JNU" *http://www.telegraphindia.com/1130801/jsp/frontpage/story_17182272.jsp#.UspEkNIW28o*
18. Vishaka and others V. State of Rajasthan and others [1997 (6) SCC 241].